ENVISIONING PUBLIC SCHOLARSHIP
FOR OUR TIME

ENVISIONING PUBLIC SCHOLARSHIP FOR OUR TIME

Models for Higher Education Researchers

Edited by

Adrianna Kezar, Yianna Drivalas,

and Joseph A. Kitchen

Foreword by Lorelle L. Espinosa

STERLING, VIRGINIA

COPYRIGHT © 2018 BY STYLUS
PUBLISHING, LLC.

Published by Stylus Publishing, LLC,
22883 Quicksilver Drive Sterling, Virginia 20166-2102

Library of Congress Cataloging-in-Publication Data
The CIP for this text has been applied for.

13-digit ISBN: 978-1-62036-775-9 (cloth)
13-digit ISBN: 978-1-62036-776-6 (paperback)
13-digit ISBN: 978-1-62036-777-3 (library networkable e-edition)
13-digit ISBN: 978-1-62036-778-0 (consumer e-edition)

Printed in the United States of America

All first editions printed on acid-free paper
that meets the American National Standards Institute
Z39-48 Standard.

Bulk Purchases
Quantity discounts are available for use in workshops and for
staff development.
Call 1-800-232-0223

First Edition, 2018

I want to dedicate this volume to and acknowledge my colleagues at the University of Southern California who do public scholarship and who have helped me develop into a public scholar. I also wish to thank my parents, who had a strong commitment to social justice and equity. And finally, I dedicate this book to my many friends who have fostered my sense of public scholarship, particularly Michelle Gilliard and Vasti Torres, who introduced me at the 2016 American Educational Research Association Vice Presidential lecture on public scholarship. They are both excellent examples of public scholarship.

—*Adrianna Kezar*

I dedicate this volume to Kyle, Gidget, my parents, my wonderful coeditors, and to my colleagues and mentors at the University of Southern California, Harvard University, and Ohio State University. Their unyielding support has made this work possible. I also dedicate it to the contributors to this volume and to emerging public scholars everywhere who work to advance public scholarship and the public good.

—*Joey Kitchen*

For the emerging scholars who know that there is more listening and giving to be done.

—*Yianna Drivalas*

CONTENTS

FOREWORD

Like others in this volume, I found my way to public scholarship via a professional pathway that started on the ground. My lived experience and the experiences of the students I have worked with over the years has served a meaningful catalyst to find my public voice and my quest to add needed nuance to the many discussions being had in Washington, DC, and around the country. One outcome of the current societal and political divisiveness around us is the production and perpetuation of absolutes and boiled down truths. Yet as social scientists, we know that the world is much more complex. Harnessing that knowledge in a way that informs decision makers and everyday citizens is at the heart of public scholarship.

As a field, higher education risks irrelevancy if we are not able to make good on what drove so many of us here in the first place: to not just see difference but to make a difference. The scholarly community finds itself at a critical juncture, always empowered but not always knowing how to harness that power and turn it into action. This pivot represents a paradigm shift for the academy and indeed frightens some who think a move to action means abandoning the tenets on which higher education has built its scholarship. To the contrary, public scholarship does not render theoretical underpinnings irrelevant: it requires them. But what scholars and their institutions must do is leave behind their own echo chambers, speak beyond their peer review walls, and become translational entrepreneurs with a public purpose.

The opportunity for influence is before us, although the window is in need of widening. Public scholarship is well poised to return national attention to evidence and its role in sound policymaking and other judgments, while at the same time pushing for needed reforms such as those outlined in this volume. In an era of "fake news," scholarship is not less but more relevant than ever before. The dangers of anti-intellectualism demand scholarship that is accessible and welcoming of engagement. Lest it be deemed elitist or irrelevant, today's public scholarship must widen its audience, meet stakeholders where they are, and find its way into a multitude of information channels.

I would argue that there are five imperatives (and surely more) to ensuring effective public scholarship in higher education:

1. Public scholarship requires a recognition that knowledge comes in many forms and is not the sole domain of the academy. In an information age, the transfer and take up of knowledge knows few boundaries. The role of the public scholar is to apply needed rigor and historical, sociocultural, and other contexts and to help sort, translate, and make use of knowledge in its many forms.

2. Similarly, public scholarship does not flow in one direction but is void of hierarchy. The notion that public intellectualism occurs from the academy down is as antiquated as the typewriter. While some may prefer this mechanism, even cling to it, the internet and social media render this view not only obsolete but also ignorant. Entire (including evidence-based) movements begin on the ground by everyday citizens, ripe for engagement by public scholarship as a vehicle, not the sole driver.

3. The language of public scholarship is multidisciplinary. Public scholarship is well served by interdisciplinary structures and professional relationships, including when it comes to the type of data utilized to communicate one's message. While there is a time and place for experimental research, most policy decisions are still made with descriptive and anecdotal evidence. This begs for public scholarship that is multimethod and easily translatable by a variety of advocates.

4. If public scholarship is to truly inform policy and practice in a long-lasting way, the academy as a whole must embrace it. This does not mean adding a few classes to graduate coursework, but transforming the *entire* curriculum such that the tools for public scholarship are embedded throughout. This is only possible if there exist complementary incentives for faculty members to engage in public scholarship; yet another needed departure from an antiquated tenure and promotion system that reinforces the very echo chambers we need to get away from.

5. In order to realize what it means to trade in public scholarship, the higher education field itself must be diverse and inclusive of the very communities its research aims to serve. This is especially true of those who study higher education policy research, a small and far too elite group that is nearly as homogenous as its policy-making audience (read: mostly White and male). It is no wonder we are often viewed as out of touch.

Those aspiring to public scholarship would be wise to seek out individual and collective impact outlets. The intermediary organizations touched upon in this volume can provide a space for both, as can local and national opinion editorial pages, blog platforms, and social media outlets. So can newly formed, independent and nonpartisan channels such as the Scholars Strategy

Network, an association that connects university scholars and their research to policymakers, members of the media, and the public. Also powerful is engaging policymakers on the ground, inviting them into the educational setting. The American Youth Policy Forum's long-running "study tour" program seeks to do just that, providing policymakers with a firsthand look at schools, classrooms, and evidence-based programs.

In a fast-paced world of competing information streams, public scholarship and its ability to transcend false narratives and physical and virtual spaces emerges a bright light. A beacon for truth and sense-making. A foundation for sound policy and practice at national, state, and local levels. Such a call to action is not new, and while its import underlies the very foundation of our field, the need for scholars of higher education to look beyond the walls of academe has never been more critical to the advancement of American society.

Lorelle L. Espinosa, PhD
Assistant Vice President for Policy Research and Strategy
American Council on Education

PART ONE

CONTEXT FOR PUBLIC SCHOLARSHIP

DEFINING THE EVOLVING CONCEPT OF *PUBLIC SCHOLARSHIP*

Adrianna Kezar, Yianna Drivalas, and Joseph A. Kitchen

George Keller (1985), a higher education scholar, published an article that was critical of higher education research when higher education was still a young field of study that had just emerged in the 1970s. Keller challenged researchers, saying that their studies were not read by policymakers and practitioners and were not informing higher education, and as a result, their studies were trees that bore no fruit. This analogy has remained a part of our discourse in higher education. Adrianna Kezar has used it when noting the limited way our research has been translational; reaching and; we hope, transforming practice. Over the years, occasional concerns have been raised about the gap between research and practice. At other times, scholars in our field have disregarded the calls for relevance as anti-intellectual and antitheoretical.

In this volume, we wish to explore the idea of public scholarship as a goal and a way to overcome the lack of impact that the work in higher education has on practice and policy. Public scholarship addresses traditional concerns about the gap between research and practice and policy, bridging the divide. We argue that public scholarship should be the norm in higher education. George Keller (1985) and other critics have typically had a narrower vision of translational research, primarily expecting elites to shape and frame practice and policy from the top down. But this view of engaging the public is far too limited and renders short the possibilities for more bottom-up change when other groups are armed with our research. We hope to involve you the reader in public scholarship for our time, guided by a vision that advocates for and supports diverse democracy, equity, and social justice.

Defining *Public Scholarship*

For the editors of this volume, public scholarship is connected and closely related to the words *diverse democracy*, *equity*, and *social justice*. We conceptualize our stance with our publics, whether the general public, society, or community, in an ethical way. One might try to work with and change policy, but the policy might ultimately be faulty or wrongheaded. The act of reaching out is not by itself the goal of public scholarship as we envision it. Rather, the objective is to support an equitable, diverse democracy and to promote social justice. Thus, it is not enough to be a scholar who simply interacts with policymakers, teachers, or the general public unless those interactions are tied to supporting a diverse democracy. We believe diversity strengthens democracy because more voices are heard, and in an equitable and diverse democracy, those previously marginalized voices become acknowledged. This idea of democratic inclusiveness means recognizing diversity on the grounds of race, class, caste, creed, religion, ethnicity, gender, sexual orientation, age, disability, geographical isolation, socioeconomic status, and other characteristics of difference (Banks, 2004). Public scholars, then, should work with as many stakeholders as possible in a diverse democracy like ours, especially with members of marginalized communities whose voices are often not heard through traditional research.

By social justice, we mean promoting a just society by actively challenging and working to correct injustice. All people have a right to equitable treatment, support for their human rights, and a fair allocation of community resources.

We align with thinkers such as Rawls (2009) who emphasize that social justice is about ensuring the protection of equal access to liberties, rights, and opportunities, as well as taking care of the least advantaged members of society. Whether something is just or unjust depends on whether it promotes or hinders equality of access to civil liberties, human rights, and opportunities for healthy and fulfilling lives, as well as whether it allocates a fair share of benefits to the least advantaged members of society (Rawls, 2009).

Our conception of public scholarship imagines a much wider public than Keller (1985) and other higher education critics did. We envision public scholarship as service to a diverse democracy and social justice, which are interconnected and necessary to build an equitable society. The broad reach and multiple types of public scholarship, then, are not merely different strategies but are intentionally linked to, and in service of, reaching the most powerful as well as marginalized and often forgotten groups. Moving toward justice is best served when scholars work closely and mutually with these diverse public groups.

The *public scholarship* defined in this chapter and described in this volume moves beyond informing policymakers, faculty, and administrators. It also includes populations such as students and parents, media, the general public, and particularly groups that may have had little or no access to our research. Public scholarship compels us to consider the ways we can connect to and involve the public with our research in its creation, dissemination, and application. It represents a departure from stale research to practice dissemination concepts, which might mean forming a partnership with a community agency to design a research project and disseminate results. It might also mean writing for practitioner or policy venues and magazines outside the traditional academic journals. It could be serving on boards for national groups vested with the authority to make important decisions related to an area where one conducts research. Public scholarship can also consist of sharing results over social media, which is accessible and widely understood by the general public. We have tried to capture the essence of public scholarship in Figure 1.1.

Our vision of public scholarship builds on John Dewey's (1916/2004) work that maintained scholars must engage democratically with *publics* in ways that raise awareness of social problems (in education and beyond) and

Figure 1.1. Public scholarship.

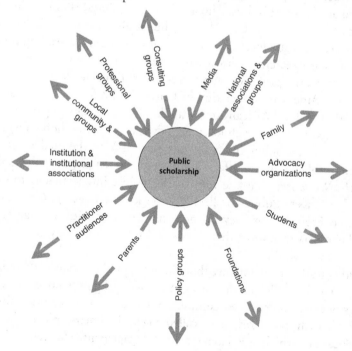

foster a democratic and public solution to those problems. Dewey argued that science could contribute best to social progress, including educational progress, through a process of sustained public inquiry rather than by being asserted by, or trickling down from, professionalized and technical fields of study embedded within sanctioned institutions. He directly critiqued the traditional research dissemination model and suggested much more direct involvement with our research stakeholders (Dewey, 1916/2004). We now turn to two of the major movements in higher education since Keller's (1985) critique that have challenged and redefined the entire enterprise of higher education—the growth of the public intellectual and the idea of the engaged scholar.

It's likely that while reading these first few pages, the idea of the public scholar conjured up images of the public intellectual, that is, someone who works extensively with the media. For example, one might picture Cornel West appearing on one of Bill Maher's television shows, or the *Daily Show*, or *Meet the Press* or engaging in lively radio program exchanges or with followers on social media. But public scholarship is much broader than the in-fashion notion of the public intellectual. Although using social media, blogging, and appearing in the media are all ways to be involved in public scholarship, there are also less media-focused avenues involving community partnerships, policy dialogues, and local and national leadership roles that also are forms of public scholarship (Small, 2008). Public scholarship includes the example of Cornel West, but it also includes scholars working with teachers at a local school to develop an intensive reading program based on their research, a scholar who testifies before Congress on the value of Pell Grants, the professor who serves in a national leadership role as the head of the American Association of University Professors, or the scholars who work with local African American families to develop a parent organization to make sure their children are advocated for in school. The public is not the general public in an abstract way vis-à-vis the media but rather multiple publics that are affected and could be empowered through our research. We worry that the idea of the public intellectual is too much a one-way street. Public intellectuals speak to a larger *public* audience, broadly conceived, but they do not truly interact with a range of public stakeholders to inform their views and research the way we envision a public scholar would.

Other readers may not have thought of the public intellectual but instead of Boyer's (1996) idea of the engaged scholar, a figure who is involved in university extension services, community-based research, or other forms of public outreach. Boyer originally called engaged scholarship the scholarship of application, which was later renamed engagement, and referred to the responsibilities of a faculty member to those outside the university. Boyer's public engagement also involves the application of disciplinary expertise and research on the complex problems and issues of policy, practice, and the like. He noted how the scholarship of application addressed the following key questions: "(a) How can knowledge be responsibly applied to consequential problems?; (b) How can it be helpful to individuals as well as institutions?; and (c) Can social problems themselves (and the public sphere) define an agenda for scholarly investigation?" (Boyer, 1996, p. 21). Although the *scholarship of application* is most often considered to be aligned with the realm of service in higher education, the idea has expanded since Boyer and is defined as research that involves the community. In later years, groups such as the New England Resource Center for Higher Education (NERCHE), further elaborated on this definition, suggesting that the

> term redefines faculty scholarly work from application of academic expertise to community engaged scholarship that involves the faculty member in a reciprocal partnership with the community, is interdisciplinary, and integrates faculty roles of teaching, research, and service. While there is variation in current terminology (public scholarship, scholarship of engagement, community-engaged scholarship), engaged scholarship is defined by the collaboration between academics and individuals outside the academy— knowledge professionals and the lay public (local, regional/state, national, global)—for the mutually beneficial exchange of knowledge and resources in a context of partnership and reciprocity. The scholarship of engagement includes explicitly democratic dimensions of encouraging the participation of nonacademics in ways that enhance and broaden engagement and deliberation about major social issues inside and outside the university. It seeks to facilitate a more active and engaged democracy by bringing affected publics into problem-solving work in ways that advance the public good with and not merely for the public. (NERCHE, n.d.)

Engagement, as described earlier, emphasizes mutuality and bidirectional communication that are not captured in Boyer's (1996) original idea of scholarship of application. Boyer and later works on public engagement also emphasize that scholarship is more than just research alone and can include service and teaching.

Engaged scholarship is a relevant concept and is incorporated into our vision of public scholarship. Engaged scholarship as a form of research is often more mutual and involves deep relationships between researchers and their communities. There has been a significant movement in the past two decades called the *engaged university* that is built on Boyer's (1996) model of scholarship and this model of community engagement. Many associate engaged scholarship with applied fields because this form of scholarship comes from the history of university extension services and agriculture, but it is used across all fields in higher education. From 1980 to 2000, engaged scholars fought for legitimacy. But there is now much greater acceptance by institutions and other scholars of engaged scholarship than in the past (Van de Ven, 2007).

These two movements (i.e., public intellectual and engaged scholarship) redefine the work of the scholar to be more public and extends the idea of scholarship beyond the confines of the proverbial ivory tower. However, we find each to be too narrow to encompass the many ways we have seen public scholarship unfold and the other ways we imagine scholars should be engaging with the public; the movements belie particular approaches rather than invite scholars into a broad set of activities that can have a greater impact on policy and practice. This broader set of activities also honors and respects a field of study like higher education that is multidisciplinary with scholars in very different types of work such as policy, administration, leadership, student development, teaching and learning, finance, and history. In this book, we set out to define *public scholarship* as a multifaceted set of activities on a continuum ranging from less mutually engaged to more mutually engaged.

The continuum in Figure 1.2 is a visual representation of the varied engagement levels of public scholarship. For example, although circulating policy reports and briefs is an important practice for researchers, it is frequently a one-directional activity. Even if the audiences receiving the information can benefit from it, it is not very mutually engaging and often does not involve critical input from the publics the reports or briefs intend to inform and serve. Practice embedded educational research (which is described later in the chapter) and other forms of participatory work such as participatory action research, community-based research, and arts-based research, however, are more mutually engaging because of their collaborative nature. Researchers and participant communities alike contribute to and benefit from this sort of activity and research. Each example along the continuum in Figure 1.2 is

Figure 1.2. Varied engagement levels of public scholarship.

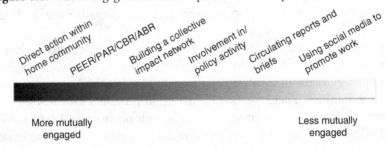

some form of public scholarship, and this volume is committed to exploring the range of possibilities for public scholarship.

Several books related to the notion of public scholarship have been published, but they do not define *public scholarship* in the way we do, and the objectives of those books are quite different from ours. Therefore, we thought it might be valuable to explain how this volume is different from these prior works. Gasman (2016) provides practical advice for scholars on how to be public intellectuals, writing and speaking for lay audiences. Perna (in press) focuses on whether academics should interact with the public, and if they do, how to do so in a way that does not compromise the work by crossing a line and becoming an advocate and shares the perspectives and related decision-making of various scholars regarding whether and how to take one's work public. Shaker (2015) examines faculty-engaged scholarship, service, and teaching as contributors to the public good, and describes the greater potential to do such work but does not devote much time to exploring scholarship and instead focuses on service. Our perspective is quite different in that we believe it is the scholars' responsibility to bring their research to the public; it is not their choice but an obligation driven by the mores of equity, social justice, and a diverse democracy. We also argue for much broader approaches than Gasman, who is largely concerned with what we would consider a more public intellectual–oriented definition of *public scholarship*. Finally, we connect public scholarship to an ethical professional commitment and to serving the public good in very specific ways: supporting social justice and a diverse democracy.

Importance of Public Scholarship

Public scholarship, as we envision it, works toward supporting the public good, which is a core mission of faculty as professionals (Kezar, Chambers, & Burkhardt, 2005). For instance, we as scholars have an inherent responsibility to inform public debates on key policy and practice issues that affect education. It is not enough for those in the field to simply produce research. Because we are the ones who examine the issues in methodologically rigorous and ethical ways, we therefore have the responsibility to bring our findings to those forums wherein the public good is debated. We also have a responsibility to be actors in that public sphere. Dissemination of research is key, but we must also be active in terms of testimony. We can activate our research in public spheres by serving on national commissions and petitioning our policymakers, for instance. It is also important to train our graduate students in this tradition through modeling and by getting them involved in the work. We argue that this dissemination and action is embedded in the work of scholars and is part and parcel of conducting quality research with integrity. Although some avenues described in this chapter are more likely to be counted as faculty service than others, we believe it is important to go beyond the considerations of formal service and to work with the intention of doing right by the research and the communities that contributed to and will be served by the research.

This is the challenge we present to the reader: Consider public scholarship as we have defined and explored it. Is it how we as a community—faculty, graduate students, and others in our field—define *research*? Or, is it not? Our history as a field suggests that we have been largely unsuccessful in being engaged with the broader public. We hope to inspire scholars to reframe their research so that it can be consistently seen as public scholarship. We also encourage scholars to consider new modes of public scholarship that move beyond the work of a public intellectual (an often a self-serving role) and into a position that supports a diverse democracy, equity, and social justice. Through public scholarship, we have the potential to shape important policies and decisions, reshaping public dialogue and transforming our educational settings.

Evolving Methods to Enhance Public Scholarship

New research models are emerging in education that embed public scholarship into the research process. These models build on traditions of action and participatory research that developed in the 1970s from the work of Paulo Freire (1970/1996) and in fields of social work and sociology. These methods—particularly action research—are tied to goals of social justice. At present, these are marginalized methods in higher education that could serve as beacons for the future. These newer models embed practitioners, policymakers, and the publics of our research directly into the research process. From the beginning, this form of engagement allows the publics to define the study and participation parameters, review and interpret the data and findings, and disseminate the results at different levels to various constituencies and stakeholders. Through this direct engagement, the separation between researcher and publics is completely broken and reconceptualized.

Networked improvement communities are one such model. The Carnegie Foundation for the Advancement of Teaching is advocating for this approach under the leadership of Anthony Bryk (2015). In examining the history of school reforms and the very minimal uptake of research-based ideas in reform efforts, Bryk concludes, "We undervalue the importance of systemic and organized methods of learning to improve" (p. 467). In the networked improvement communities model, scholars work on the ground with practitioners on problems of practice, and they are part of the research and inquiry process, which incorporates learning practice-based evidence. The assumption in this research is that systems are incredibly complex, and issues are often tied to a particular context; thus, generalized findings from typical research studies do not represent key institutional context variables that shape the implementation of research-based practices and policies. This approach also assumes variability of performance. Instead of seeing variations as problems or aberrant findings to be ignored, researchers learn from variations to alter the system, and variations are much more present and identifiable in the context-based research done as part of networked improvement communities. In higher education, the Bay View Alliance is an example of a networked improvement community. Nine universities work in partnership to improve teaching in science, technology, engineering, and mathematics (STEM) using evidence-based teaching practices (see bayviewalliance.org). Scholars on campus work with STEM faculty to conduct studies in research clusters across these various institutions. They develop insights in the context of the institution, easing implementation and ensuring it is responsive to the institutional context. These networked improvement communities involve dozens of faculty and practitioners who have been conducting ongoing research for many years with no plan to end the work. We challenge members of networked improvement communities to consider the extent to which they think about their communities. For example, students and parents are often not brought into the research process, but they are important community stakeholders. We challenge researchers in this model to think even more expansively about the notion of community and who we invite in.

Practice-embedded educational research is another model showcased by Catherine Snow (2015) in which research studies begin with an urgent problem of practice jointly defined by practitioners and researchers. Practitioners and researchers collaborate closely on an educational issue in an educational setting and interactively. Researchers become much more familiar with issues in practice, and practitioners become much more knowledgeable about research-based forms of practice. Practice embedded educational research is a form of community-based research in which community participation is an integral component of the research process, and social justice and social science are linked (Taylor & Ochocka, 2017). Community-based research comes in many nuanced methodological forms and has many names (e.g., practitioner research, collaborative action research), but each is rooted in action. (For a thorough explanation of the distinctions among community-based research models, see Taylor & Ochocka, 2017.)

The work of Estela Bensimon on the Equity Scorecard is an example of participatory action research, another form of community-based research

(USC Rossier School of Education, n.d.). In the scorecard work, researchers partner with teams of staff, faculty, and administrators on college campuses to examine institutional data on student outcomes, disaggregated by race and gender, to determine gaps in performance and develop relevant interventions. The approach to this work is embedded in the campus context and uses data from that context rather than generalized data from studies of other educational contexts. Moreover, the researchers in this model work collaboratively with practitioners on the resulting data-based interventions.

Collective impact is another way researchers and publics can engage in shared research and action (Hanleybrown, Kania, & Kramer, 2012; Kania & Kramer, 2011). Collective impact brings together stakeholders invested in the same agenda, often in social justice, to work together toward one goal. This mode of organizing and working stands in contrast to the more commonly seen isolated efforts of stakeholders, where many individual groups and agents are working independently, without sharing resources, toward the same or very similar goals. Public scholarship can look like building or participating in collective impact networks so that research agendas are mutually created and employed by as many relevant publics as possible.

Throughout this volume, the chapter contributors describe methods that involve bridging the gap between our current modes of research and the publics that use and are informed by that research. But even as we develop new research modes, some areas of study may never be fully realized through networked improvement communities, participatory action research, or practice embedded educational research, so we will need other translational approaches. Additionally, we can always complement these newer methodological approaches with other stances as a public scholar through media, partnerships, translational writing, advocacy and activism, local policy making, community development, and leadership roles. We all have different strengths and approaches, so we want to emphasize the many ways one can be a public scholar, making it seem accessible and enticing to scholars doing very different types of research.

Situating This Volume in the Public Scholarship Conversation

This book is organized into three parts. In part one, the contributors define and describe *public scholarship*; in part two, they provide examples of what public scholarship can look like in higher education. Part three describes ways to institutionalize the adoption of public scholarship into higher education as a field of study. Together, the chapters in this volume provide you, the emerging or established scholar, with an opportunity to reflect on your own strengths, talents, passions, and values as you find your place within public scholarship. Regardless of your experience with this mode of scholarship, we hope this collection of chapters will serve as a guiding resource as you begin your journey into public scholarship or help mentor others as they begin theirs.

Much of the responsibility to promote public scholarship can and should fall on graduate schools. The replication and socialization processes that occur in most institutions almost guarantee that the next generation of higher education researchers will not be public scholars unless faculty and administrators make intentional choices to break the cycle.

In chapter 13, Angela Clark-Taylor, Molly Sarubbi, Judy Marquez Kiyama, and Stephanie J. Waterman describe how embedded holistic approaches in graduate training are necessary components to cultivating PhD students as public scholars. On a similar note, Michael Lanford and William G. Tierney identify course assignments as an important tool toward this goal in chapter 12. They argue that diverse writing assignments and genres in PhD course work can prepare emerging scholars to use appropriate methods for diverse communities and audiences.

As young scholars move beyond their doctoral studies and into their first faculty positions, they have the opportunity to define themselves as public scholars. In chapter 14, Jamie Lester and David Horton Jr. describe how public scholarship can change across faculty career stages and provide suggestions that align with the different phases of one's career. Adrianna Kezar uses her own experience and deep knowledge of the field in chapter 2 to describe how different modes of public scholarship can be used for different purposes while also sharing the challenges faculty face when committing to that work. For the emerging public scholars who choose to pursue other career routes, Lesley McBain provides examples of ways to engage with higher education and conduct meaningful research outside of academia in chapter 15. Regardless of the career path researchers choose to follow, the ethics of their work are always important. Cecile H. Sam and Jarrett T. Gupton describe the ethical dilemmas of public scholarship in chapter 3 and encourage professionals to be mindful about how they respond to those concerns. Their chapter includes research and practical perspectives, covering the creation, dissemination, and application processes of research.

Traditional academic journals serve a very important role in higher education scholarship, but their audiences are narrow. In chapter 5, Charles H.F. Davis III, Shaun R. Harper, and Wilmon A. Christian III explore the responsibility to reach their varied communities and audiences in cost-free, accessible ways. They describe the methods they employ, including a multimedia platform for circulation of reports and policy briefs, to reach their constituencies and other relevant audiences. Although social media is an immediate and useful way to connect with others, it is not consistently used by academics. In chapter 10, Constance Iloh describes the important role social media can play in dismantling structures that limit the reach of public scholarship, particularly for underrepresented scholars, and its impact on societal inequities

The dissemination phase requires researchers to consider many valuable and important options available to them. However, the work of the public scholar begins sooner, as early as developing the research question, sample and setting, and methods. Home campuses and local communities are important sites for the public scholar. Amalia Dache-Gerbino's chapter 8 describes direct activism at an individual's home institution and in the surrounding community through national movements while simultaneously developing a scholar-activist identity. When working in local communities, the arts can serve as a way to share and conduct research because they are more accessible than traditional methodologies and modes of dissemination. In chapter 11, Yianna Drivalas and Adrianna Kezar argue that arts-based education research, currently underused in education's academic spheres, can contribute to engaging the public as the beneficiaries and agents of higher education research.

Public scholarship must also be sensitive to working with historically marginalized populations that have been taken advantage of by the research enterprise through colonization of thought, lack of reciprocation, and more. Action research provides researchers with another opportunity to serve and work with marginalized populations. In chapter 6, Estela Mara Bensimon shares her experiences with action research, including the challenges of creating specialized tools, cultural differences, and just-in-time response pressures.

Often, engaging in public scholarship requires a shift beyond methodology to one's research agenda. In chapter 4, Sylvia Hurtado describes her experience evolving from a traditional researcher into a public scholar through her work to inform a Supreme Court case on affirmative action. Direct participation in policy development is another way for public scholars to engage with important stakeholder communities. Kim Nehls, Oscar Espinoza-Parra, Holly Schneider, Travis Tyler, and Elena Nourrie in Chapter 7 write about connecting research and policy at the state level at the University of Nevada, Las Vegas College of Education. Their chapter recounts the dean's call for setting an agenda and writing a white paper on topics relevant to the state legislative body.

Public scholarship as described and discussed in this volume is relatively new, but elements of public engagement have been a cornerstone of higher education for years. Universities have a history of conducting research relevant to and serving the public's needs. Casey D. Mull, Jenna B. Daniel, and Jenny Jordan describe in Chapter 9 the public scholarship of cooperative extension and the mutual impact of this scholarship on university systems and communities, focusing on how it has responded to changing student population and university needs.

To Be or Not to Be a Public Scholar?

Some have argued that scholars should remain separated from the public so they can remain objective. Others have argued that it is not the responsibility of scholars to disseminate but only to generate knowledge. Intermediary organizations like higher education associations and other organizations that work directly with various publics are best suited to the role of involving publics in the work produced by scholars, or so the argument goes. Certainly, these groups play a key role. But concern is increasing that these organizations are overwhelmed by so many information sources and are becoming less well equipped to identify and play their crucial role. There is also the concern that these groups may play gatekeeper for what knowledge is considered worthy to investigate and disseminate. Scholars are being called on to curate and make publics aware of their work in their own capacities. Although we are cognizant of the vision of disengaged scholarship—often considered the traditional norm or perspective—we believe that actively considering the idea and possibility of public scholarship is an ethical obligation.

We advocate for a public scholarship guided by, and embedded in, ethics. One might attempt to change policy, but the resulting policy might ultimately be faulty or misguided. Purely making an effort is not the goal; it is important to tie it to supporting a diverse democracy and social justice. Ethics is a theme that appears throughout this volume and is a particular focus of chapter 3. There are ethical considerations in all research, but as scholars move into new ways of working they need to revisit and understand the particular ethical dilemmas that emerge for public scholarship.

Conclusion

Derek Bok (2009), president of Harvard, warns of the dangers of detachment in the following:

> Armed with the security of tenure and the time to study the world with care, professors would appear to have a unique opportunity to act as society's scouts to signal impending problems long before they are visible

to others. Yet rarely have members of the academy succeeded in discovering the emerging issues and bringing them vividly to the attention of the public. The very complexity of modern life requires more, not less, information; more, not less, participation. (pp. 76–77)

We believe that framing public scholarship broadly is important to including a diverse range of stakeholders, goals, and audiences and to promoting social justice. Narrow definitions that do not allow us to fully meet the needs of a diverse democracy have too often characterized public scholarship. Dewey's (1916/2004) writing reminds us that multiplicity and complexity are inherent in better serving the complex demands of democratic ideals. Furthermore, as editors, we think this broad definition also better captures the good work of many researchers in the field of higher education that often gets overlooked. And in reframing our research as a field, we might bring to light many examples of good research that do not receive attention under our current norms.

Like Boyer (1996), we believe that when the academic communities (fields and disciplines) embrace this collectively, only then can faculty fully embrace public scholarship. Faculty live in communities and need a shared vision of scholarly work. Part three of this book directly addresses norms and socialization into the field of higher education.

Are we doing our job adequately if we only write journal articles and make presentations at research conferences? We say no, but we are not sure what those in the field envision for it. Do we want to hold ourselves to the standards of public scholarship? If we do, how do we better prepare scholars by educating them about the multitude of options to be a public scholar and for the challenges we have described? What models in graduate programs for training public scholars may already exist? Can we better prepare scholars for the messiness of public scholarship? How can scholars do this work and be rewarded with our current tenure and promotion processes?

By working to change our professional norms with an eye toward ethics and guided by a responsibility to work toward social justice, equity, and a diverse democracy, we commit to working together toward a new vision for our work, one that we are proud to align with. Research that does not take into account the importance of diverse democracies and public scholarship risks perpetuating cycles of marginalization and oppression. Researchers must make a conscious effort to ethically and appropriately contribute to and serve the communities they study. Without this deliberate focus, even the most significant, timely, and methodologically rigorous study will miss the important opportunity to critically engage with diverse publics.

References

Banks, J. A. (Ed.). (2004). *Diversity and citizenship education: Global perspectives*. San Francisco, CA: Jossey-Bass.

Bok, D. (2009). *Beyond the ivory tower: Social responsibilities of the modern university*. Cambridge, MA: Harvard University Press.

Boyer, E. L. (1996). *Scholarship reconsidered: Priorities of the professoriate*. Lawrenceville, NJ: Princeton University Press.

Bryk, A. S. (2015). 2014 AERA distinguished lecture: Accelerating how we learn to improve. *Educational Researcher, 44*, 467–477.

Dewey, J. (2004). *Democracy and education: An introduction to the philosophy of education*. Mineola, NY: Dover. (Original work published 1916)

Freire, P. (1996). *Pedagogy of the oppressed* (M. B. Ramos, Trans.). New York, NY: Continuum. (Original work published 1970)

Gasman, M. (Ed.). (2016). *Academics going public: How to write and speak beyond academe*. New York, NY: Routledge.

Hanleybrown, F., Kania, J., & Kramer, M. (2012). *Channeling change: Making collective impact work*. Retrieved from ssir.org/articles/entry/channeling_change_making_collective_impact_work

Kania, J., & Kramer, M. (2011). *Collective impact*. Retrieved from ssir.org/articles/entry/collective_impact

Keller, G. (1985). Trees without fruit: The problem with research about higher education. *Change, 17*(1), 7–10.

Kezar, A., Chambers, T., & Burkhardt, J. (Eds.). (2005). *Higher education for the public good: Emerging voices from a national movement*. San Francisco, CA: Jossey-Bass.

New England Resource Center for Higher Education. (n.d.) Definition of engaged scholarship. Retrieved from http://www.nerche.org/index.php?option=com_content&view=article&id=265&cati=28

Perna, L. W. (Ed.). (in press). *Advancing equity, inclusiveness and social change in higher education: How scholars connect research, advocacy, and policy*. Baltimore, MD: Johns Hopkins University Press.

Rawls, J. (2009). *A theory of justice* (Rev. ed.). Cambridge, MA: Harvard University Press.

Shaker, G. G. (Ed.). (2015). *Faculty work and the public good: Philanthropy engagement and academic professionalism*. New York, NY: Teachers College Press.

Small, H. (Ed.). (2008). *The public intellectual*. Hoboken, NJ: Blackwell.

Snow, C. E. (2015). 2014 Wallace Foundation distinguished lecture—rigor and realism: Doing educational science in the real world. *Educational Researcher, 44*, 460–466.

Taylor, S. M., & Ochocka, J. (2017). Advancing community-based research in Canada. *International Journal of Knowledge-Based Development, 8*, 183–200.

USC Rossier School of Education. (n.d.). *The equity scorecard: Balancing educational outcomes*. Retrieved from rossier.usc.edu/the-equity-scorecard-balancing-educational-outcomes

Van de Ven, A. H. (2007). *Engaged scholarship: A guide for organizational and social research*. Oxford, England: Oxford University Press.

2

THE MANY FACES OF PUBLIC SCHOLARSHIP

Opportunities, Lessons Learned, and Challenges Encountered From the Journey of a Public Scholar

Adrianna Kezar

In chapter 1, we defined *public scholarship* and described why it is important. In this chapter, I describe my own journey as a public scholar as a vehicle to demonstrate the various approaches to public scholarship. More detailed examples of these approaches are provided in the chapters in part two. By highlighting several different modes of public scholarship in a single career, I hope to demonstrate how scholars can evolve over time, how different projects may lend themselves to different forms of public scholarship, and how different points in one's career provide different opportunities to engage in public scholarship. Serendipity and opportunities presenting themselves can also play an important role in the evolution of a public scholar. At times, a more formal version of public scholarship, like a network improvement community model, works best in one project, but in another, the researcher may decide a less formal partnership is best.

In addition to discussing different modes of public scholarship, I review lessons learned along the way that can assist other scholars as they consider doing this type of work. I also note ethical dilemmas, challenges, and the ways I navigated each. I write about some challenges particular to instances of public scholarship in the sections where I describe the ways I have acted as a public scholar, and I also summarize some key challenges that cut across the examples of public scholarship I have engaged in over the course of my career.

Writing for and Presenting to Practitioner Audiences

My first work as a public scholar focused on translating higher education research for the general public through my role as director of the Educational Resources Information Center (ERIC), a nationwide information network on higher education. One of my first endeavors was developing a guide titled *The Path to College: Making the Choices That Are Right for You* (Kezar, 1997), aimed at parents, students, and community groups—my publics. I decided it would be a helpful resource if I summarized the research on college choice and transition to help inform students, counselors, and parents because at the time college access was a growing national concern. Groups that exist today to provide information about college access simply did not exist then. College guides were available if you paid for them, and their advice was not research based. I thought a guide that was rooted in research would be an indispensable resource, and the staff at the U.S. Department of Education agreed. With their support and funding, we printed and disseminated 10,000 copies of the guide, which I thought was amazing. This was much more than the typical academic book that averages about 2,000 readers or journal articles whose readers range in the hundreds. I thought I had identified an important and large public to inform about the good research being conducted in higher education. But I had no idea there would be such a thirst for our scholarship when written in an accessible and jargon-free way. A staff member from the U.S. Department of Education later contacted me and said it wanted to print 50,000 more guides, and then another 50,000; ultimately more than 300,000 guides were printed. Eventually the money ran out, and the guide was made available online. It is sad to say that one of my first publications was my most widely read publication, but I am sure it is the truth.

I learned from this experience how valuable our research is to people if we can package it in ways our publics can access. Shortly after the publication of *The Path to College*, I was stopped by a staff member at the American Council on Education who said, "This guide is unlike anything I have ever seen related to college access—it is research based. It tells about the complexity of higher education college choice, but without making it seem complex." I learned that to be an effective public scholar, we have to be willing to address our language, formats, and the ways we describe and package our research with our audiences in mind.

My next major lesson in public scholarship relates to the value of obtaining feedback from your publics as a way to help develop more instructive and useful research applicable to a wide and inclusive range of audiences. For example, many church groups were calling ERIC to ask for more copies of

The Pathway to College. Interestingly, many of these groups were also eager to offer their advice on the guide, such as the following, which I received in a letter from a church group:

> Thank you so much for producing this informative college guide. We put them out for our Sunday school group and they went immediately and we would like more copies. If you are revising or reprinting, it would help to have different student voices represented. (Anonymous, personal communication, 1998)

Former students who worked at ERIC offered me advice from the student perspective, but they were middle-class White students who did not represent the diversity of experiences I described in the guide. The guide did not feature advice from anyone at community colleges or from low-income students, for example. It is one thing to talk about issues for disabled students or students of color in a report like this, but it is another thing to showcase their college-going experiences. I realized then that had I sent a draft of the guide to some of the communities and stakeholders I was aiming to help in advance, I could have made sure that the stories told were inclusive of all type of students. This echoes the points made in chapter 1, advocating for greater breadth, diversity, and richness, which can be achieved in public scholarship when many voices are included.

My work at ERIC also lead to the development of a project and book titled *Moving Beyond the Gap Between Research and Practice in Higher Education* (Kezar & Eckel, 2000), which was based on a research study I conducted at ERIC that addressed what it might mean to be a public scholar. I conducted focus groups with the research stakeholders I identified, including national higher education organizations, policymakers, and administrators. A couple of findings really struck me. Mirroring what Keller (1985) had noted three decades before, individuals in the focus groups did not find our research in higher education accessible in terms of language (e.g., too much jargon and not succinct enough), formats (e.g., they do not read journal articles, few scholars write for general public audiences), or objectives (e.g., work includes mostly theoretical or literature insights, the contribution of research to practice or policy was opaque). This reinforced my belief in the need for scholars to attend to language, format, and objectives. Still, I also understood that scholars are not trained in graduate school to write in more accessible formats, which often makes it a difficult challenge to overcome.

Despite the challenge, it is possible and imperative for the public scholar to make a serious effort to broaden the reach and accessibility of scholarship to achieve a wider readership and bring more stakeholders into the fold.

For instance, one area I know many scholars struggle with (and perhaps question whether it is possible) is making ideas from critical theory, postmodernism, or constructivism accessible to lay people. I have striven to make concepts of power, privilege, racism, intersectionality, inequality, neoliberalism, and hierarchy accessible to any audience. My book about low-income students (Kezar, 2010) aimed at campus staff used poststructuralism as a conceptual guide, but it did not use the complex jargon of poststructuralism. It was a conscious undertaking on my part to accomplish my objectives as a public scholar. Many campus staff members have thanked me for translating these complex ideas and making the often difficult concepts of agency, deconstruction, local power dynamics, history, and embedded relational power easy to understand (i.e., accessible).

Conducting the research study for Kezar and Eckel (2000) at ERIC was an influential force in my development as a public scholar, and it helped reshape my future direction and commitments. I committed to writing a practitioner article for every journal article I wrote, a compendium piece that I could ensure would be read by the publics I was conducting the research for. I have mostly kept true to this commitment my entire career with an extensive publishing record in practitioner magazines such as *About Campus, Diverse, Change, Academe, Liberal Education, Trusteeship, The Presidency, NASPA magazine*; dozens of newsletters such as the *League of Innovation*; and more recently, blogs and other online media. I intentionally try to write for very different audiences so that my work on supporting low-income students, for example, is read by a range of relevant publics including community college administrators, trustees, policymakers, Federal TRIO Programs staff, and parents.

So 20 years ago, my first major venture into public scholarship consisted of translating our research in higher education for various practitioners and policy audiences. By publishing in venues they read, we obtain direct access to publics that make decisions and create policies in higher education. We open a dialogue with these publics that typically also leads to invitations to conference presentations and to further work with groups on matters related to the ideas we share from our research in accessible ways. We open the door to ongoing exchanges that help these publics rethink and inform their perspectives in their own work. I have also found that these exchanges help me to learn enormously by redirecting my research agenda and approach over the years and improving my interpretation of results in my studies. For example, in exchanges with adjunct faculty I have come to a deeper understanding of their day-to-day working conditions, and in discussions with administrators, I have come to understand their struggle to reprioritize funding to support faculty.

Forming Partnerships With Groups on Research and Research Translation

Another way I have been a public scholar is through partnerships and work with national organizations and groups to design, disseminate, present, and implement my research findings. Although this is maybe not something you can do in your first years as a scholar the same way you can write for practitioner audiences, it is the type of public engagement that can be fairly accessible early in your career through networking or attending conferences for national organizations. I regularly present papers at national conferences and meetings, serve on advisory boards for organizations, help with projects for these organizations, and publish my scholarship with them. These opportunities were often a direct result of the accessible writing I was doing. I have worked with various groups spanning policy, practice, and consulting, and I have worked with nongovernmental agencies and for-profit organizations. I have chosen to work with powerful groups ranging from those that represent presidents and boards to organizations that support marginalized voices such as the TRIO Clearinghouse on Educational Opportunity; the New Faculty Majority, a group that represents adjunct faculty; and the Student Aid Alliance, which is a grassroots student advocacy group. This partnership work started early in my career as director of the ERIC clearinghouse where I regularly worked with higher education organizations to provide them with translational documents of our research. For example, one of the regular requests we had at ERIC was for key resources listing research written for practitioner audiences.

Another lesson I learned working with practitioners is the power of diagrams, charts, pictures, stories, and videos to capture and communicate my work. Adopting tools from other modes of communication in cinema, journalism, or public policy can be helpful in communicating our research messages in higher education. In my work with the Delphi Project on the Changing Faculty and Student Success (which I describe later), I used infographics as a helpful tool to digest and communicate the research and trends about adjunct faculty. Kezar and Maxey (2013) features a menu-based option using dollar signs like a restaurant guide to designate the cost associated with providing support for non-tenure-track faculty. This guide is quite popular with administrators and faculty for providing ways to support non-tenure-track faculty (NTTF). But I have struggled over the years to create tools and resources that capture the essence of my research. If it were not for the brilliance of my coauthors, I am sure my public outreach efforts would have faltered. So we need to learn to work in partnership with others who possess the relevant communication and framing skills and bring them into our projects to complement the work we do ourselves. We can be partners with other professionals who are more experienced in visual modes to ensure our work is accessible to our audiences. This is yet another area where we could use more skill development in graduate school.

Working on Our Own Campuses and in Local Contexts

Another way I have worked as a public scholar is by providing leadership at my own campus on critical issues like supporting diverse students or adjunct faculty. Often we can engage publics locally on our own campuses or in or neighborhoods and towns. By involving our local communities, we often have the most readily available context for implementing and gaining the public's interest in our research ideas. For many readers, this is the first logical and most direct place to achieve local involvement. The advantage, of course, is that changes at the local level are often the most easily accomplished and are where we have the most control and potential. Furthermore, this is an easy place to begin playing a public role early in one's career; I began this work as an assistant professor. Given that our research is on higher education, we are often able to implement our ideas locally.

In one community example, I worked with a local chapter of the National Urban League on a project called Neighborhood Works. The project examined ways that Los Angeles neighborhoods characterized by high unemployment, violence, and low educational achievement could be systematically altered by addressing multifaceted issues of safety, health care, employment, and education simultaneously. Over time, the project became embroiled in local politics and mired in challenges that led to its dissolution.

In an example from higher education, I served for the past 10 years on our university senate subcommittee on NTTF and had a term as chair of our faculty council in our school of education. While chair of the faculty council, I advocated for the right of NTTF members to attend meetings and be part of the life of the college. I presented research on the benefits of such a move, and eventually our school became a much more inclusive environment. Although I was able to use our research to make changes for NTTF at our university and in the school of education, it came with a political cost. Some senior faculty disagreed with this stance, and I knew for years they were not happy with the changes or with me. As our school has moved to online approaches to learning and more standardized curricula offered largely by adjuncts, I have questioned our sheer growth, quality of learning experience for students, and ability of the faculty we hire to provide enough support for students, again based on research across these areas. But this has not put me in good favor with our leadership.

I learned that it is harder to avoid politics and power in one's local context compared with other settings. So as we act on our ideas within our communities, we risk career stability and progression, potentially in the form of promotion, salary raises, tenure, contract renewal, colleague support, and the like. But we also have to balance this with being true to our own views and values. I was able to leverage my tenured status to take bold action, so I did not approach this type of work when I was pretenure. Thus, one's career stage is important to consider if the work challenges institutional norms.

Working With the Media

I have also worked with various media outlets to discuss my research and engage the public, another venture into public scholarship. The use of blogging and social media can be started early in your career, and as your expertise builds, opportunities for working with newspapers, radio, and TV will follow. I probably speak to a journalist every week, and each year I am invited to appear on several radio and television shows. Working with media is a way to reach the general public and broadly shape views and, perhaps, ultimately inform decisions. I think opportunities for this type of public scholarship are largely understood through working with and informing media personnel, and engagement with public debates. However, I think the challenges of working with the media and the kinds of lessons I have learned from doing so are not well understood.

There are multiple challenges to doing this kind of work. Journalists have no problem talking to you for an hour and deciding not to do the story, or they may decide to use it only as background. They easily distort or change your intended meaning, and they almost never send anything back so you can check the accuracy. So far, I must admit, compared to other scholars I have spoken with, I have had few major distortions that made me wary of speaking to reporters, but this is a very real challenge. I have learned that if you develop relationships with media they are more likely to fairly represent you. Like in life, once trust is developed, individuals are loathe to destroy it. Making yourself a valuable resource to media is a way to develop those relationships. I often get back to reporters at 6:00 p.m. on a Friday when they are on a deadline and they appreciate knowing I am working late for them. One way to avoid potential distortion is writing opinion pieces. It can be an excellent way to help communicate your research findings in your own voice, but they are very hard to get published. Any colleague who has written one will tell you they can take as long to write as a journal article and require a real art to succinctly communicate complex research ideas.

The media is typically interested in stories that are sensational in some way or focus on polarized issues and will likely ignore research that doesn't fit into this paradigm. Therefore, it is often a difficult resource for disseminating ideas from your research. My research on adjuncts fits well into the polarized narratives (administrators versus faculty), so journalists are interested in this area of my research agenda but not the rest of my work. So in reality, the media has been quite a limited approach for my overall research agenda and will be for others unless your work fits the narrow parameters of the current journalistic paradigm. A lesson learned is that you need to realize when the media can work for your topic and when it might be better to work with organizations or communities that have better access to the publics you want to communicate with.

Of course, blogs allow any scholar to publish an opinion and control the message, but most are not widely read. Still, blogs are an important area for scholars to consider, particularly through partnerships with other organizations or by writing for the blogs of other groups; these are possibilities to increase readership for your scholarship. I also realize that social media provides immense possibilities for public scholarship. Although I have written blogs and I have websites for my research, I have not tapped into the full power of social media as many other scholars in our field have. One of the most exciting trends I have seen in recent years is the strategic and thoughtful use of social media by scholars to communicate their research, projects, and informed views. That is why several chapters in this volume focus on social media as an important venue for the future of public scholarship, a tool that was not readily available for most of my career.

Teaching and Training

I serve as a faculty member for several national academies, seminars, and workshops. These opportunities provide me with the ability to bring my research to leaders and campus change agents across the country. The examples of teaching, training, and consulting that I describe next are typically practices for later in your career as you have become better known for your expertise. For example, I speak every year at the Higher Education Research Institute's Diversity Research Institute. I address 75 leaders who are advancing diversity agendas on college campuses and help them consider the best approaches to change, navigate politics, and achieve acceptance for their ideas. I also speak annually at the Western Association of Schools and Colleges's (WASC) Assessment Leadership Academy where about 50 leaders implementing assessment on campuses gather for a year-long seminar to become change agents. I have also been a regular speaker at the Higher Education Resource Services Summer Institute for women leaders usually aspiring to presidencies or provost roles. I helped create and taught in the now defunct National Association for Women in Higher Education's Emerging Woman Leader's Institute. This institute was designed specifically to target underrepresented women and women from sectors such as community colleges or institutions serving underrepresented populations like historically Black colleges and universities, which are often overlooked for leadership positions and development. In almost all these settings, I discuss my research on change, and over the years I have worked with thousands of change agents in higher education, bringing them advice from my research to guide their own work.

This has been some of the most rewarding work I have done. Although it is more difficult to see the direct impact or results of this work, the engagement and interest in your research are authentic as is the possibility for more direct use of your research. Also, in these settings, there is a mutuality that can serve to create learning for teacher and participant, setting the stage for long-lasting relationships. For example, participants in the training setting are typically leaders in the field of higher education who bring critical knowledge of campus challenges. I often have participants who share a passion for diversity, equity, new teaching approaches, or community engagement leading to the formation of long-term and mutually sustaining relationships. Forging these kinds of networks is important for influencing policy and practice, and training and teaching opportunities can help create a large and diverse network capable of broadening the reach of your public scholarship. Through the networks created by these training opportunities, I have been asked to consult, evaluate, present, be a partner, and conduct research.

Consulting

Another way one can be a public scholar is to consult with or advise campuses or higher education organizations. By working directly with campus administrators, I have helped implement new curricula, more inclusive practices to support underrepresented minorities, policies to support hiring more scholars of color, and strategies that help support first-generation college students. By working directly with campuses or on national projects aimed at supporting campuses, I directly implement my research findings. Not all research areas lend themselves to consulting. My work on organizational leadership, student success, and change make such possibilities more likely, so this avenue may not be as open to all scholars. In representing my partnerships, which I write for and present to higher education publics, I also learn a tremendous amount by consulting work with campuses, and I have developed a better understanding of challenges on the ground. A lesson I have learned in consulting is to try to determine if the interest in change is authentic among groups that contact you. Often consultants can be brought in to work on untenable situations, or they serve as window dressing to make it appear that a leader is addressing an issue but has no real interest in undertaking the research. By asking questions up front, I have been able to make better choices about spending time with institutions authentically interested in and willing to engage in change.

A challenge with consulting that has emerged for me is equity related to sharing my expertise. Usually wealthier institutions are able to hire consultants to connect with and support them. Over the years, as more groups have contacted me for consulting, I have begun to consider the pro bono role I should play for organizations unable to pay for me to help them translate my research for their purposes. Otherwise, you run into the problem of having your research only support those publics that can pay for it. Thus, I have worked with many groups for free. Because this option is not more apparent, I do wonder how many groups have not contacted me over the years because they were unaware that I accepted pro bono work. What responsibility do we have for making our expertise more transparently available to groups that have less privilege? Without a conscious consideration of this issue, we may be providing consultation in inequitable ways, which works against the fundamental character of public scholarship as we have defined it in this book.

National Leadership and Service

Another way to play a role as a public scholar is by taking a leadership or service role that uses your research knowledge. For example, I was recently a commissioner for WASC. In the past, I have served as a fellow for the Teachers Insurance and Annuity Association of America–College Retirement Equity Fund Institute, served on panels for the National Academy of Sciences, and have been a member of the Board of Visitors for the National Science Foundation. I have also worked with foundations such as Bill & Melinda Gates, Lumina, Alfred P. Sloan, Spencer, and Teagle, helping advise them on funding, program direction, and evaluation. Through national service, you work with organizations that are influential and can dramatically shape policy and practice. Most likely this type of service and leadership are roles played later in your career. But like consulting, there may not be an authentic interest in change, and your role can sometimes also be window dressing. Additionally, an organization may be so committed to a line of thinking that its administrators are unwilling to deeply apply your work or perspective.

In one example, WASC administrators asked me to serve as commissioner based on my knowledge about change processes, quality assurance, and the changing role of faculty. I have had the opportunity to present my research to the commission about the problems of the changing faculty, particularly the increase in number and types of adjuncts and their poor working conditions. If I had not agreed to take this role, I could not have obtained access to WASC and its many influential leaders (mostly college presidents) and policymakers. WASC leaders have asked me to present papers at retreats and conduct workshops with presidents, board members, and academic leaders such as provosts about the changing face of faculty. Yet, I have faced some challenges here as well. As a commissioner, I have certain authority and have to be careful how it is used. I have been asked by several faculty unions to make public comments rebuking accreditation agencies' stance on faculty and the agencies' loosening standards. I have made such public comments to the media because I truly do believe accreditors need a higher standard and need to be more supportive of faculty to ensure quality. My research suggests academic quality and student outcomes are negatively affected by changes to the composition of the faculty (e.g., a majority of adjuncts), but when you serve in a leadership role, you also have to think about the consequences. Accreditors are under tremendous scrutiny from Congress, and the House Committee on Education and the Workforce is floating proposals to change or eradicate accreditation agencies. I also know from research the important role that accreditation has historically played in improving quality in higher education and supporting institutional learning and improvement. Therefore, when you speak out and voice your opinion as a leader, you have to balance it with consequences. It would be tragic if my comments were used to undermine the legitimacy of the accreditation process. Therefore, in leadership roles you may face conflicts among your research and positions and those of the groups you are leading and serving.

Policy Forums

We can also serve as public scholars by presenting papers in political and policy forums. I recently had the opportunity to make a presentation to a congressional committee about adjunct faculty working conditions. In giving testimony, scholars are able to have a direct impact on legislators' views and on drafting and revising policies that can affect thousands and often millions of individuals. Earlier in my career, I conducted a policy study of the federal Individual Development Accounts (IDAs) program, and my findings suggested that the only way to support low-income students well through this policy, which provides students with additional financial support and financial literacy training, would be to make changes to the Higher Education Act of 1965 during its 2013 reauthorization. Students were essentially penalized for saving money for college, given the language on financial aid in 2006 through 2009. I met with dozens of key people who helped me to appreciate the difficulty of altering the language, partly because the U.S. Department of Housing and Urban Development, which created the IDA policy, did not work closely with the U.S. Department of Education, which facilitated the reauthorization. I also did not have the relationships in the various government agencies to effect this change. I even had the support of major national higher education organizations, but making this a priority given other issues on the table for reauthorization was difficult. I did learn from this experience that policy, particularly at the state and national levels, are vexing and complex arenas to make changes.

I am still new to the policy arena, and as I do little direct policy-related research, this may not be a major avenue for me as a public scholar. As I have tried to emphasize, our research can direct us to different forms of public scholarship. Those doing research on financial aid, access, and affirmative action will certainly find that policy is a more natural avenue for their outreach. But as I do my work I continue to consider the question of whether there is a local, state, or federal form of outreach I might be conducting to get my research results to the right audiences. I encourage readers to ask these questions as well.

Bringing These Approaches Together: Community-Based Research Paradigm

In recent years, I have begun to use many of these aforementioned approaches all at the same time to maximize impact and to work within the participatory research paradigm we presented in chapter 1. As I have become more involved in being a public scholar, I have embedded my research more into methods that directly link me to practitioners and policymakers. It may be easier to bring together multiple avenues of public scholarship later in your career as you build expertise working in certain venues and larger networks.

About 5 years ago, I started the Delphi Project on the Changing Faculty and Student Success (see www.thechangingfaculty.org) by inviting more than 50 policy-making, practitioner, and professional organizations; unions; non-tenure-track advocacy groups; and students and disciplinary societies to participate in a discussion about faculty roles. Over the years, I have learned the value of bringing in as many diverse voices as possible to inform my research.

The project was developed with and from a diverse group of stakeholders focused on faculty roles, ranging from the more grassroots to the highest and most powerful levels. I should thank Dan Maxey for his work on the Delphi Project in its first four years. We designed the research and project together using a community-based action research format, which is another form of public scholarship. Together, all the stakeholders formed the research study, project directions, and have continued working as a network for the past five years. They have continued their involvement in three different studies related to the changing faculty including the most recent survey study about new faculty models called the professoriate reconsidered (Kezar, Maxey, & Holcombe, 2015). The partners also ask me to speak and write for their stakeholder groups.

I am a partner with the Association of American Colleges & Universities (AAC&U) to provide some visibility, thought partnership, and dissemination for the research. I make presentations each year at the AAC&U conference and publish in the AAC&U's various outlets related to the project. Through partnerships with these national associations and groups, we have published 45 practitioner- and policy-based articles and opinion pieces about the challenges facing NTTFs and the need for new faculty models. In addition to the articles, we created resources and tools aimed at helping campuses better support NTTFs. These tools were developed through retreats with various stakeholder groups that discussed what would be most useful to help reshape campus policies; the stakeholder groups have also actively reviewed materials and resources that emerged from the project.

I have testified before congressional subcommittees on behalf of the New Faculty Majority and spoken in various state policy forums. I regularly contact media related to our research results and have been featured in *Inside Higher Education, The Chronicle of Higher Education, New York Times, Wall Street Journal,* and many local papers. Dan Maxey, my colleague in this work, used Twitter to get the word out about our work and to encourage more dialogue on adjuncts and new faculty models. As I noted earlier, my own campus is now using our work to redesign our policies related to NTTFs. I have several national leadership roles working in support of addressing the changing faculty, such as my WASC commissioner role in which I am actively working to change accreditation standards and policies related to faculty.

Through my engagement with policymakers, national organizations, unions, adjunct faculty, and sometimes individual campuses, I have helped reshape state and institutional policies related to NTTFs affecting hundreds of campuses so far and, I hope, thousands in the near future.

Different Career Stages and Different Projects Lead to Different Possibilities

Over my career trajectory or stages, I have taken different avenues to engage in public scholarship, some of which (e.g., national leadership or consulting) required more experience and expertise, whereas others were available to me at the beginning of my career (e.g., writing for practitioners, forming partnerships with organizations, or being active in my local campus context).

Some projects lent themselves to particular approaches, such as the federal IDA policy I was studying and working on lent itself to policy work; the work on change through consulting, advising foundations, and training; the work on low-income students through forming partnerships with national organizations; my work with adjuncts by working with the media; and my work with community engagement leading to work and leadership on my own campus. Because there are lessons to learn across each of these avenues for public scholarship, there is a value to specializing in areas that best serve the issue you are focused on as long as these avenues can support diverse stakeholders. One meta lesson I have learned is that you improve in your work in each of these areas over time—you become a better consultant, a better writer for media or practice, and a better research partner or policy advocate as you practice. Engaging in the work of public scholarship on financial aid might seem best approached through policy. However, it might be that working in partnership with groups that support marginalized voices such as the Student Aid Alliance could also be an important avenue so that your public scholarship can include the voices of students who can be empowered through your research. My advice is to learn deeply a set of strategies for public scholarship but to think expansively enough so that you consider the diverse and marginalized voices that often go unheard.

Challenges for Public Scholarship

I do not mean to suggest that this work is without challenges and struggles, some which have already been mentioned. I also want to note that challenges are not inherently bad and often lead to some of the most important lessons learned. It is critical that through this work you address and recognize challenges and learn lessons that help to do this work better over time. Next, I discuss a few challenges in depth that have cut across my work in public scholarship.

Simplifying and Removing Nuance

I have often received feedback on my writing and presentations of research to simplify my message, shorten and delete important details, and make the ideas seem a bit more linear. Take my research on change: All of it points to the impact of context and culture; to iterative, nonlinear change processes; to customizing and designing unique strategies; to the variation that exists for change agents based on their power and authority, to name a few. Those messages typically did not resonate with audiences.

For example, in a review of my book, *How Colleges Change* (Kezar, 2013), a practitioner noted a desire for more direct advice, concreteness, and less balance in my work between theory and practice. Over time, I grappled with offering simpler change approaches and merely sprinkling in culture and emphasizing the importance of customizing approaches and local contexts. I often leaned on simpler rubrics like Bolman and Deal's (2003) four frames, which leaders found so much easier to understand. So I found myself trying to connect with and engage my public by altering my message, sometimes more than I wanted to, so I could be heard. There is nothing wrongheaded with this advice, yet I often was not able to stay true to my research findings. I have found over time, though, that I have reshaped the dialogue, and change agents are increasingly open to more complex models of change. Although it may take time for your publics to be open to your message, I learned it may not be bad to meet them halfway for a while to keep the lines of communication open and to create a bridge for understanding. So even the most basic level of translating research for practitioners presented challenges.

Power and Politics

As I evolved to working more directly with organizations, the challenges became more political and complex. I have been working in partnership with the AAC&U, and our report, "Adapting by Design," included critiques of the adjunct model as well as the tenure-track model (Kezar & Maxey, 2015). The AAC&U asked us to take out these critiques of tenure and a discussion on Western Governors University, which we used as an example of new faculty models. Instead, we chose to publish the document without the changes and without the AAC&U's endorsement so we could maintain our message. Although I am not against tenure, I felt it would be disingenuous to leave out legitimate existing criticisms of it. As a partner with groups, you might be asked to alter your research and findings to suit their boards or to avoid upsetting publics they work with. By not leveraging our partnership with the AAC&U, however, we lost out on exposure and visibility for our ideas. There are always hard choices that need to be made. Additionally, as I note in the section on working with and providing leadership in your local context, you can experience power conditions that require you to examine the costs of continuing this work, such as losing your job or promotion opportunities.

Then there is the issue of power and politics in our findings. Many practitioners shy away from direct discussion of the political nature of our campuses and prefer to view them as rational entities. Many times my research has demonstrated negative power dynamics, particularly my work on grassroots leadership, and this is something many practitioners ask me to downplay when presenting my results. But I try to create a dissonance and ask them to challenge themselves and their audiences. Sometimes we need to make our publics uncomfortable so they can learn and develop too.

Taking a Position With Mixed or Nuanced Findings: Altering for Audience Clarity

In recent years I have been an advocate for faculty off the tenure track, mostly adjuncts who are paid roughly $24,000 a year on average, have no benefits, are excluded from the professional community, are unable to be part of decision-making, are isolated, and live with working conditions that make it extremely hard for them to be successful. I have summarized research to advocate on their behalf. Truth be told, the research picture is not as clear as I present it, and in higher education more generally, often it is not. One position to take is if the research is not clear, do not say anything. But over the past 20 years of observing the trends, I see that research just cannot document effectively enough how the growth of adjuncts is damaging our enterprise. Piecing together the evidence and designing studies that can show this is not often possible. Our colleagues across the country have developed some compelling evidence suggestive of problems, but it is certainly not definitive. However, if I speak to administrators, policymakers, or the media and say—like a typical academic—"Well, the research is mixed in some areas, in others there are some minimal negative impacts, and still other data trends are indicative of some potential problems," they will just not listen. But I do not present that framing of the research. Admittedly, I present less complex and nuanced pictures. I note there are demonstrated negative impacts on student outcomes from more courses being taken with adjuncts, and I veer from the nuanced picture of the data. When I was asked to appear before a congressional committee about NTTF issues and their impact on student learning, I presented a couple of bullet points that made the issue seem fairly definitive as it relates to student learning.

I am okay with my choice, but I am also okay with people questioning my decision. A very nuanced discussion was not understandable in that context of testifying before a congressional committee, and I also knew the research was unable to demonstrate the full problem. I feel deep down that if the research was perfect, it could paint the picture that I feel is true, that the expansion of adjunct faculty has affected student access to mentors, made learning less engaging for first-generation students who need engagement the most, and that our institutions suffer because of fewer dedicated faculty serving on committees and who can be involved in governance, drive curricular and pedagogical reform, nurture student success, and perform basic tasks like writing recommendations. But research is imperfect, and it is not always able to provide insights on issues. Because of this, most researchers would say they cannot comment on areas where they cannot come up with research to argue a specific policy. But I worry that so many important issues will be left without being informed by our research and insights, even if they are imperfect, and we have to shave away some of the nuances to make it more understandable.

Given my concerns about practitioners oversimplifying the research on change, clearly there are some inconsistencies in my thinking. I am fine with presenting research on NTTFs that glosses over nuance in favor of cleaner, more simplified messages, but I am worried with oversimplified models of change. So, as I said, working in this space, one has to wrestle with questions of what is right and where lockstep answers may not be available. In wrestling with these issues, I ask myself: What is in the service of the public good, and what is socially just?

Rewards Structure

Most will say the challenges I have noted skirt the largest challenge to being a public scholar; that is, this type of research is not rewarded in our current promotion and tenure systems. I went through those systems and still maintained a role as a public scholar, and honestly I never felt pressure that this role compromised my possibilities for tenure or promotion. I am a person with some privilege, I am White and heterosexual, so I speak from that positionality. It is likely that this work is riskier for faculty of color or members of oppressed groups. Still, I think these partnerships and engagement can lead to more opportunities for funding and collecting research. Once you begin learning to write in more accessible ways and formats, the learning curve is much lower. And yes, we need to ensure that promotion and tenure do not get in the way of this obligation, and certainly it is necessary to consider changing campus policies to embrace new standards. But I often feel senior faculty overexaggerate the barrier of promotion and tenure, paralyzing scholars who want to do this work. I hope to present a case for agency that also acknowledges the risk for some scholars. It is worth noting that some research universities are beginning to emphasize consequential and translational research in promotion processes. Moreover, many campus administrators have long viewed their institutions as having a community-engaged mission that aligns well with public scholarship.

Conclusion

Public scholarship provides the opportunity to take our research into communities we care about in a multitude of ways, reshaping policy and practice. It is certainly not new and has had many names over the years, for example, engaged and applied scholarship (Boyer, 1996). I do not want us to consider this as just another form of scholarship, but instead I suggest that everyone is obligated to the public good and to being a public scholar. To not become involved is a morally questionable stance in a field like education.

I found my way to public scholarship only by happenstance, starting off directly in the role of public engagement through ERIC. Had I not, nothing in my graduate experience would have prepared me for this role. I am encouraged by younger scholars and their activity on social media that is more systematically connecting them to the public and their commitment to social justice. We need to incorporate graduate training opportunities to help students become public scholars and develop the habits of mind that will carry them through their scholarly ventures. We also need to provide information, like what is contained in this book, to help promote the public scholarship mind-set among emerging and established researchers.

I hope I have intrigued you enough to consider ways you might be a public scholar, or for those already playing this role, to consider new ways of approaching public scholarship. I also hope I have challenged us as a field to consider what our obligation is to the public good and our diverse democracy. I want to end with the following comment from Dewey:

> The only way to prepare for social life is to engage in social life. To form habits of social usefulness and serviceableness apart from any direct social need and motive, apart from any existing social situation, is, to the letter, teaching the child to swim by going through motions outside of the water. (as cited in Hickman & Alexander, 1998, p. 248)

Our research should be directly engaged in the social lives we are trying to shape and the publics we are hoping to benefit and transform. As Dewey encourages us, let's jump in the water!

References

Bolman, L. G., & Deal, T. E. (2003). *Reframing organizations: Artistry, choice, and leadership*. Hoboken, NJ: Wiley.

Hickman, L. A., & Alexander, T. M. (Eds.). (1998). *The essential Dewey*. Bloomington, IN: Indiana University Press.

Keller, G. (1985). Trees without fruit: The problem with research about higher education. *Change, 17*(1), 7–10.

Kezar, A. (Ed.). (1997). *The path to college: An analysis of research and literature.* Retrieved from https://archive.org/details/ERIC_ED413886

Kezar, A. (Ed.). (2010). *Recognizing and serving low-income students in postsecondary education: An examination of institutional policies, practices, and culture.* New York, NY: Routledge.

Kezar, A. (2013). *How colleges change: Understanding, leading, and enacting change.* New York, NY: Routledge.

Kezar, A., & Eckel, P. (Eds.). (2000). *Moving beyond the gap between research and practice in higher education.* San Francisco, CA: Jossey-Bass.

Kezar, A., & Maxey, D. (2013). *Dispelling the myth: Ways to pay for support for non-tenure track faculty.* Los Angeles, CA: Pullias Center for Higher Education and Changing Faculty and Student Success.

Kezar, A., & Maxey, D. (2015). *Adapting by design: Redesigning faculty roles for the 21st century.* Los Angeles. CA: Pullias Center, Association for American Colleges & Universities.

Kezar, A., Maxey, D., & Holcombe, E. (2015). *The professoriate reconsidered: Stakeholder views of new faculty models.* New York, NY: TIAA-CREF Research Institute.

3

CULTIVATING ETHICAL MINDFULNESS

Using an Activity Theory Framework to Address Ethical Dilemmas in Public Scholarship

Cecile H. Sam and Jarrett T. Gupton

Public scholarship, with its goal of supporting an equitable, diverse democracy through social justice (Kezar, Kitchen, & Drivalas, 2017) is one of the ways higher education institutions can meet their responsibility to contribute to the public good (Kezar, Chambers, & Burkhardt, 2005; Shaker, 2015). Although the goal of public scholarship may be grounded in the idea of the ethical good, it does not ensure that the decisions we make as researchers engaged in public scholarship will always be ethical or good. Because much of research involves working with numerous stakeholders with varying interests and degrees of privilege, the potential for ethical complexity is abundant. It is important to try to maintain ethical integrity throughout the process of public scholarship, lest we undermine our own intended goals and the trust between scholar and stakeholders. Some of the choices we face will be simple (although perhaps not easy), for example, choosing to do what is morally right over what is morally wrong. Meanwhile, other choices will have no perfect solution, and some ethical principle will be compromised (Cooper, 2012).

As the academy continues to produce and socialize more scholars, some who will choose to become engaged in public scholarship, we have to be thoughtful about the ethical implications of our work and the precedents we set. One way to be more cognizant of the ethical dimensions of scholarship is through ethical mindfulness, a reflective practice that attunes the researcher to the potential ethical decisions that may arise during the public scholarship process (Guillemin & Gillam, 2015). The purpose of this chapter is to orient academics toward ethical mindfulness in their public scholarship and to provide examples from the field. Rather than seeking to provide definitive answers, we argue that the real bulk of the work happens when scholars start asking the right questions.

The choices we make as public scholars have important consequences. First, thoughtless decisions can leave the door open for potential harms that may undermine the very good we are trying to do. These harms can take the form of replicating similar structures of oppression, continuing the disenfranchisement of marginalized groups, or perpetuating dominant social narratives. Harms also include undermining the groundwork of trust that exists between the researcher and stakeholders. Second, the ethical manner in which leaders in public scholarship conduct their work establishes expectations for others in the field. Research indicates that people who have ethical role models in their career tend to be ethical role models themselves (Brown & Treviño, 2006). Third, researchers run the risk of failing to learn from prior experience if they are not reflective in their practice. Even if past decisions were appropriate in one context, it may not follow that they would be appropriate in another.

In what follows, we discuss ways to integrate ethical mindfulness into the process of public scholarship. Further, we suggest ways to deal with ethical dilemmas that may occur. We close with a discussion on the need to be courageous when endeavoring in the work.

Procedural Ethics and Ethics in Practice

Before we examine the ethics of public scholarship, we want to acknowledge the difference between procedural ethics and ethics in practice (Guillemin & Gillam, 2004; Kubanyiova, 2008). Procedural ethics are formalized external codes of ethics that usually entail an approval process to conduct research or a professional code of ethics (Guillemin & Gillam, 2004). For researchers, the internal review board (IRB) approval process serves in this role of procedural ethics, as do the codes of ethics from professional organizations like the American Association of University Professors. The IRB focuses on obtaining consent, maximizing benefits while minimizing harm, and equitable selection. Procedural ethics are necessary because they provide a minimum threshold to determine if decisions are unethical rather than if they reflect the highest ethical standard, a distinction similar to the difference between do no harm and do good. In terms of public scholarship, procedural ethics speak in some part to a diverse democracy and social justice but do not provide specifics about the relationships we build and maintain through the process. It does not address how we determine which topics to study or how we interact with those in our community. Procedural ethics do not cover ethics in practice.

Ethics in practice focuses on day-to-day decision-making as we engage in public scholarship from conception to dissemination. It concerns "everyday ethical dilemmas that arise from the specific roles and responsibilities that researchers and research participants adopt in specific research context" (Kubanyiova, 2008, p. 504). With ethics in practice, we can use procedural ethics as guidelines, but ultimately we rely on our own ethical paradigms and personal principles to make the choice for good or ill (Shapiro & Stepkovitch, 2016). Although formal procedural ethics are an important aspect of the research process, in this chapter we focus on the gray areas where we are forced to make our everyday decisions and choices.

Public Scholarship as a Process

In this chapter, we conceptualize public scholarship as a process that results in a product or outcome, rather than as the outcome itself. As discussed in chapter 1, we conceptualize *public scholarship* to include creation, dissemination, and application of the research. We chose this expanded definition because it emphasizes the many opportunities for ethics in practice over the course of a study before research questions have been confirmed and long after the final manuscript.

If public scholarship is a process, then we can see that it includes many interconnected components that interact. These interactions are also potential ethical decision points. The interconnected components include the human aspect: researchers, staff, and various stakeholders. It also includes the means and resources for research. There are also less tangible aspects such as the tacit or explicit rules and regulations, divisions of labor, sociocultural norms, mental schemas, theoretical frameworks, standard operating procedures, and explicit policies. To have a holistic perspective of the research process and the various interconnections means we can have a different scope to examine potential ethical decision points.

Ethical Mindfulness

We propose ethical mindfulness as an epistemological paradigm to understand our practice of public scholarship. In addition to being a practice, ethical mindfulness is a way to explain how we come to see the world, and more specifically for this chapter how we come to see our work. According to Guillemin, McDougall, and Gillam (2009) and Guillemin and Gillam (2015), the five key aspects to ethical mindfulness are: being sensitized to ethically important moments, acknowledging these moments as significant, articulating the ethical implications, being reflexive and recognizing standpoints and limitations, and being courageous.

To illustrate ethical mindfulness in approaching public scholarship, we have chosen examples within our own research practice. Even though public scholarship includes all methodologies across disciplines, our examples focus more on qualitative research methodologies in social science to align with our experiences. However, the content can be extrapolated beyond discipline and methodology.

Being Sensitized to Ethically Important Moments

There is a difference between making decisions with ethical consequences and ethical decision-making, and that difference is where we focus our attention. People make mundane decisions often without taking into consideration the potential ethical consequences of their actions. In the research sphere, this can be as simple as choosing to print data for analysis or determining where to purchase laboratory supplies. Each decision has potential ethical implications depending on one's stance on the environment or labor conditions. These types of decisions become ethical decisions when we first become aware that there is an ethical issue at hand. Some scholars begin the ethical decision-making process with developing an ethical sensitivity, (Sirin, Brabeck, Satiani, & Rogers-Serin, 2003; Welfel, 2015) but most begin with the individual identifying the ethical problem (Cottone & Claus, 2000; Craft, 2013; O'Fallon & Butterfield, 2005). When we do not recognize there is an ethical decision to be made, other factors can influence our decision instead.

The challenge comes in being able to see the ethically important moments when they arise. Guillemin and Gillam (2004) note that ethically important moments are "the difficult, often subtle, and usually unpredictable situations that arise in the practice of doing research" (p. 262). When we think about the three phases of the public scholarship process, we can see the myriad of potential ethical decisions we may face. Interacting with stakeholders or using resources are potential situations for ethical decision-making. Even the seemingly innocuous choice of a research topic can have some ethical implications given that human beings have limited resources, time, and energy. Our choice of topic means there is an opportunity cost for all the other topics we chose not to research, but we have determined that for the time being our chosen topic has priority and is worth our dedication.

In our own practice, we acknowledge that we most likely have missed more ethically important moments than we recognize, which on retrospection are missed opportunities; for example, the times we did not make advocating for others a priority.

Ethically important moments can occur in all forms of public scholarship and throughout the research process. As primarily qualitative researchers, we focus on examples that derive from our experiences in the field. Much of that work relates to the study of vulnerable or marginalized student populations. In one instance, at the outset of a project involving housing vulnerable students, an important ethical moment occurred when considering how the participants would benefit from the study. This question was in contrast to the do no harm directive of most IRBs. Although many public scholarship projects pose little to no harm (e.g., minimal risk), it is difficult to articulate how they directly benefit the populations or communities that participate.

To address the issue of benefit, we began by asking ourselves what type of relationship we wanted to have with the community and the participants. Once we had a clear understanding of our responsibilities to the students and school, we went to the specific schools and community agencies to talk about how a project could benefit them. We began by finding community partners and learning about their concerns and values during several meetings with our partners' staff members and youth leaders prior to data collection. These meetings allowed us to better understand the ethical landscape of the school and the community. At these meetings, we shared the goal of our research and what we felt our obligations were to the organization and the participants. The preliminary meetings provided the community agencies with a chance to revise responsibilities in a manner that was respectful of their workflow and organizational boundaries. For example, one community agency had hired an educational coordinator who was assisting students with building an educational plan that included obtaining a high school diploma or general equivalent degree, making plans for any necessary or desired postsecondary education, or starting career or vocational training. All questions students posed that related to postsecondary planning were referred to the coordinator. Forging an understanding of our responsibilities to each group was one way to develop and practice ethical mindfulness.

Beyond the creation phase, ethically important moments occur during the application of public scholarship. We have encountered multiple ethically important moments that required us to consider how our responses might affect the well-being of the individuals or the communities. In many instances community-engaged research blurs the lines of objectivity or the line between researcher and participant. In that light, ethically important moments take on a different connotation. Although still upholding the IRB principle of beneficence, the researcher considers what is ethically relevant from within the context of the community or the organization under study.

For example, in working with homeless youth agencies it became clear that our responsibilities to the youths, the organization, and the institution required different ethical outlooks. Trying to negotiate those ethically important moments means recognizing the various, and sometimes contradictory, ethical boundaries of each domain. As we stated earlier, the first step in addressing such situations is recognizing that there is a moral landscape. Second, it is important to consider what the relationship is between or among the researcher, community, and participant. The third step, as we discuss later, is addressing each situation in an appropriate way given the information, resources, and time available. We are not suggesting that this process leads to a correct decision; rather, it is a way of building ethical mindfulness into the process.

In regard to the dissemination phase, ethically important moments arose with decisions of what to do with the final product and resulting data. Determining ways to discuss the challenges and inequities that emerged from the data without undermining the communities we worked with was difficult. Understanding our own final role with the community as advocates or critical friends or passive observers was something that each person had to come to terms with.

Acknowledging These Moments as Significant

We recognize that we have numerous opportunities to make ethical decisions, and according to Guillemin and Gillam (2015), we also have to acknowledge that these opportunities are significant. Another way to conceptualize this aspect of ethical mindfulness is to think of the first phase as realizing the frequency of ethical decision-making moments and the second phase as recognizing the importance of those moments. The goal is to not take our ethical decisions lightly because they illustrate the values we care about. If we do not see these events as important, it is possible to cease seeing them as ethical events altogether (Tenbrunsel & Messick, 2004). Because we tend to believe in our better nature (that we are good, able, and deserving), it can be more difficult to overcome our personal bias to really explore the ethical dissonance that we experience (Chugh, Bazerman, & Banaji, 2005). Rather, it would be easier to justify our actions in hindsight or to ignore the issue completely. Studies indicate that we can divert the ethical significance of a moment in many ways. Tenbrunsel and Messick (2004) discuss the phenomenon of *ethical fading*, which is when a person shifts attention from the ethical implications of decisions until he or she no longer takes into account those implications in decision-making. In his model of moral disengagement, Bandura (1999) illustrates different ways people justify their unethical behavior, separating themselves from the discomfort they may feel about their decisions. We resort to actions such as making advantageous comparisons, diffusing or displacing responsibility, disregarding the effects of our actions, and dehumanizing or attributing blame to others. Even as we make unethical decisions, studies indicate we can still maintain our self-concept of being ethical people (Mazar, Amri, & Ariely, 2008).

To give weight to our qualms and concerns and to take a moment to reflect on the reasons we may be feeling uncomfortable can be a way to at least limit the effects of our self-serving bias. To be thoughtful about ourselves as we experience these ethical moments may play a role in the final decision we make. Studies indicate that when people are more self-aware, they may also be more honest (Bateson, Nettles, & Roberts, 2006; Haley & Fessler, 2005). For example, Mazar and colleagues (2008) found that in their experiment, as people attended to their own internal standard of honesty, they were less likely to be dishonest in a given situation. We tried to be thoughtful in our work by building in time for discussions with the research team and colleagues about our personal and professional standards of ethics and integrity and any ethical discomfort we may be feeling. These discussions provide opportunities for us to be accountable to others in addition to ourselves.

Articulating the Ethical Implications

However, once we recognize the significance of the moment, what is next? As scholars, our work often involves the articulation and clarification of ideas and concepts to the public, and the same should also apply to our ethical moments. The next step is to articulate what is "ethically at stake" (Guillemin & Gillam, 2015, p. 729). In Guillemin and Gillam's (2015) discussion emphasizing the role emotion plays in ethics in medicine, they discuss the importance of moral emotions and having the emotional intelligence to recognize the differences among them. For example, they mention discerning between feelings of moral regret, the feeling of doing something "prima facie wrong, but ethically justified overall," and moral distress, the feeling of doing something morally unjustified (Guillemin & Gillam, 2015, p. 729).

We want to add to Guillemin and Gillam (2015) the recognition of moral emotions and ethical dilemmas and articulating the ethical stakes of those decisions. Not all ethical problems are in fact ethical dilemmas, rather, these are specific problems with no ethically satisfactory solutions. Ethical dilemmas are usually thought of as problems that have no good moral solutions (Childress, 1994). A dilemma has three criteria. The first is personal agency in which the individual is able to make the choice without being under undue duress or using instinctual behavior. Second, there must be alternative courses of action. Third, regardless of the choice the person makes, an ethical principle is compromised (Cooper, 2012).

We want to emphasize ethical dilemmas in public scholarship because, as noted earlier, equity, democracy, social justice, and the public good are implicit in public scholarship. However, the public good is not the only value found in scholarship. Other values may be security, autonomy, connectedness, justice, dignity, truth, compassion, order, or freedom, which sometimes can be in conflict with one another.

In our public scholarship work, ethical dilemmas do occur. One example is the tension among dignity, compassion, and veracity. In our work related to studying students who experience trauma (e.g., homeless students) we had to keep in mind that some of the participants will provide a false narrative of events. As researchers, we are put in a position of thinking about our want for veracity and the dignity of our participant.

Although making decisions when faced with an ethical dilemma may be difficult, many scholars of applied ethics suggest several common steps to help make that decision (e.g., see Cooper, 2012; Hamrick & Benjamin, 2009; Newman & Brown, 1996). Those steps include clarifying your short-term and long-term goals, gathering facts about the situation, determining all the options available, considering consequences, making a decision, and monitoring the outcomes of your decision and modifying as needed.

In terms of the previous example, as researchers, we had to think about our work in relation to the participants, in this case the students. Through the course of our study, when we found a discrepancy or major inaccuracy, one goal was to address the issue, but another was to maintain the dignity of our participants. We had to take into consideration different facts about the situation such as the type of false narrative, potential ways those narratives could harm others, and the ways we could be encouraging or discouraging the participant. We also had to learn more about trauma and youths from a psychosocial perspective, for example, the use of a false narrative as a coping mechanism or preservation of self. As scholars, we had to think about the demands of our own research and any benefits it could provide. Of our options, we decided to try to build trust with the participants before addressing any factual inaccuracies. Once the trust was built, we revisited some of the areas that may have been modified. For the study, we purposefully structured the research design to allow having multiple formal and informal meetings. This practice allowed the participant to see the researchers outside the formal interview context to build a level of trust with them. We were also cognizant of which staff members assist in recruiting participants. In one instance, a staff member told a student "You can trust him," referring to Jarrett T. Gupton. This endorsement made it easier to build trust and a rapport with the participant. For those participants who never reached that point with us, we decided not to push and instead tried to find alternative means of obtaining the information. To address those inaccuracies, we used several forms of triangulation to gather an accurate account of the informant's experience. Although it is never a perfect system, being able to articulate what is at stake in an ethically significant moment is also part of being able to evaluate the experience.

Being Reflexive and Recognizing Standpoints and Limitations

As we think about the choices to make when faced with an ethically significant moment, we also may need to take a moment to recognize the emotions, standpoints, and experiences that shape our responses (Guillemin & Gillam, 2015). Our standpoints can play a role in the theories and constructs we apply to understand a phenomenon, direct our focus of attention to some events and not others, and shape how we analyze and interpret the data. This recognition can be similar to how qualitative studies emphasize the need for transparency and acknowledgment of standpoints and limitations (Warin, 2011). Qualitative methods such as journaling or bracketing (the research reflects and describes an individual's own experience with the phenomenon, and the person puts that understanding aside to be open to other thinking) are opportunities for scholars to be reflexive and explore their standpoints. However, this practice need not be limited to only qualitative methodologies.

What this feature may look like in practice can vary from scholar to scholar. For example, several scholars use reflexivity as a means for achieving ethical mindfulness (Etherington, 2007; Warin, 2011). An important aspect of reflexive practice is being reflective. To be reflective is to think about oneself in relation to the situation in terms of privilege, standpoint, and context. However, to be reflective in a way that results in change in practice or person is reflexive.

For example, Warin (2011) examines her own ideas of self and the other when studying children and young adults. She recommends several guidelines on how to "do reflexivity" while conducting research such as "recognizing the complexity of consent" (p. 812) and being aware of any agendas of gatekeepers beyond the scope of the study. Other scholars used more of a reflective practice approach, taking time to examine the decisions made afterward and determining alternative courses of action for future opportunities. Carr (2012) presents his own experiences in an action research project involving a public skateboarding facility as a critical reflection piece exploring his ethical frameworks, tracing his decisions, and evaluating his choices in different ethical lights.

Being reflexive and recognizing standpoints can also be a more private affair that can happen through all stages of the public scholarship process. Taking a moment to acknowledge personal standpoints and the standpoints of the research team does not have to result in a paper, but is a way to be reflective. As scholars begin to develop research questions and design, it can be a good place to take a moment to explore how personal lived experience has influenced the process. As dissemination plans begin, this may be a good place to explore the narratives that our knowledge may be creating or supporting. In application, we may have to be honest in our intentions and about the potential risks or harms that may result and be honest with why we would continue to support the application. Especially when being an outsider working with populations that historically have experienced marginalization or disenfranchisement, acknowledging our standpoints and privilege can serve as a means for scholars to be thoughtful and not continue to marginalize further.

The role of reflexivity is vital to public scholarship. To do good people must understand their relationship or the type of relationship they want with others. Thus, we return to our earlier suggestion that public scholars work to clarify and articulate the type of relationship they want to have with the public.

In our work with housing vulnerable populations, we acknowledged that our experiences were shaped by housing and familial stability. During the project, we worked to meet with representatives from the community and organizations who conducted a vetting process and asked us questions about our backgrounds. Through this process, community partners helped bring attention to assumptions and biases that we missed. Once the project was completed we held community forums to discuss findings and to share some of the assumptions that arose during the project. Further, these meetings provided an opportunity for the public to call attention to any suppressed assumptions they saw in the findings. In our experience, a benefit of openly sharing the findings of a public scholarship project is that it provides various constituent groups with the chance to organize and create new opportunities for collaboration.

Being Courageous

As we end this chapter, we left the final aspect of ethical mindfulness for this space. In a time of uncertainty and upheaval, being mindful of the ethics of our work becomes even more important because we must become

beacons of light in the darkness for others to find their way. If public scholars ignore the ethics, then we undermine the core tenet that underpins the
work we do.

We find the final aspect, being courageous, particularly important. One
of the consequences of ethical mindfulness is realizing that for almost all
decisions, there are ethical implications. For some public scholars, this may
result in removing the veneer of neutrality that sometimes coats our research
and requires us to take a stand in one direction or another. For example,
Lundy and McGovern (2006) discuss "truth telling" in their work in Northern Ireland and how in the face of injustice and marginalization it would
be unethical for researchers to be "detached and silent" (p. 49). Kidder and
Born (2002) define *moral courage* in broad terms as the courage "to be honest, to be fair, to be respectful, to be responsible, and to be compassionate"
(p. 16).

Developing ethical mindfulness also means that we must grow accustomed to the uncomfortable space where we must reexamine our motivations, our options, and the consequences of our actions, and ultimately make
a choice. That understanding alone places a daunting task on the individual
to be cognizant of his or her decisions, but it can also place a moral imperative on the person to do the right thing, whatever that may be. In our studies, to do what is right—engaging with the community through different
forums, providing transparency, and giving voice to research participants—
is a costly process in terms of time and money. It would be easier to bypass
everything to complete a project and get the results published; however,
to do so would be to acknowledge that we prioritized expediency and efficacy over justice and care. Especially when working with different constituents, as our public scholarship increases in complexity the chances that our
research may not turn out as expected also increases, either with unintended
consequences or less-than-stellar results. Depending on the stakes involved,
scholars may feel pressure to present reality differently or ignore problems
completely.

Although the process to ensure the most ethical outcome can never be
flawless, ethical mindfulness as a practice to use with public scholarship can
be a way to continue our own personal vigilance to ensure that the work that
we do while serving the public good is also the ethical good. It recenters our
perspective of the scholarship process as being filled with a myriad of ethical
opportunities. Through reflexive practice found in ethical mindfulness, we
can continue to grow and learn personally and professionally. As scholars,
we will not always make the best ethical decisions at the time, but we can
learn from our past decisions and develop insights that may be shared with
our community. For example, in our work with homeless youths we learned

that practicing ethical mindfulness during the process of designing, conducting, and disseminating research enhances our ability to create positive social change. Ethical mindfulness helped us create space to clarify our responsibilities to better serve our informants, the field, and the public.

References

Bandura, A. (1999). Moral disengagement in the perpetration of inhumanities. *Personality and Social Psychology Review, 3*, 193–209.

Bateson, M., Nettle, D., & Roberts, G. (2006). Cues of being watched enhance cooperation in a real-world setting. *Biology Letters, 2*, 412–414.

Brown, M. E., & Treviño, L. K. (2006). Ethical leadership: A review and future directions. *Leadership Quarterly, 17*, 595–616.

Carr, J. (2012). Activist research and city politics: Ethical lessons from youth-based public scholarship. *Action Research, 10*(1), 61–78.

Childress, J. F. (1994). Principles-oriented bioethics: An analysis and assessment from within. In E. R. DuBose, R. P. Hamel, & L. J. O'Connell (Eds.), *A matter of principles* (pp. 72–98). Valley Forge, PA: Trinity Press International.

Chugh, D., Bazerman, M. H., & Banaji, M. R. (2005). Bounded ethicality as a psychological barrier to recognizing conflicts of interest. In D. Moore, D. Cain, G. Lowenstein, & M. Baxerman (Eds.), *Conflicts of interest: Challenges and solutions in business, law, medicine, and public policy* (pp. 74–95). Cambridge, England: Cambridge University Press.

Cooper, T. L. (2012). *The responsible administrator: An approach to ethics for the administrative role.* San Francisco, CA: Wiley.

Cottone, R. R., & Claus, R. E. (2000). Ethical decision-making models: A review of the literature. *Journal of Counseling & Development, 78*, 275–283.

Craft, J. L. (2013). A review of the empirical ethical decision-making literature: 2004–2011. *Journal of Business Ethics, 117*, 221–259.

Etherington, K. (2007). Ethical research in reflexive relationships. *Qualitative Inquiry, 13*, 599–616.

Guillemin, M., & Gillam, L. (2004). Ethics, reflexivity, and "ethically important moments" in research. *Qualitative Inquiry, 10*, 261–280.

Guillemin, M., & Gillam, L. (2015). Emotions, narratives, and ethical mindfulness. *Academic Medicine, 90*, 726–731.

Guillemin, M., McDougall, R., & Gillam, L. (2009). Developing "ethical mindfulness" in continuing professional development in healthcare: Use of a personal narrative approach. *Cambridge Quarterly of Healthcare Ethics, 18*, 197–208.

Haley, K. J., & Fessler, D. M. (2005). Nobody's watching? Subtle cues affect generosity in an anonymous economic game. *Evolution and human behavior, 26*, 245–256.

Hamrick, F. A., & Benjamin, M. (Eds.). (2009). *Maybe I should—: Case studies on ethics for student affairs professionals.* Baltimore, MD: University Press of America.

Kezar, A., Chambers, T., & Burkhardt, J. (Eds.). (2005). *Higher education for the public good: Emerging voices from a national movement*. San Francisco, CA: Jossey-Bass.

Kezar, A., Drivalas, J., & Kitchen, J. (2018). Defining the evolving concept of public scholarship. In A. Kezar, J. Drivalas & J. Kitchen (Eds.), *Envisioning public scholarship for our time: Models for higher education researchers* (pp. 3–17). Sterling, VA: Stylus.

Kidder, R. M., & Born, P. L. (2002). Moral courage in a world of dilemmas. *School Administrator, 59*(2), 14–18.

Kubanyiova, M. (2008). Rethinking research ethics in contemporary applied linguistics: The tension between macroethical and microethical perspectives in situated research. *Modern Language Journal, 92*, 503–518.

Lundy, P., & McGovern, M. (2006). Participation, truth and partiality: Participatory action research, community-based truth-telling and post-conflict transition in Northern Ireland. *Sociology, 40*, 71–88.

Mazar, N., Amir, O., & Ariely, D. (2008). The dishonesty of honest people: A theory of self-concept maintenance. *Journal of Marketing Research, 45*, 633–644.

Newman, D. L., & Brown, R. D. (1996). *Applied ethics for program evaluation*. Thousand Oaks, CA: Sage.

O'Fallon, M. J., & Butterfield, K. D. (2005). A review of the empirical ethical decision-making literature: 1996–2003. *Journal of Business Ethics, 59*, 375–413.

Shaker, G. G. (Ed.). (2015). *Faculty work and the public good: Philanthropy engagement and academic professionalism*. New York, NY: Teachers College Press.

Shapiro, J. P., & Stefkovich, J. A. (2016). *Ethical leadership and decision making in education: Applying theoretical perspectives to complex dilemmas*. New York, NY: Routledge.

Sirin, S. R., Brabeck, M. M., Satiani, A., & Rogers-Serin, L. (2003). Validation of a measure of ethical sensitivity and examination of the effects of previous multicultural and ethics courses on ethical sensitivity. *Ethics & Behavior, 13*, 221–235.

Tenbrunsel, A. E., & Messick, D. M. (2004). Ethical fading: The role of self-deception in unethical behavior. *Social Justice Research, 17*, 223–236.

Warin, J. (2011). Ethical mindfulness and reflexivity managing a research relationship with children and young people in a 14-year qualitative longitudinal research (QLR) study. *Qualitative Inquiry, 17*, 805–814.

Welfel, E. R. (2015). *Ethics in counseling & psychotherapy*. Cengage Learning. Belmont, CA: Cengage Learning.

PART TWO

APPROACHES TO PUBLIC
SCHOLARSHIP

4

LEGAL ARENAS AND PUBLIC SCHOLARSHIP

Sylvia Hurtado

We were assembled as a research team to provide evidence for expert testimony. It was our first meeting with the legal team representing the University of Michigan in the cases on affirmative action in college admissions. A lawyer asked, "What difference does it make to have diverse students in a classroom?" This clearly was an open question for social science research. Savoring the thought, ideas flashed in our heads. Thinking about research and the data we had developed to address diversity in college settings, we responded: "We think we can answer that question." On reflection, it was essentially a research question of great practical value to colleges that would be weighed against other arguments in a legal arena. The lawyers provided no guidance about how to answer the question or about the types of findings that would constitute acceptable evidence for the courts in defining the educational benefits of diversity. As social scientists, it was up to us to determine the types of tests we could perform with existing data, using established parameters for social science research evidence. This is what we do for a living, and we do our best to make our work public (i.e., publish and disseminate findings). However, this did not make us public scholars, and the legal arena was a new environment for us.

Little did we know that this key question would turn into a seven-year journey working as a collaborative research team, require us to learn how to

An intense collaborative experience with a great group of colleagues was life changing. I am forever grateful to my colleagues Patricia Gurin, Gerald Gurin, and Eric Dey when we were all at the University of Michigan. Each brought incredible strengths to the team. We learned much from each other, about ourselves, and our commitment to social justice.

become public scholars, and eventually lead to a developing area of social science research. The collaborative work on this question started an evolution in my own research, yet it was also tied to my sense of purpose as a young scholar. Drawing parallels with the transformative paradigm, the aim of this chapter is to provide an example of a transition to public scholarship that may be compared with other forms of scholarship and decision points in a research trajectory, offering key elements that reflect the experience of becoming a public scholar in collaboration with lawyers who represented the interests of communities of educators and the diverse students they sought to serve.

Distinguishing Between Policy Research and Public Scholarship

I have never considered myself to be a policy researcher, nor do I study specific policies as the basis of my work. I find that *public scholarship* is probably a more fitting term than *policy research* for the work I do on behalf of marginalized communities, along with diverse communities, and in collaboration with those servants of the public good or the institutions intending to serve diverse communities. Many policy analysts often study policy alternatives and weigh the costs and benefits of each alternative. The researcher and the study are distanced from those who will be most affected by the policy, and the researcher assumes that people in power (and powerful people) will make the right choice for the public good based on the research. This assumption ignores power dynamics, the systems of oppression (e.g., racism, sexism) that are in place, and new forms of repression. Value-free research assumes that people will make rational decisions based on facts rather than values. However, much of what is weighed in decision-making is based on competing values, and not all values, worldviews, or perspectives hold equal legitimacy in specific circumstances or contexts. Moreover, historically marginalized and newly minoritized communities are often excluded from, victimized, or scapegoated in the policy discourse and social constructions of the public good (e.g., implementing a Muslim travel ban to the United States in the interest of national security). The lack of attention to inequality and power dynamics are limitations of the research conducted under the postpositivist and the pragmatist "what works" (Hurtado, 2015, p. 293) paradigms; which often dominates policy research.

In contrast, the transformative paradigm fosters a concern for social justice that "permeates the entire research process, from the problem formulation to the drawing of conclusions and use of results" (Mertens, 2003, p. 159). The transformative paradigm, which arose because researchers and members of marginalized communities were dissatisfied with dominant paradigms and practice, is intended to serve as an umbrella for all scholarly approaches that may employ different research methods, but are rooted in a critique of the power relationships with emancipatory goals for individuals and transformative goals for institutions and systems of oppression. (Hurtado, 2015, p. 286)

Research that falls under the transformative paradigm acknowledges the power dynamics that shape ontology or lived realities, epistemology, or differences in ways of knowing and approaches to knowledge and focuses on equity outcomes for marginalized communities.

An element of inclusiveness is essential in the transformative paradigm that has an important parallel with public scholarship in the research process. It involves the willingness of the researcher to interact with communities and public advocates to inform them about results (at minimum), implement findings, frame the research, or even teach them how to collect data and carry out their own studies. Public scholars are aware of differences and may convene diverse groups, use a variety of methods to reach diverse audiences, and often are an effective bridge between communities that differ in background, training, worldview, or social status. This is consistent with the transformative research paradigm and is illustrated here in my personal and professional case of public scholarship.

Ikigai and Public Scholarship

One of the key requirements of becoming a public scholar is to be willing to engage in the work, without fully knowing your impact or immediate reward, because it fulfills your sense of purpose. I did not begin as a public scholar or transformative paradigm researcher. I was trained in the typical research paradigms of the time (postpositivist and social constructionist) and through my graduate research socialization processes found no opportunity to be critical of my training. I knew that my sense of purpose and reason for learning how to conduct research differed from what my instructors in college and graduate school thought and felt. As a former staff administrator, I needed to learn research to support programs for underrepresented groups in college. However, the distance I was taught to maintain in conducting research during graduate school initially made me forget how I was connected with the experiences of research participants. In writing the dissertation, I found my *ikigai*, a Japanese term for one's sense of purpose in life that converges with passion, mission, and vocation. I wanted to document the experiences of underrepresented groups in higher education. I only fully realized I was unpacking my own story as a woman of color educated in a predominantly White college environment when I was finishing a journal article on the campus racial climate from my dissertation research. I was free to write about and openly critique with research evidence the system in which I was educated. With new research methods in my toolbox, I also found it empowering to ask questions and find answers that would advance the progress of underrepresented groups in higher education. I wanted to do this my entire career.

Role Models of Public Scholarship in the Legal Arena

Fortunately, there are some clear public scholar models that are nationally recognized, which I consider early adopters of the transformative paradigm. My master's degree adviser, John Williams (1988), worked on understanding the legal issues and the long-term progress of desegregation cases in 18 states with dual systems of higher education. Michael Olivas (2006) wrote the book on legal issues in higher education and played a pivotal role in the formation of several state policies for the education of undocumented and nonresident students. He was an expert witness and provided testimony in more than a score of legal cases in education (Olivas, 2012). Walter Allen (my postdoctoral mentor), Jomills Braddock, and William Trent, similarly have long been involved in scores of cases in K–12 and higher education and have studied the long-term effects of desegregation (Braddock, Dawkins & Trent, 1994). Despite their demanding careers, they collaborated with legal teams to advance the use of social science research and formulate policy. Each modeled their commitment to social justice and conveyed the value of this work, influencing how I became involved in the practice of public scholarship.

More specific to affirmative action cases, Gary Orfield (2001), professor at the University of California, Los Angeles, was also an early adopter of the transformative paradigm focused on social justice and a model public scholar. He orchestrated a meeting between young researchers working on diversity in higher education and lawyers representing universities in affirmative action cases in Washington, Texas, and Michigan. He sought funds from foundations to support both groups and commissioned papers from scholars, which were published (Orfield, 2001). At this early meeting, as the group attempted to determine which cases would likely arrive on the U.S. Supreme Court docket, we quickly realized that the researchers did not grasp the legal arguments, and the lawyers were frustrated by the methods, language, and academic style used by the researchers. The implications of the research were not clear. We were like two distinct cultures speaking different languages in the same room, and somehow we had to work together. Orfield became the chief translator, talking with lawyers to understand arguments in the case and serving as an effective bridge between academics and the legal community.

He also employed legal experts to help frame some of the work for the Civil Rights Project, which was his major research endeavor. Most important, he oriented many young scholars to begin to align their work with the needs of the legal teams representing the universities. I was one of the young scholars who began to learn how my research on diverse college student populations could be important for the court cases, even though I could not anticipate my role at the time.

Elements of Public Scholarship in the Legal Arena

Each legal case and each relationship with the legal teams differed. Here I describe our professional relationship and begin to illustrate essential elements. After the lawyers met with several of us individually, we were each asked to be one of several researchers involved in the Michigan cases to deliver expert testimony. Two external expert historians were selected to detail the context and background for Latinas and Latinos and African Americans in terms of underrepresentation and exclusion from higher education in the region. Another group of scholars focused on issues of access and how students were selected for admission. Our research team focused on the compelling interest for diversity and included two senior scholars (Patricia Gurin and Gerald Gurin) and two assistant professors (Eric Dey and myself), working together for the first time. We were brought together because of our expertise with longitudinal data and research on diversity, but legal issues were not our area of scholarship. Patricia Gurin, interim dean of the college of Arts and Sciences at the University of Michigan, was selected to be the expert witness, and the research team participated in her training for deposition and testimony after results were submitted. The process of learning to become a public scholar involved at least three elements: mutual learning and collaboration; attention to language and presentation; and dissemination, including educating the press to engender public support for the issues. In each area, this involved some learning through trial and error until we achieved a satisfying outcome.

Mutual Learning and Collaboration

Working with individuals from a different discipline, and their respective norms for scholarship, can pose a challenge, but we had a common goal, which was to support the university's case for diversity. Mutual learning and collaboration require a great deal of respect for each party's work and for building trust in the relationship to achieve understanding. Free-flowing questions and conversations were central to sharing how we were trained to

think in our disciplines about the problem. To be an effective public scholar
in the legal arena meant we had to become familiar with the legal arguments
and how the evidence fits within the legal tests established by precedent in
similar cases. First, we had to learn their method and way of knowing to
understand how social science evidence fits within the framing of arguments.
Many court cases use hypothetical arguments, are based on reasoning, and
do not necessarily have social science research evidence in the legal decisions. Such was the case when Justice Lewis F. Powell wrote in *Regents of the
University of California v. Bakke* (1978) that attainment of a diverse student
body broadens the range of viewpoints collectively held by those students,
allows a university to provide an atmosphere that is "conducive to specula-
tion, experiment and creation—so essential to the quality of higher education"—(p. 438), and improves the chances that the training of tomorrow's
leaders will gain wider exposure to a robust exchange of ideas. The Michigan
cases provided evidence for the first time regarding the compelling interest
test in the case and expert testimony for why including race in college admissions was necessary to achieve desirable college outcomes.

Second, we also helped to frame legal arguments based on theory and
empirical evidence. We had free reign to develop the theoretical rationale
and the empirical analyses focused on the central question of the educational
benefits of diversity. We met periodically to show progress in the development of the social science evidence. I recall when we met to present the
theory of diversity in higher education, the lawyers were excited and intel-
lectually stimulated by what they learned. The theoretical rationale advanced
their thinking about how diversity works in education (based on cognition,
development, and learning theory) and advances democratic goals (Gurin,
Dey, Hurtado, & Gurin, 2002). The legal team members also became familiar with statistical tests of the data, and we helped them grasp our approach
to the analyses. However, when we met to discuss the written results of the
analyses across race and ethnicity, levels, and time periods (four years in college and nine years after college entry), we had to rethink our presentation
of data.

Attention to Language and Presentation

Any researcher would likely struggle to present a series of replication studies that included findings across samples in the classroom, a cohort at the
University of Michigan (using the Michigan Study), and institutions
nationally (using data from the Higher Education Research Institute at the
University of California, Los Angeles). Moreover, we analyzed 88 educational
outcomes, disaggregated by race and ethnicity, and two longitudinal time

points. We wrote the results as we would typically for any scholar to review, and at the next meeting with the legal team, we announced that the findings were consistent. The lawyers were frustrated about the written results and did not understand our statement. We explained that it is rare to take different student samples; follow them longitudinally at two different time points across race, institutions, and a host of outcomes; and show consistent findings in social science. There were some variations but overall the findings were amazingly consistent: Students who had contact with diverse peers in college showed distinct and improved college outcomes compared with those who did not. We helped the legal team understand how we arrived at the conclusion that it is important to be educated with a diverse student body in predominantly White colleges.

Based on discussions about the findings from our first draft of results, we brainstormed the ways the results could be understood by judges, clerks, and Supreme Court justices. The lawyers helped us understand how evidence was reviewed and summarized in court decisions. We proceeded to make the research process and results accessible to people who are not social scientists. Rewriting was painful but necessary to convey the weight of the findings. First, we explained analyses in baseball terms to help the reader understand how significant findings are determined above all other alternative explanations. Second, we opted for graphics and summaries of results. Third, we limited tables, presenting results in readable sections with key headings acting as signposts for summaries of the findings in the text. All the tables and about 35,000 pages of computer printouts were submitted separately as evidence that the opposing counsel and experts could review. Suffice it to say that no results from these analyses were contested at any level of court review of the cases.

Dissemination and Working With the Media

Another element of public scholarship that quickly became part of our role was conveying information to various audiences, including students who had started their own activist organizations, campus forums, and various media organizations about aspects of the case that were central to the work of the university. Later, we made presentations at a variety of external organizations whose members were interested in understanding the benefits of diversity. It was important to understand each audience and its level of understanding regarding social science research. The theory of how diversity works in education was central to communicating the rationale, whereas the graphics were effective in communicating main points of the findings. We made presentations to any group that wanted to hear about the empirical evidence for diversity in higher education. As a result of this experience, I am comfortable with addressing a wide variety of audiences and educating the public and the press about diversity in higher education. It also helped to have a team involved in the process of dissemination. This led to several journal articles and a book about the research findings and the experience (Gurin et al., 2002; Gurin et al., 2004; Hurtado, Dey, Gurin & Gurin, 2003).

We did not anticipate, however, the use of the media by the opposing groups of individuals who were behind the court cases. This required us to write opinion pieces in response because once the opposition planted a false story, a newspaper was not going to publish another story with our version of events. I was surprised how newspapers published those perspectives without seeking a balance of views or perspectives. Where were the fact checkers? We tried to get ahead of the news and release some of our own statements with the university. We also learned the value of taking the time to educate reporters who were intent on using an angle that did not support data on college students and diversity in higher education. This seemed endless, but we took on the tasks over the years as the cases wound their way through the courts. In 2003 a Supreme Court decision supported the educational benefits of diversity but ruled out point systems for race in admissions in favor of holistic reviews of applicants that considered race (as one of many factors), which had been the practice at the University of Michigan Law School (*Grutter v. Bollinger et al.*, 2003). This was not the end of the issue, as opponents later mounted a successful campaign in Michigan for a ballot initiative to ban the use of race in contracting, employment, and higher education, but it was the end of our collaboration as a team.

Public Scholarship for Whom?

In the Michigan cases, mutual learning and the collaborative process were productive, research results could be understood by many audiences, and all research was directed toward actions that would be important in preserving opportunity for underrepresented groups. These elements were strongly rooted in the transformative paradigm approach. However, issues arose that began to question the extent to which the best interests of marginalized groups were represented by the university. From the beginning, students felt their experiences were not fully reflected in the university's case and mounted their own case as intervenors, hiring other scholars to conduct new studies on their behalf. This was designed to bring forward more evidence regarding past and continuing discrimination that warrants a remedy. We saw this as a healthy development in the cases; the students could provide their own rationale independent of that framed by the university's lawyers. Although the university provided expert witnesses who submitted testimony about the history of discrimination and underrepresentation in the region, it was criticized for not emphasizing past or current injustices enough to compel a public university to better serve underrepresented communities. The lawyers felt that remedies for past discrimination were no longer acceptable arguments based on the arguments in *Regents of the University of California v. Bakke* (1978), and technically they represented the university and indirectly represented the communities most affected. However, the lawyers began to build a rationale for the need for a critical mass of students, based on research, to help avert continuing discrimination and stereotyping because of underrepresentation. Looking back, this became an important development for future challenges.

As scholars working in a variety of circles, we also faced some criticism for following the arguments as framed by precedent in other cases. Given the level of effort, and knowing the the level of commitment to social justice by the individuals who were involved in the collaboration for the University of Michigan, this felt unfair. In our own minds, we did this work because we believed it would prevent African Americans and Latina and Latino students from losing ground in access to the university. We also went to great lengths to disaggregate the findings (published later in Gurin, et al., 2002) to show educational benefits for each racial and ethnicity group in interacting with diverse groups during college evidenced in educational outcomes. Thus, the benefits of diversity were not limited to White students but were evidenced in each racial and ethnic group. Although a separate campus climate report had been submitted as evidence, leaving out more complex details about discrimination and bias for underrepresented groups in support of the benefits-of-diversity argument was a compromise we debated. Eventually, I had a second chance to rectify this situation as a direct result of the outcome of these cases. Ten years after the decisions in the Michigan cases (*Gratz v. Bollinger*, 2003; *Grutter v. Bollinger*, 2003), another Supreme Court case on affirmative action arose, *Fisher v. University of Texas at Austin* (2013). My colleagues and I at the University of California, Los Angeles, were able to demonstrate that African Americans and Latinas and Latinos experienced higher levels of discrimination and harassment as a result of attending a less diverse college. I was able to present the data as part of the amicus briefs submitted by social scientists for the case, reinforcing the value of a critical mass of underrepresented students to avert racial isolation. The groundwork for the logic surrounding the necessity of a critical mass had been established in the Michigan cases and could be expanded in subsequent cases. With each case, I learned we were able to refine our arguments, produce more focused research, and create a complete portrait of underrepresented groups in higher education. There is more work to be done as the saga continues.

Conclusion: Public Scholarship and the Public Good

Acting on our sense of purpose (*ikigai*), we put our best work toward the task of understanding the compelling interest for diversity in higher education. As educators, we believed that each admitted class was enhanced by diversity in the student body, and we acted on those beliefs in psychology and education classrooms. As researchers, we had developed the theory of why diversity enhances learning in college and created a series of replication studies to empirically show how interactions with diverse peers resulted in educational and democratic outcomes over four years of college and nine years after college entry. As public scholars, we collaborated with the legal team, worked to inform the campus, and addressed many audiences to shape and disseminate these results. We did not initially anticipate the impact of the work until it reached the Supreme Court. We provided a strong rationale for diversity in the student body, advanced the conversation about diversity among college educators, and advanced the research in our fields. It is gratifying to see many more studies follow our initial theoretical framing and find confirming results with numerous college student samples and advanced techniques (Bowman, 2010; Bowman, 2011). Although court challenges to affirmative action continue, we have a firm empirical grounding now to support campus efforts to continue to diversify the student body, create the conditions that result in educational outcomes for a diverse democracy, and diversify the college-educated leaders and the workforce for the nation.

From a personal and professional standpoint, the work created a strong sense of the reward that can come from collaboration toward a common goal. My own work was advanced in light years. How long does it take to publish a single scholarly article and show impact? Because we worked on replication studies with multiple outcomes, it would have taken years to produce most of these findings without a team of capable colleagues. The effort led to another large project sponsored by the U.S. Department of Education, Preparing College Students for a Diverse Democracy, which enabled campuses to replicate the *Michigan Student Study* (Office of Academic Multicultural Initiatives, University of Michigan, 2017) and focus on outcomes related to diversity in the first two years of college (Hurtado, 2005). It was intended to advance the goal of liberal education, to move students from their own embedded worldviews to broaden their perspectives with interactions among diverse peers (Hurtado, 2007). That project resulted in many dissertations and articles that accelerated the careers of young scholars who are now in higher education. My public scholar mentors will be pleased to know that I am paying it forward and providing a model for others to follow.

After leaving the University of Michigan, I continued to see the need for campuses to collect data for educational purposes about campus diversity. This led to summer institutes sponsored by the Higher Education Research Institute on creating and using diversity research on college campuses. The legal and educational rationale is shared with administrators so that they can improve their climates for diversity and also assess the impact of their diversity efforts on student outcomes. It also led to the development of the Diverse Learning Environments Survey (Higher Education Research Institute, 2017) with many reliable measures of student experiences of campus climate and positive interactions with diverse peers that are associated with competencies for a diverse democracy. Much of this work that started with the Michigan cases can be replicated on many college campuses. I always return to my original *ikigai*, which is helping institutions improve practices for the success of underrepresented groups in college. I have learned that public scholarship is a personal career choice that integrates research, policy, and practice and is driven by notions of the public good. It is not always easy work to do, but the rewards can be tremendous.

References

Bowman, N. A. (2010). College diversity experiences and cognitive development: A meta-analysis. *Review of Educational Research, 80,* 4–33.

Bowman, N. A. (2011). Promoting participation in a diverse democracy a meta-analysis of college diversity experiences and civic engagement. *Review of Educational Research, 81,* 29–68.

Braddock, J. H., Dawkins, M. P., & Trent, W. (1994). Why desegregate? The effect of school desegregation on adult occupational desegregation of African Americans, Whites, and Hispanics. *International Journal of Contemporary Sociology, 31,* 273–283.

Fisher v. University of Texas at Austin, et al. 133 S. Ct. 2411 (2013).

Grutter v. Bollinger, et al., 539 U.S. 306 (2003).

Gurin, P., Dey, E. L., Hurtado, S., & Gurin, G. (2002). Diversity and higher education: Theory and impact on educational outcomes. *Harvard Educational Review, 72,* 330–366.

Gurin, P., Lehman, J. S., Lewis, E., Dey, E. L., Gurin, G., & Hurtado, S. (2004). *Defending diversity: Affirmative action at the University of Michigan.* Ann Arbor: University of Michigan Press.

Higher Education Research Institute. (2017). *Diverse learning environments survey.* Retrieved from heri.ucla.edu/diverse-learning-environments-survey

Hurtado, S. (2005). The next generation of diversity and intergroup relations research. *Journal of Social Issues, 61,* 595–610.

Hurtado, S. (2007). ASHE presidential address: Linking diversity with the educational and civic missions of higher education. *Review of Higher Education, 30,* 185–196.

Hurtado, S. (2015). The transformative paradigm: Principles and challenges. In A. Aleman, B. P. Pusser, & E. Bensimon (Eds.), *Critical approaches to the study of higher education* (pp. 285–307). Baltimore, MD: Johns Hopkins University.

Hurtado, S., Dey, E. L., Gurin, P., & Gurin, G. (2003). The college environment, diversity, and student learning. In J. Smart (Ed.), *Higher education: Handbook of theory and research* (Vol. 18, pp. 145–189). Amsterdam, The Netherlands: Kluwer Academic Press.

Mertens, D. M. (2003). Mixed methods and the politics of human research: The transformative-emancipatory perspective. In A. Tashakkori, & C. Teddlie (Eds.), *Sage handbook of mixed methods in social and behavioral research* (pp. 134–164). Thousand Oaks, CA: Sage.

Office of Academic Multicultural Initiatives, University of Michigan, (2017). *Michigan student study*. Retrieved from oami.umich.edu/about/research/michigan-student-study

Olivas, M. A. (2006). *The law and higher education: Cases and materials on colleges in court* (3rd ed.). Durham, NC: Carolina Academic Press.

Olivas, M. A. (2012). *No undocumented child left behind: Plyler v. Doe and the education of undocumented children*. New York, NY: New York University Press.

Orfield, G. (Ed.). (2001). *Diversity challenged: Legal crisis and new evidence.* Cambridge, MA: Harvard Education Publishing Group.

Regents of the University of California v. Bakke, 438 U.S. 265 (1978).

Williams, J. B., III. (Ed.). (1988). *Desegregating America's colleges and universities: Title VI regulation of higher education.* New York, NY: Teachers College Press.

5

BLACK DATA MATTER

Connecting Education Research to
the Movement for Black Lives

Charles H. F. Davis III, Shaun R. Harper, and Wilmon A. Christian III

A s scholars in a metropolitan city, we are constantly thinking about ways to connect our research to the publics beyond the often-exclusionary boundaries of higher education. This includes not only the nearby neighborhoods where our institution is located but also similar urban areas with predominantly Black communities across the nation. These considerations have led us not only to focus our research in areas we believe to be useful for improving the life and educational outcomes of Black folks but also to make our best attempts at making our work responsive, timely, and accessible to a broader public beyond the academy.

Over the past few years in particular, our intellectual and political commitments to this praxis have illuminated the potential contributions research can make to vulnerable communities that are resisting various forms of state violence. We begin this chapter by introducing the origins of Black Lives Matter (BLM), the Movement for Black Lives (M4BL), and some of the issues with which they are concerned. Then we discuss three different examples in which we produced and used research on the racial inequities at the educational epicenters of M4BL's community organizing and direct action work. First, we describe the development of a rapid response research project intended to critically shift the discourses about 2014 school closures in Ferguson, Missouri, after the killing of Black teenager Michael Brown. Second, we detail our analysis and public reporting of data on racial disparities in school discipline practices contributing to the school-to-prison pipeline. Third, we recount the development and use of documentary film to socially inform and professionally develop educators teaching Black students.

BLM and M4BL

In 2013, a year after unarmed 17-year-old Trayvon Martin was unjustly killed on his way home from a convenience store in Sanford, Florida, George Zimmerman, the killer, was exonerated of second-degree murder by a Seminole County court. In the wake of this gross miscarriage of justice, just before the Dream Defenders, an organization of young adult Black and Brown organizers, initiated its 31-day occupation of the Florida capitol, Alicia Garza created the social media hashtag #BlackLivesMatter with Patrisse Cullors and Opal Tometi, all of whom are Black women. As a call to action for Black people, Garza (2014) defines *BLM* as

> an ideological and political intervention in a world where Black lives are systematically and intentionally targeted for demise. It is an affirmation of Black folks' contributions to this society, our humanity, and our resilience in the face of deadly oppression. (para. 2)

In collaboration with artists, designers, cultural workers, and others, the hashtag moved beyond social media to the streets of Ferguson. After Darren Wilson, an officer in the St. Louis Police Department, killed 18-year-old Michael Brown, also unarmed, Cullors and Darnell Moore organized a national BLM ride to Missouri to support local on-the-ground efforts. In the aftermath of the unrest in Ferguson, organizers from 18 different cities returned home to start local BLM chapters in their own communities (Kahn-Cullors, 2016). Now, several years later, what was once seen as a movement unto itself has emerged clearly as an international network of activists, organizers, and social movement organizations. BLM has committed itself to develop Black leadership as well as create a movement network "where Black people feel empowered to determine our destinies in our communities" (Kahn-Cullors, 2016, para 6).

On another broader level of the social movement ecology, M4BL has recently emerged to define the collective contemporary resistance of everyday Black people. *M4BL* (2016) defines itself as a

> collective of more than 50 organizations representing thousands of Black people from across the country [that] have come together with renewed energy and purpose to articulate a common vision and agenda. We are a collective that centers and is rooted in Black communities, but we recognize we have a shared struggle with all oppressed people; collective liberation will be a product of all of our work. (Movement for Black Lives, 2016, para 2)

The collective's six-point platform, A Vision for Black Lives, takes on the maladjustment of Black communities resulting from the "named and unnamed wars" (M4BL, 2016, para. 1) against Black people (i.e., the criminalization, incarceration, and killing of Black people by the state). More specifically, the platform demands redress for historic and systemic disenfranchisement from human and citizenship rights that includes, but is not limited to, socioeconomic freedom and the discontinued exploitation of Black labor, divestment from exploitative forces (i.e., police, prisons, and fossil fuels), investment in Black communities (e.g., affordable housing, universal health care, and quality education), and control and shared governance to exercise political power in the best interests of Black communities.

Race and the Ferguson-Florissant School District Closure

On August 9, 2014, unarmed Black teenager Michael Brown was killed by a White St. Louis Police Department officer, Darren Wilson, after being stopped for jaywalking, a commonly cited offense under the broken-windows approach to policing in Ferguson. In the week following Brown's death, which was scheduled to be the start of the 2014–2015 school year, the Ferguson-Florissant School District was forced to remain closed because of unrest in and around the city of Ferguson, which shares its public school district with neighboring Florissant. According to the district administration, the leadership of which is overwhelmingly White, local law enforcement officials and school security staff were consulted on this decision before it was finalized. What remained unclear, however, was the extent to which parents and families of students in the district were engaged in the decision-making process.

Once we learned of this decision, as educational researchers, we were immediately interested in the implications of the school closures on students in the two suburban St. Louis communities. In particular, we were concerned with the disparate impact that delaying the academic year would have on the Black youths in the district. However, neither of these issues seemed to be present in the discourse about what was referred to as the Ferguson Uprising and remained unaddressed by the research community. Therefore, we found it critically important to engage in a rapid response effort to answer several research questions and publicly report our findings. This involved contacting our colleagues and friends we knew to be natives of the St. Louis area and who had attended schools in nearby districts. We did this as a short-order form of determining the validity of our otherwise presumptive concerns. Specifically, this process ultimately involved informal and unstructured interviewing, more similar in style to investigative reporting, which allowed some of our presumptions about the ways area school districts were likely to be racially (and socioeconomically) composed to be interrogated. Once we were able to confirm some of our presumptions (and eliminate others), we

Figure 5.1. Race and the Ferguson-Florissant school district closure.

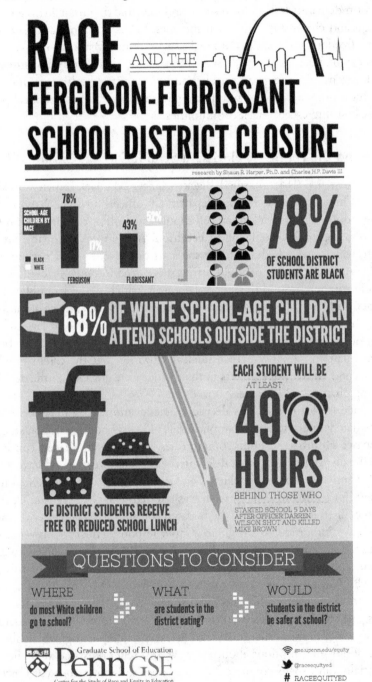

spent two days rigorously mining publicly available databases to empirically determine possible racial inequities resulting from the district's closure.

Matching U.S. Census data in conjunction with statistics from the U.S. Department of Education, Harper and Davis (2014) first examined the extent to which schools were reflective of the children who live within the boundaries of the Ferguson-Florissant School District. Not surprisingly, despite being 60% of the school-age population, Black youths represented 78% of all students in the district. This finding led to further analyses, which ultimately determined that 68% of White children living within the district boundaries actually attended school elsewhere. When considered together, the data made clear that district school closures would disproportionately affect Black youths, whereas most White children would remain unaffected. More specifically, it was determined Black youths would miss at least 49 hours of instruction compared to their White peers enrolled outside the district. Black parents, some of whom partially rely on school as a form of child care during business hours, would also be forced to determine how their children would be cared for during the time they were usually in school. Furthermore, district-level data indicated 75% of students in the district received free or reduced lunch, a commonly used proxy for the socioeconomic composition of students and their home communities. This indicated that Black youths relying on subsidized food programs administered through their school would also be disproportionately affected and could possibly go hungry.

Once these disparities were uncovered, the question of how best to disseminate our findings to be most accessible to the broader public needed to be answered. Ultimately we determined to develop an infographic (see Figure 5.1), rather than a journal article or research brief, to succinctly report the key findings of the study and publish it online on the University of Pennsylvania Center for the Study of Race and Equity in Education's website and social media platforms. In doing so, we first sent the infographic to our database of more than 20,000 teachers, principals and school leaders, school district administrators, and superintendents. We also worked directly with our school's communications office on a press release with a descriptive summary of our findings, as well as the infographic, which subsequently was picked up by several national education media outlets (e.g., *Education Week* and *Inside Higher Ed*) and other news organizations.

Disproportionate Impact of K–12 School Discipline Practices on Black Students

Numerous scholars have studied the impacts of K–12 school discipline practices such as in-school suspension, out-of-school suspension, and expulsion

(Skiba, Michael, Nardo, & Peterson, 2002). For more than two decades, education researchers have consistently found the administration of school discipline to disproportionately affect Black students more than their peers from other racial and ethnic groups generally and their White peers in particular. Much of the school discipline problem is connected to the adoption of zero-tolerance policies, which were suggested to create safer learning environments for all students (Kang-Brown, Trone, Fratello, & Daftary-Kapur, 2013; Skiba & Rausch, 2006). However, these policies are often rigidly applied to students with predetermined, high-stakes consequences that limit professional discretion for individual cases (including those with extenuating circumstances), remove students from schools (and thus opportunities to learn), and involve law enforcement personnel. Displacement from school and the increasing reliance on police to address perceived behavioral issues are regularly cited as major contributing factors to the overcriminalization and incarceration of Black and Brown youths, a process more commonly referred to as the school-to-prison pipeline.

The implementation of zero-tolerance discipline practices has dramatically increased the number of suspensions and expulsions to address low-level issues such as dress code violations and challenging the authority of teachers and administrators to weapons possession or the sale of drugs and other controlled substances (Monahan, VanDerhei, Bechtold, & Cauffman, 2014). Although such punitive approaches have been found to be terribly ineffective, they also have a disproportionate impact on students of color, students with disabilities, and low-income students (Fabelo et al., 2011; Giroux, 2003; Harry & Kinger, 2014; Kennedy-Lewis, 2014; Kim, Losen, & Hewitt, 2010; Losen, Ee, Hodson, & Martinez, 2015; Losen & Skiba, 2010; Noguera, 2003; Skiba & Knesting, 2001; Toldson, 2011; Vincent, Swain-Brady, Tobin, & May, 2011).

In 2015, we examined data on the out-of-school suspensions and expulsions of students in K–12 schools. In our report (see Figure 5.2), Smith and Harper (2015) found that nationally, 1.2 million Black students were suspended from public schools during the 2011–2012 academic year. Nearly 60% of those suspensions occurred across 13 southern states: Alabama, Arkansas, Florida, Georgia, Kentucky, Louisiana, Mississippi, North Carolina, South Carolina, Tennessee, Texas, Virginia, and West Virginia. In their findings, Smith and Harper reported the following disproportionalities in school suspensions from the 3,022 school districts they analyzed:

- In 132 southern school districts, Black students were suspended at rates 5 times (or higher than) their representation in the student population.

Figure 5.2. Disproportionate impact of K–12 school suspension and expulsion of Black students in southern states.

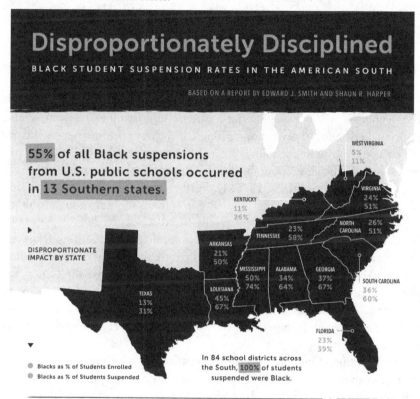

Disproportionately Disciplined

BLACK STUDENT SUSPENSION RATES IN THE AMERICAN SOUTH

BASED ON A REPORT BY EDWARD J. SMITH AND SHAUN R. HARPER

55% of all Black suspensions from U.S. public schools occurred in **13 Southern states.**

DISPROPORTIONATE IMPACT BY STATE

WEST VIRGINIA
5%
11%

VIRGINIA
24%
51%

KENTUCKY
11%
26%

NORTH CAROLINA
26%
51%

TENNESSEE
23%
58%

ARKANSAS
21%
50%

MISSISSIPPI
50%
74%

ALABAMA
34%
64%

GEORGIA
37%
67%

SOUTH CAROLINA
36%
60%

TEXAS
13%
31%

LOUISIANA
45%
67%

FLORIDA
23%
39%

● Blacks as % of Students Enrolled
● Blacks as % of Students Suspended

In 84 school districts across the South, **100%** of students suspended were Black.

Some recommendations...

■ Black families, religious congregations, and others concerned about racial justice must hold schools accountable and partner with educators to identify alternatives to policies and practices that sustain the school-to-prison pipeline.

■ Zero tolerance discipline policies do not make schools safer. School leaders need to eliminate them, offer more professional development for educators on managing student behaviors, and lead district-wide conversations about racial equity.

■ Teaching more about implicit bias and other racist forces that lead to disproportionality in school discipline must occur in schools of education, as well as other sites where teachers are prepared and educational leaders are certified.

More recommendations are offered in the report.

Read the full report, including suspension rates for every school district in the South, at **gse.upenn.edu/equity/SouthernStates**

Graduate School of Education
PennGSE
Center for the Study of Race and Equity in Education

- In 84 districts, Blacks were 100% of the students suspended from public schools.
- In 346 districts, Blacks were 75% or more of the students suspended from public schools.

- In 743 districts, Blacks were 50% or more of the students suspended from public schools.
- Blacks constituted 74% of suspensions from public schools in Mississippi, which was the highest proportion among the states.
- Florida schools suspended the highest total number of Black students ($n = 121,468$).

The report was primarily created to better equip those concerned with the school-to-prison pipeline (i.e., parents and families, educators and policymakers, and grassroots organizing collectives) with district-level data, which could be used to hold teachers, school leaders, school boards, and other elected officials accountable for the "educational mistreatment of Black youth" (Harper & Smith, 2015, p. 1). Furthermore, the report was intended to assist consciousness-raising of faculty in schools of education, and other entities that prepare and develop teachers and school leaders, in regard to racial biases in school discipline and the systemic effects resulting from the prejudicial perspectives of Black youths as criminals. To that end, intentional efforts were made to disseminate the report widely through the Center for the Study of Race and Equity in Education's extensive e-mail database, press and media contacts provided by school and university communications offices, and through interpersonal relationships of center staff with community stakeholders.

For example, Davis had preexisting relationships with several organizing collectives in Florida, 1 of the 13 states examined in the report. More specifically, the Dream Defenders (dreamdefenders.org), with chapters in 6 cities throughout the state, and the Power U Center for Social Change (poweru.org), an organization dedicated to developing leadership among Black and Brown youths and Black women, were collectively engaged in organizing efforts to dismantle the school-to-prison pipeline. Immediately following publication of the report, tweets and direct messages from Davis were sent to both organizations' Twitter accounts. The messages included a link to the report as well as annotations for the subsets of data in key Florida school districts where actions have taken place or were forthcoming (e.g., citizen testimony at local school board meetings). As intended, community groups like Dream Defenders and Power U were provided almost immediately with substantive data to support their efforts to change policy in their communities. In the case of Power U in particular, the data were reported to be useful and to have filled an important but challenging dimension of fully understanding the severe impacts of school discipline on Black youths. This was particularly true for districts whose access to such data was either restricted, not publicly reported, or not analyzed for racial disparities by district officials.

Documentary Film and the Professional Development of K–12 Teachers

In October 2015, our center was approached to be a partner in the production of a documentary film focused on innovative solutions to the formidable challenges facing Black youths in urban education. In partnership with TVOne, a Black-owned and operated national television network, and Lighthouse Films, staff from our center took the role of consultant to determine the film's general direction, issues for investigation, stakeholders, and on-camera contributors. An important background detail worth sharing is that sometime after initially being approached about the film, it was revealed that the network was also in partnership with a for-profit university, the University of Phoenix, which was to serve as the film's underwriter. Naturally, we harbored concerns about how the project may be influenced by the University of Phoenix's agenda, which we discussed collaboratively and at length before engaging any further. However, we were also forced to consider the extent to which for-profit institutions generally, and the University of Phoenix more specifically, had reached and built relationships with publics historically disenfranchised from traditional colleges and universities. In this particular case, the University of Phoenix was easily the most well-known and broadest reaching for-profit institution in the marketplace. In that way, we considered how our perspectives, informed by decades of education research and practice, had an important opportunity to determine the narrative of a film that would have an extensive reach. And so, staff at the center proceeded to participate in the production as a partner, which further involved Davis serving as a writer, executive producer, and the documentary's host.

In December 2015, *Saving Tomorrow, Today* (Mysak & Davis, 2016) went into production on location in three metropolitan cities: Miami, Philadelphia, and New York. Each city had a specific focus on an area we felt was critically important to elevating the work of communities, schools, and educators invested in the future of Black youths. To confirm that our foci were geographically and organizationally appropriate, we scheduled individual calls with each of the prospective groups we intended to work with. On each call, we provided an overview of our broader vision for the film and the tentative production schedule. However, and this is important, we also solicited direction and feedback from each prospective partner to determine the best way to capture their work, schools, and communities in relation to our vision. This required us to remain flexible and open to changing our schedule to not disrupt and to better align with the existing structures in which each organization, classroom, or educator operated.

For example, in Miami the focus was on community-based, youth-serving organizations and the educators who provided co- and extracurricular learning opportunities outside and away from schools. Specifically, organizations like the Power U Center brought together high school students to discuss their organizing work on moving schools toward restorative justice practices and away from punitive forms of punishment. We also reached out to contacts at the Overtown Youth Center and Belafonte Tacolcy Center in Liberty City to understand out-of-classroom and extracurricular learning programs for Black youths in the Miami-Dade area. These community educators, who were either teachers or former teachers, along with several of their students and a few parents gathered to share their experiences working with the programs provided by the community centers. In Philadelphia, researchers from the Center for the Study of Race and Equity in Education presented evidence from our various reports, including the aforementioned racial disparities in school discipline as well as strategies and practices employed by urban high schools to encourage and support Black students' admission to college. In New York, we worked with colleagues from Columbia University Teachers College to visit classrooms in the Bronx, some of which were existing research or practicum sites. This made accessing and filming in the school a less arduous process to navigate rather than attempting to cultivate a new relationship with a school. In addition, we directly contacted elementary school leaders in Brooklyn to highlight the development of community schools and use of technological innovation to enhance pre–K and early childhood learning. In both settings, educators and students shared strategies and pedagogical practices used to improve Black student engagement in the classroom and various measures of academic achievement.

In February 2016, the promotional trailer debuted on TVOne during a broadcast of the National Association for the Advancement of Colored People Image Awards. The next month, the 22-minute film was nationally broadcasted on the same network and subsequently released online on a dedicated platform. Because the film was well received on its release, the film was soon requested for screenings by a variety of audiences, including the National Action Network, a community-based organization founded by Al Sharpton, for its national meeting; the National Network of State Teachers of the Year; the State of Black Arizona for its statewide meeting; and the Philadelphia Forum on Advancing Black Male Education Success. Additionally, during the screenings in Arizona, our center's researchers and an affiliate used the film to facilitate two professional development programs for teachers in Phoenix and Tucson high schools.

By and large, the film has been one of the most publicly useful and accessible productions of our center. Beyond the initial release, the film has continued to be used as a tool for faculty in schools of education, in professional development for teachers and school leaders, and for parents and community-based educators. The film's impact in breadth and depth has been deeply encouraging to us as we think about ways to do more work with film as we take on new and important topics related to equity in education.

Conclusion

Long before we ever became scholars and certainly before codirecting a national research center, we were Black boys from the American south. In many ways, our experiences as Black youths and adolescents drew us to specifically investigate the racial inequities in education. More important, however, we had a desire to produce research in ways that could not only be timely but also useful and accessible to the communities from whence we came. And as the political landscape and racial climate have intensified in recent years, we have found ourselves wanting to be even more intentional about ensuring that the impetus for our work is not lost among the many professional demands of academic life.

The three cases in this chapter are but a few examples we hope illuminate the possibilities for public scholarship in this and future sociopolitical moments. In part, the duty of public scholarship is one of timeliness in regard to the issues it addresses. However, implicit in the duty of timeliness is ensuring that the often lengthy processes and systems for conducting and disseminating scholarship do not limit our ability to connect research to practice in real time. A second duty of public scholarship is accessibility, specifically in regard to the formats used to present research. Ideally, research should be translatable into multiple publication types (e.g., scholarly essays, reports, and policy briefs) and media communications (e.g., infographics, digital videos, and films) that are publicly accessible. In some cases, however, and in those we present here, the production of research can begin as a public endeavor in which the format is predetermined in the same way scholars write journal articles for peer review.

We realize what we are suggesting is not easily attainable. The current reward structure for many scholars and researchers, particularly within the academy, fails to consider many forms of public scholarship as valuable. Conversely, the publications that result in the most awards have little value to epistemologically and materially disenfranchised publics beyond academe. Therefore, we invite scholars to reimagine our commitments to the conventions of our profession, particularly those that may reinforce the very relationships of power we challenge in our research. To be clear, our invitation is not meant to imply doing away with one form of production for others.

Rather, we are advocating centering the intentions and purposes of our work as we carefully consider its production and dissemination. We believe doing so restores agency not only to ourselves as researchers but also to the communities where we hope our scholarship will be the most valuable.

References

Fabelo, T., Thompson, M. D., Plotkin, M., Carmichael, D., Marchbanks, M. P., III, & Booth, E. A. (2011). *Breaking schools' rules: A statewide study of how school discipline relates to students' success and juvenile justice involvement.* New York, NY: Council of State Governments Justice Center.

Garza, A. (2014). *A herstory of #Blacklivesmatter movement.* Retrieved from www .thefeministwire.com/2014/10/blacklivesmatter-2

Giroux, H. (2003). Racial injustice and disposable youth in the age of zero tolerance. *International Journal of Qualitative Studies in Education, 16,* 553–565.

Harper, S. R., & Davis, C. H. F., III. (2014). *Race and the Ferguson-Florissant School District closure.* Retrieved from www.gse.upenn.edu/sites/gse.upenn.edu.equity/files/CREE%20Ferguson%20School%20District%20Infographic.jpg

Harper, S. R., & Smith, E. J. (2015). *Disproportionate impact of K–12 school suspension and expulsion on Black students in southern states.* Philadelphia: University of Pennsylvania, Center for the Study of Race and Equity in Education.

Harry, B., & Klinger, J. (2014). *Why are so many minority students in special education? Understanding race & disability in schools* (2nd ed.). New York, NY: Teachers College Press.

Kahn-Cullors, P. (2016). *We didn't start a movement, we started a network.* Retrieved from medium.com/@patrissemariecullorsbrignac/we-didn-t-start-a-movement-we-started-a-network-90f9b5717668

Kang-Brown, J., Trone, J., Fratello, J., & Daftary- Kapur, T. (2013). *A generation later: What we've learned about zero tolerance in schools.* New York, NY: Vera Institute of Justice.

Kennedy-Lewis, B. L. (2014). Using critical policy analysis to examine competing discourses in zero tolerance legislation: Do we really want to leave no child behind? *Journal of Education Policy, 29,* 165–194.

Kim, C. Y., Losen, D. J., & Hewitt, D. T. (2010). *The school-to-prison pipeline: Structuring legal reform.* New York, NY: New York University Press.

Losen, D. J., Ee, J., Hodson, C., & Martinez, T. E. (2015). Disturbing inequities: Exploring the relationship between racial disparities in special education identification and discipline. In D. J. Losen (Ed.), *Closing the school discipline gap: Equitable remedies for excessive exclusion* (pp. 89–106). New York, NY: Teachers College Press.

Losen, D. J., & Skiba, R. J. (2010). *Suspended education: Urban middle schools in crisis.* Los Angeles, CA: UCLA Center for Civil Rights Remedies, the Civil Rights Project.

Monahan, K. C., VanDerhei, S., Bechtold, J., & Cauffman, E. (2014). From the school yard to the squad car: School discipline, truancy, and arrest. *Journal of Youth and Adolescence, 43*, 1110–1122.

Movement for Black Lives. (2016). *A vision for Black lives.* Retrieved from policy .m4bl.org/platform

Mysak, C. (Director), & Davis III, C. H. F. (Executive Producer, Writer). (2016, March 3). *Saving tomorrow, today* [Video file]. Retrieved from newsone.com/ watch/3664448/watch

Noguera, P. A. (2003). Schools, prisons, and social implications of punishment: Rethinking disciplinary practices. *Theory Into Practice, 42*, 341–350.

Skiba, R. J., & Knesting, K. (2001). Zero tolerance, zero evidence: An analysis of school disciplinary practice. *New Directions for Youth Development, 92*, 17–44.

Skiba, R. J., Michael, R. S., Nardo, A. C., & Peterson, R. L. (2002). The color of discipline: Sources of racial and gender disproportionality in school punishment. *Urban Review, 34*, 317–342.

Skiba, R. J., & Rausch, M. K. (2006). Zero tolerance, suspension, and expulsion: Questions of equity and effectiveness. In C. M. Evertson, & C. S. Weinstein (Eds.), *Handbook for classroom management: Research, practice, and contemporary issues* (pp. 1063–1089). New York, NY: Routledge.

Toldson, I. A. (2011). *Breaking barriers 2: Plotting the path away from juvenile detention and toward academic success for school-age African American males.* Washington, DC: Congressional Black Caucus Foundation.

Vincent, C. G., Swain-Bradway, J., Tobin, T. J., & May, S. (2011). Disciplinary referrals for culturally and linguistically diverse students with and without disabilities: Patterns resulting from school-wide positive behavior support. *Exceptionality, 19*, 175–190.

6

THE REMAKING OF MY RESEARCH PRACTICE

From Creating Knowledge to Creating Equity-Minded Competence

Estela Mara Bensimon

In the simplest terms, my work focuses on exposing racial inequality in higher education. I want to make it public to practitioners, leaders, policymakers, and scholars. My aim is to create practitioners' awareness of the fine-grained details of racial inequality and build their capacity to adopt racial equity as a norm in their classrooms, departments, curricula, hiring practices, evaluations, and accountability systems. Essentially, the public in my scholarship is exemplified in the use of research tools, not simply as methods to gather data but as instruments to develop equity-minded competence (Bensimon, 2007; Bensimon & Harris, 2012; Bensimon & Malcom, 2012). By describing my own journey as a scholar who moved from traditional research methods to research methods that are intentionally designed to attain racial equity in higher education outcomes, I reflect on the experiences, knowledge, and politics of social justice that help me practice critical action research methods. For those of you who share my concerns and have aspirations to do research that does much more than describe the contours of racial inequity (or other forms of injustice), my story offers a window into how you might develop the methods of critical action research. However, I caution that the experiences I describe as influential in the development of my critical action research agenda and methods are not intended to suggest that only those who have similar life experiences can engage in critical action research. My story shows there are many ways of being a public scholar. Most important, my story illustrates what helped me put action into public scholarship.

In the spirit of being instructive I return to the question that might be in your mind—So, how can I do this?—and provide some practical advice.

How I Developed a Research Practice Focused on Equity Mindness

To those who did not know me before I became a professor of higher education, I decided 16 or so years ago to adopt what may have appeared to be a radical paradigmatic shift from traditional methods of producing knowledge. In choosing to dedicate myself to critical action research aimed at eliminating racial inequality in higher education, I embraced what some view as activist methods of social action. In reality, doing research that has an explicit racial equity focus represents a return to an agenda that represented my work many decades ago. Polkinghorne (2004) said our practices are informed by knowledge that lives in the background below our conscience. This knowledge, as Romm (2010) suggests, is the product of "our ways of living and being" (p. vi). My turn toward racial equity through the methods of critical action research draws on the ways of living and being as a community organizer and advocate. For me, graduate school and subsequent faculty appointments required new ways of living and being, and the know-how of being a community organizer and activist receded into the background—below consciousness— but thankfully was reawakened by a series of important events.

Doing Social Change

The foundation for my turn to critical action research and the pursuit of an agenda centered on the attainment of racial equity in higher education was laid a long time ago, before I even knew what being an academic meant, and for sure before I knew how to become one.

I came of age in the 1960s, and after finishing college, imbued by the ideals of the anti-Vietnam War Movement, the Civil Rights Movement, and the emergence of the Black Panthers and the Young Lords, I became professionally involved in community-oriented organizations that advocated for the rights of the children and youth of the Puerto Rican diaspora in New Jersey. As an educational advocate, my role was to persuade state education officials and policymakers that bilingual education was a legitimate pedagogical approach for the dominant Spanish-language students who swelled enrollments in the public schools of Newark, Jersey City, Hoboken, Vineland, Perth Amboy, Paterson, Union City, Weehawken, and Camden. These cities were undergoing a major racial and ethnic transformation. Whites moved out to the suburbs, and Puerto Ricans and Cubans moved into the cities, turning predominantly White working-class neighborhoods into culturally and linguistically Puerto Rican and Cuban enclaves.

Much of my work then consisted of the kinds of activities that Adrianna Kezar, Joseph Kitchen, and Yianna Drivalas describe as public scholarship. I presented testimony in the New Jersey legislature, I served on educational boards and committees where my job was to represent the interests of the Puerto Rican community, I reviewed policy and legislation to assess their impact on Puerto Ricans, I collaborated with other community organizations to join as an amicus curiae in the famous legal case of *Robinson vs. Cahill* (1973) to equalize public school funding, I drove miles and miles from Trenton, the capital of New Jersey, to the southern farms of Vineland to the industrial towns of Perth Amboy and Elizabeth to Hoboken and Jersey City in the north and to the Puerto Rican neighborhoods in Newark and Paterson. My work consisted of meeting with grassroots organizations and informing them about educational policies, providing them with the tools to demand bilingual education and to advocate for data transparency. From 1969 to 1979, my professional life involved power struggles, conflict, and compromise. With my colleagues at Congreso Boricua, a statewide community and political organization I participated in meetings with policymakers and institutional leaders where discussions were focused on institutionalized and overt racism, low-performing schools and teachers' insensitivity toward Puerto Ricans, and higher education policies and practices that limited access to higher education.

Thinking back on it, my work aimed to provide Puerto Rican community groups with the know-how to advocate for educational rights. We were outsiders trying to fight our way into the institutions that had an impact on educational opportunity and political power for a community that was just starting to make itself seen and heard. For the most part, this work involved battling and arguing with the leaders of institutions and government offices who believed that a meritocracy worked equally well for all. Their standpoint was that recent Puerto Rican arrivals should learn English and that the institutionalization of bilingual education would retard their assimilation.

In 1999, I founded the Center for Urban Education (CUE; cue.usc .edu), whose mission was to create tools to remediate institutional structures and develop equity-minded agency among practitioners and leaders. I wanted to transform racial equity from an ideal that was embraced in the abstract to something that was actionable and measurable. In my community work, I advocated for bilingual education and other reforms aimed at Spanish speakers on the grounds of fairness and justice. As an academic, however, I learned to frame advocacy for racial equity in higher education in the language of theory, evidence, and empiricism.

Engaging in advocacy based on a moral appeal for justice has helped me develop a practice of research that is based on the ideals of justice and is pursued through methods of participatory critical action research (Kemmis & McTaggart, 2000). The change agenda I pursue today is not all that different from the one I pursued in my twenties, but the methods and knowledge base I draw from are very different.

From Community Activism to Academic Assimilation

I wish I could say that throughout my doctoral work I was planning on how to use my knowledge for emancipatory work. But as I describe in another work (Bensimon, in press), graduate school and subsequent appointments at the Ford Foundation; postdoctoral work at the University of California, Los Angeles's Center for the Study of Community Colleges; research with the National Center for Postsecondary Governance and Finance; and finally my appointments to the faculty at Pennsylvania State University and the University of Southern California resulted, I am self-conscious to admit, in a too-successful assimilation. In graduate school I learned to be dispassionate and to view higher education through the lens of male authors who considered the research university an institution that had to continuously protect itself from federal government regulations that required compliance (e.g., with affirmative action), from students who expected the university to take a public stand against social injustice (e.g., South Africa apartheid), and from pressures to make curricula more inclusive (e.g., the establishment of women's and ethnic studies). The discriminatory practices of historically White institutions were never discussed or studied. The curricula I was exposed to taught me to view higher education structurally, not culturally or critically.

The seductiveness of the life of the mind and the privileges enjoyed by professors at research universities are hard to resist, so I conformed to the rules of doing research that met the criteria of objectivity and to pay more attention to the particularity of the studies I conducted than to their social value. I bought into the pursuit of knowledge for its own sake, the separation between theory and practice; I even bought into the idea that gender was irrelevant, and in the first few studies I published on leadership I used the generic *he* to describe women and men (see Bensimon, 1989, for a feminist reconstruction of my studies). Compared to the moral urgency and political tensions associated with community advocacy, academic life felt cloistered and far away from the emotionally charged power struggles in advocacy work.

Fortunately, a series of circumstances reawakened my interest in social causes. At Penn State in 1989, along with my colleagues and friends Bill Tierney, Bobby Wright, Kevin Allison, Sabrina Chapman, Tony D'Augelli,

Sue Rankin, and many others, I became involved in a movement to include sexual orientation as one of the categories protected by Penn State's nondiscrimination statement. We used our research skills to bring to light through surveys and narratives the existence of lesbian and gay students and faculty in an overtly homophobic environment (Bensimon, 1992).

From that point on, my work increasingly veered toward feminist research. Although still an untenured assistant professor at Penn State, I organized a lecture series of feminist scholars, leading to harsh criticism from some of my colleagues in a department that was all White and male. I created a course on women in academe and introduced my students to the works of bell hooks, Gloria Anzaldúa, Sandra Harding, and many others. And when I moved to the University of Southern California (where I am now a full professor), I developed a course titled Politics of Difference, a lecture series on the metro Latinization of Los Angeles, and a PhD seminar on urban education.

But these efforts, even though they addressed critical issues of identity, oppression, and subjugated knowledges, were performed according to academic norms and within the walls of the university. It was not until 1999 that I made a dramatic shift in my research practice and founded CUE, where social action research became a strategy to address inequality in the higher education outcomes of students whose relationship with the United States was mediated by enslavement, colonization, and territorial invasion. Despite the democratic intents of civil rights legislation and the many subsequent compensatory interventions to level the racial playing field, African Americans, Latinos and Latinas (particularly from Puerto Rico and Mexico), and Native Americans continued to be failed by a system of higher education that was racially unconscious. With few exceptions, much of the higher education scholarship that focused on the educational participation and outcomes of African Americans, Latinos and Latinas, and Native Americans were quantitative and concerned with the search for variables that would explain why the outcomes of these student populations were different from the outcomes of White students. Race was just one more variable, no different than gender, age, and other personal characteristics that go into the cocktail mix that produces correlational studies.

As a researcher, I felt most at home with theories of organization and leadership, so instead of approaching the problem of racial inequity as a behavioral, motivational, aspirational, efficacious, and academic preparation, I chose to frame it as a problem of organizational learning. Obviously, organizations do not exist without people, so practitioners, including faculty, staff, and leaders, needed to understand the manifestation of racial inequality in their own institutions and ask themselves why there is a consistent pattern

THE REMAKING OF MY RESEARCH PRACTICE

of unequal educational outcomes among racially minoritized students and how practices, structures, and policies are implicated in the production of these inequalities. I chose to treat racial inequality as a problem of racism institutionalized in the routine practices that keep colleges running and in the established structures of teaching and research. This is of course not novel. A great deal has been written on the phenomenon of institutional and structural racism (Baez, 2000; Bonilla-Silva, 2010). On the other hand, the research methods I adopted to develop the capacity of institutions and practitioners to more effectively produce racial equity in educational outcomes *were* novel, to me and to the field of higher education studies. There was no shortage of studies that touched directly or indirectly on topics of racial inequality, and my interest was to conduct research that would create change (2004), so I chose to learn and apply the methods of participatory critical action research (Kemmis & McTaggart, 2000).

The Motivation to Develop a Research Practice Focused on Racial Equity

One of the motivations to re-create my research practice through the methods of participatory critical action research was an interest in establishing more enduring relationships with colleges that were struggling to improve the educational outcomes of students of color. I knew that I wanted to do research to create change rather than describe how change happens and that the change I sought to create was at the local institutional level from the inside. Inspired by the work of Donald Polkinghorne (2004), I was persuaded that individuals, not programs or best practices, should be treated as the embodiment of interventions. The severity and pervasiveness of racial and ethnic inequity called for a model of intervention that is different from typical programmatic approaches. Thus, my colleagues and I at CUE, first with the guidance of Don Polkinghorne and later with that of Robert Rueda, developed a research model that involved faculty in a structured and facilitated process of inquiry into the structures, practices, and policies that shape the institutional culture that is experienced by racially minoritized students. I mentioned earlier the importance of drawing on the work of scholars from other disciplines to establish a strong theoretical and empirical foundation for action research tools, and I provided the example of institutional racism. In my work it has also been important to draw on theories of practitioner learning and change and create tools that are informed by these theories. We invited Don Polkinghorne and Robert Rueda, both of whom are psychologists, to join our design team, which consisted of CUE staff that meets every Wednesday for two hours to design, present, and discuss tools. From them we learned to focus on the effectiveness of our tools to bring about practitioner self-change (Polkinghorne, 2004) and frame the purpose of our tools to remediate activity settings where practices are produced and reproduced (Bustillos, Rueda, & Bensimon, 2011). The deep imprints of Alicia Dowd's intellectual leadership as CUE's codirector for five years before joining Penn State's faculty are noticeable in all of CUE's tools and in particular in the analysis of impact (Dowd & Bensimon, 2015). This is all to say that I had the motivation to do critical action research, but it was made possible through collaboration with individuals whose specialized expertise enabled me to see critical action research more expansively

Learning How to Do Critical Action Research That Changes Mind-Sets

My motivation to remake my research practice was great, but I was a neophyte in action research methods, and most of my knowledge derived from the K–12 teacher inquiry literature and from my memories of the methods used in community organizing. I started out in this work thinking that by involving faculty and staff in the process of populating the Equity Scorecard (a data tool created by CUE; see cue.usc.edu/tools/the-equity-scorecard) with data disaggregated by race and ethnicity inequities in access; academic progress; representation in science, technology, engineering, and mathematics majors; grade point averages; degree completion; and other indicators of success, it would serve as a catalyst to question how things are done and to take action. I assumed that others would react to such data as I did—with shock and with the resolve to do something about it. But although some participants responded as I hoped they would, too many had a very different reaction. They absolved themselves of responsibility and came up with racialized rationalizations. Practitioners who assume that students are responsible for their own success are common among most faculty members in all sectors of higher education. The rationalizations to normalize racial inequity offered by participants in the early years of implementation of the Equity Scorecard came as a shock. Why did I not anticipate this? What made me think that faculty at Hispanic-serving institutions with large numbers of Latino and Latina and Black students would have the critical racial understanding to ask, Why is it that my or our teaching is not as effective with Latino and Black students as it appears to be with White students? Confronted with this challenge, it became obvious to me that data alone would not be a catalyst to change.

It quickly became clear that the Equity Scorecard tool by itself was not sufficient; it was a point of departure, but by itself it would not change the deficit and racialized perspectives that erupted in response to data. The deficit perspectives expressed by our partners in response to their own data required us to build action research tools that would remediate deficit perspectives among our institutional partners and assist them in adopting a critical race-conscious stance toward their own practices.

The tool-making aspect of action research has not received much attention in writings about action research or social action research. Yet tools are essential to engage participants in action inquiry that results in becoming competent as an equity-minded practitioner. Although action inquiry is the methodology through all our work, in the same way that data alone will not make practitioners more critically conscious, inquiry without a critical race understanding will not be transformative. In fact, in our work we have found that inquiry that is not grounded in an understanding of the many faces and forms of racism may mislead practitioners into thinking that being more welcoming or making greater use of active learning pedagogies represents equity mindedness (Dowd & Bensimon, 2015). In our work, we use tools to develop critical race consciousness, and this means we must be vigilant about the ways we direct our partners to *see* race in situations they do not typically think of as having race.

For example, consider James Gray, the chair of the math department at Community College of Aurora. To understand how institutionalized racism was reflected in his hiring practices, we had him think about the following questions: Who is involved in hiring? What are the rules on hiring? What are the documents and other artifacts that support hiring? and What are the specific practices on hiring? In our work these questions represent a tool to interrogate taken-for-granted activities that are repeated blindly over and over again. Posing these questions was made possible by our understanding of sociohistorical activity theory (Engeström, 2001; Roth & Lee, 2007) and institutionalized racism (Baez, 2000). The power of these questions is evident in James's reflections:

> The [Equity Scorecard] process led me to face the fact that over a ten-year period I had never hired an African American instructor, something I found very difficult to be confronted with. It became clear during a review of the hiring practices of full-time and part-time faculty that the strategies used to recruit faculty disadvantaged candidates of color. As an example, a recruiting strategy for both full-time and part-time faculty has been to contact department chairs from CCA's [Community College of Aurora] sister community colleges for referrals. While this strategy met the needs of finding faculty to fill positions, the strategy all but ensured the pool would not be diverse. (Felix, Bensimon, Hanson, Gray, & Klingsmith, 2015, p. 38)

Inquiry into his own practices led James Gray to change the rules and practices of hiring. For example, he increased the number of prescreening telephone interviews from 6 to 25, and he eliminated experiential requirements that might exclude candidates from minoritized groups. Most important, candidates who were invited for the on-campus visit were asked to do something new. In addition to having to demonstrate how they would teach a math problem, they were asked to simulate explaining the syllabus on the first day of class. A syllabus activity, another CUE tool, had helped him and his colleagues see the importance of the syllabus as a cultural practice that influences how students feel about a class, the faculty members, and their likelihood of success. This new practice helped them see that candidates of color who were first-generation students used the activity as a means of interacting with students whereas other candidates tended to just flip through the pages. The changes in the hiring process resulted in the addition of Latino and African American instructors to a department that had none prior to the implementation of CUE's Equity Scorecard.

Creating Tools to Develop Equity-Minded Competence Among Practitioners and Leaders

We provided James Gray with the tools to become an equity-minded practitioner. The tools helped him see institutional racism in his own hiring practices. My training as a researcher and teacher enables me to translate theories of change into practical tools that aim to change the minds, hearts, and practices of faculty, staff, and leaders whose collaboration is essential to achieve racial equity in higher education. The instructional design of CUE's tools consists of components to support conceptual knowledge, modeling of a competence or concept, active learning, and situated adaptation. For example, to be equity-minded, practitioners need to understand institutional racism as an endemic quality of higher education that is produced through everyday practices. Most practitioners are novices when it comes to seeing how racialization happens through routines they have learned to accept as natural and neutral. Consequently, CUE's tools include instructional content to teach practitioners the historical, economic, social, and cultural antecedents of racism. Modeling and active learning focused on institutional racism include tools that provide practitioners with protocols to see race and racialization in hiring, the curriculum, tutoring centers, honors programs, and numerical data. In addition to protocols, we create case studies and videos that capture the enactment of institutionalized racism through the experiences of students. We also use the methods of simulation and peer-to-peer observations. Interdisciplinary scholarship has been helpful to shape our tools. To provide a brief example, CUE's understanding of institutional racism derives from reading history (Wilder, 2013), sociology (Bonilla, 2010), critical race theory as applied in education (Harper, 2012; Ladson-Billing, 1998) and contemporary observers (Coates, 2016). We are mindful that participants in our projects will not have the time to read these works, so we create tools to provide the content they need to understand the theory and practices of institutional racism within their immediate context. We invest a lot of time in translating the conceptual knowledge underlying institutional racism into tools that will enable practitioners to see how institutional racism happens through what they notice and fail to notice, through what they consider good and not good, through what they say and fail to say. This aspect of the tool-making process requires the capacity to communicate concepts through images, stories, and active learning. Creativity is one of the most difficult aspects of tool making because as researchers we rely on language, spoken and written, to communicate. For example, I can explain the difference between equity, equality, and diversity in words. However, we have discovered that it is more effective to show these concepts, and after many failed trials, Debbie Hanson, one of our staff members who has the gift of turning concepts into compelling images, created a set of images that make equity, equality, and diversity easy to grasp and hard to forget (see cue.usc .edu/files/2017/02/CUE-Protocol-Workbook-Final_Web.pdf).

Learning to Do Critical Action Research

Drawing from what I have written, my advice to readers who are interested in critical action research is as follows.

Keep it small. Design a project that is confined to a small group of practitioners who have demonstrated an interest in solving a problem of inequity, for example, science, technology, engineering, mathematics courses; participation in honors programs; or faculty hiring.

Know what *critical* means in theory and practice. Throughout this chapter I use the term *critical action research*. It is very important to have a substantive understanding of the meaning of critical if your goal is to conduct research to make higher education more just for historically oppressed groups. In my work critical requires understanding how institutional racism operates to place at a disadvantage populations whose skin color is not White or whose ethnic and national origins have turned them into minoritized groups. This kind of work requires interdisciplinary study. The higher education literature is not sufficient.

Learn how to design learning tools and the skills to facilitate implementation. Critical action research requires the researcher to have the know-how to think of the details that go into creating a structure that enables a group of practitioners to conduct inquiry activities and to lay out a plan to learn about the context and the participants to design tools that start from what the participants need and want, rather than from where the researcher is or wants the participants to be. We have learned, the hard way, that it is easier to get to equity mindedness if the work is carefully scaffolded on what is familiar to the participants. We have also learned that without a detailed facilitation plan, inquiry activities will get derailed. Facilitating inquiry means knowing how to ask questions and respond in the moment. This takes practice and disciplined listening. My advice to novices is to take the role of learner, and when a practitioner says something such as, "African Americans are not doing well because they are athletes" rather than reacting by saying, "You are stereotyping," ask, "Tell me how you know they are athletes?" and "How many African Americans are there in this college and how many are athletes?" Questions like these help practitioners pause and see they are making assertions without evidence. The role of the researcher as facilitator is to create a disturbance, that is, make the practitioner less sure about the truth and more open to view stereotypical assertions as a hunch that needs to be proven.

Find sources to stimulate creative thought. Making tools is a creative process, and it is important to cultivate inspiration from the work of others or establish partnerships with others. At CUE we find inspiration in news stories, opinion pieces, fiction and nonfiction literature, music, theater, film, cartoons, TED talks, and videos. We have organized these sources into topics that are relevant to our work and stored them in a searchable database.

Assess learning and change. The purpose of critical action research is to assist practitioners to change themselves. In our work, self-change means becoming conscious of racial inequality and the role of the practitioner in creating and undoing racial inequality in his or her own practices as well as in institutional structures, policies, and practices. We measure practitioner learning and change through observations, particularly changes in language that signal equity mindedness, though pre- and postinterviews and surveys, and through evidence that show changes. For example, in the case of James Gray, which I described as an example of equity-minded change, we were able to observe learning and change in the implementation of new hiring practices as well as in the outcome of the changed hiring practices.

Learn from failures. At the start of our work I naively believed that evidence of racial inequality would move practitioners to act in socially just ways. But instead I found that they rationalized racial inequity by pathologizing students of color. My initial reaction was to blame the practitioners for implicit racism, and I had to remind myself that in doing so I was responding the way they responded to their students. I needed to ask, What is it about our approach or tools that are not working? By always asking this question, my colleagues and I at CUE have been able to persevere and stay focused in our mission.

Conclusion

The pursuit of racial equity through the methods of action research applied at the local level is quite pragmatic in that, as I showed in the example of James Gray, I seek to bring about changes in routine practices and in the activity settings where these practices take place. Treating the evidence of racial equity gaps in the outcomes produced by the math department as an indeterminate situation that can be better understood and resolved through the methods of collaborative inquiry among practitioners reflects Dewey's (1938) pragmatism. It is also a reflection of the principles of community organizing that to bring about transformation you have to start from where people are and provide them with the tools to create their own knowledge and self-change.

References

Baez, B. (2000). Race-related service and faculty of color: Conceptualizing critical agency in academe. *Higher Education, 39*, 363–391.

Bensimon, E. M. (in press). Bridging the artificial gap between activism and scholarship to form tools for knowledge. In L. W. Perna (Ed.), *Taking it to the streets: The role of scholarship and advocacy and advocacy in scholarship.* Baltimore, MD: Johns Hopkins University Press.

Bensimon, E. M. (1989). A feminist reinterpretation of presidents' definition of leadership. *Peabody Journal of Education, 66,* 143–156.

Bensimon, E. M. (1992). Lesbian existence and the challenge to normative constructions of the academy. *Journal of Education, 174,* 98–113.

Bensimon, E. M. (2007). The underestimated significance of practitioner knowledge in the scholarship of student success. *Review of Higher Education, 30,* 441–469.

Bensimon, E. M., & Harris, F. (2012). The mediational means of enacting equity-mindedness among community college practitioners. In E. M. Bensimon, & L. E. Malcolm (Eds.), *Confronting equity issues on campus* (pp. 214–246). Sterling, VA: Stylus.

Bensimon, E. M., & Malcom, L. (2012). *Confronting equity issues on campus: Implementing the equity scorecard in theory and practice.* Sterling, VA: Stylus.

Bonilla-Silva, E. (2010). *Racism without racists: Color-blind racism & racial inequality in contemporary America.* Lanham, MD: Rowman & Littlefield.

Bustillos, L. T., Rueda, R., & Bensimon, E. M. (2011). Faculty views of underrepresented students in community college settings. In P. R. Portes, & S. Salas (Eds.), *Vygotsky in 21st century society: Advances in cultural historical theory and praxis with non-dominant communities* (pp. 199–213). New York, NY: Peter Lang.

Coates, T. (2016). The case for considering reparations. *The Atlantic, 27.*

Dewey, J. (1938). *Logic: The theory of inquiry.* New York, NY: Henry Holt.

Dowd, A. C., & Bensimon, E. M. (2015). *Engaging the "race question": Accountability and equity in U.S. higher education.* New York, NY: Teachers College Press.

Engeström, Y. (2001). Expansive learning at work: Toward an activity theoretical reconceptualization. *Journal of Education and Work, 14*, 133–156. doi:10.1080/13639080020028747

Felix, E. R., Bensimon, E. M., Hanson, D., Gray, J., & Klingsmith, L. (2015). Developing agency for equity-minded change. *New Directions for Community College, 172*, 25–42.

Harper, S. R. (2012). Race without racism: How higher education researchers minimize racist institutional norms. *Review of Higher Education, 36*, 9–29.

Kemmis, S., & McTaggart, R. (2000). Participatory action research. In N. K. Denzin, & Y. S. Lincoln (Eds.), *Handbook of qualitative research* (pp. 567–605). Thousand Oaks, CA: Sage.

Ladson-Billings, G. (1998). Just what is critical race theory and what's it doing in a nice field like education? *International Journal of Qualitative Studies in Education, 11*, 7–24.

Polkinghorne, D. E. (2004). *Practice and the human sciences: The case for a judgment-based practice of care.* Albany, NY: SUNY Press.

Robinson v. Cahill. 62 N.J. 473 (1973).

Romm, N. (2010). *New racism: Revisiting researcher accountabilities.* London, England: Springer.

Roth, W. M., & Lee, Y. L. (2007). "Vygotsky's neglected legacy": Cultural-historical activity theory. *Review of Educational Research, 77*, 186–232.

Wilder, C. S. (2013). *Ebony and ivy: Race, slavery, and the troubled history of America's universities.* New York, NY: Bloomsbury Press.

7

LEGISLATIVE WHITE PAPERS

Connecting Research and Policy in Nevada

Kim Nehls, Oscar Espinoza-Parra, Holly Schneider,
Travis Tyler, and Elena Nourrie

Colleges and universities in the United States are being called on to fulfill a distinct public service function by contributing solutions to major problems facing local communities and society at large (Jongbloed, Enders, & Salerno, 2008). The traditional teaching and research functions of higher education institutions are being reassessed to include an emerging and separate mission that emphasizes social change. The political and legal changes occurring at state and federal levels signify a new era in which higher education systems have powerful constituencies and external stakeholders (e.g., state legislatures) with different societal interests and outcomes for postsecondary institutions. According to Jongbloed and colleagues (2008), "In short, the legitimacy of higher education in society will increasingly be a direct function of the nature, quality, and evolving ties with the stakeholder society" (p. 306). This chapter reflects on the shifting landscape of U.S. colleges and universities to fulfill a distinct mission and return to their origins to serve in the scholarship of engagement.

The role of higher education institutions in producing public research to help shape state policy and to respond to external accountability and societal expectations reflects an emerging function for these institutions to serve as collaborators in social issues. More than 20 years ago, Boyer (1996) reaffirmed the vital role of American colleges and universities in serving as partners with communities to solve pressing contemporary issues. In this chapter we describe a case study that models an institution's commitment to providing an infrastructure and incentives for faculty to create knowledge for the public policy arena. This type of public scholarship uses existing university structures and intentionally expands faculty reward systems to bridge the gap between research and policy making. Specifically, our case study addresses the expertise of senior administrators and faculty in producing knowledge to improve the educational system and student success outcomes for our state.

The next section provides an overview of the role of federal and state government funding for U.S. postsecondary education and the increasing governmental interest for institutions of higher education to serve as collaborative partners in addressing current societal issues. Our literature review provides the background, which is important to position our case study to draw new connections between public scholarship and policy formation, expanding traditional notions of institutional responsibility among college and university faculty. The extensive qualitative interviews we conducted with various faculty, academic leaders, and political experts describe the processes by which faculty became involved at the state level to inform and influence education-related public policies.

Expansion of Higher Education

The prevailing thought of higher education as a public good is ingrained in the history and democracy of the United States (McMahon, 2009). The Morrill Acts of 1862 and 1890 granted states land and financial support from the federal government, established and funded educational institutions, and increased access to higher education for the general American population. Higher education expanded beyond the traditional liberal arts education, establishing applied and practical arts such as agriculture and mechanical arts (Geiger, 2015). The federal government's support of higher education continued throughout the twentieth century with passage of the Servicemen Readjustment Act in 1944, the Civil Rights Act in 1964, the Higher Education Act in 1965, Title IX in 1972, and the Americans with Disabilities Act in 1990 (Wharton-Michael, Janke, Karim, Syvertsen, & Wray, 2006).

In recent years, higher education experienced a decline in federal and state financial support at the same time that institutions were instructed to better meet state and regional needs (Weerts, 2015; Wharton-Michael et al., 2006). For example, Weerts's (2014) longitudinal study analyzed state appropriations for different types of higher education institutions and the effect this had on public engagement. His study examined a 20-year period in which institutions received higher or lower than predicted state funding. From 1984 to 2004, he found that colleges and universities with higher than expected state support emphasized public engagement. Universities that received higher than expected levels of state appropriations practiced "mutually beneficial relationship[s] with their communities and local industries" (p. 159), whereas campuses with lower than expected support "framed their commitment to the state and society in more traditional terms corresponding with their liberal arts tradition (public citizen/scholars) or land-grant heritage (technology transfer, extension)" (Weerts, 2014, p. 159). Research such as this illustrates the ties between policymakers and support for public scholarship.

Concomitantly, legislative party affiliation has proved to affect higher education support. A democratic affiliation was more positively associated with support for higher education than those legislatures that were controlled by Republicans (McLendon, Hearn, & Mokher, 2009; Tandberg, 2010, 2013). The public policy process accounts for the changing nature of legislative and political actors, problems of the state, and the solutions that are considered (Radaelli, 1995). Several factors such as key political leaders and state context have the potential to determine policy outcomes. Understanding the niche where public scholarship functions in the political ecosystem remains a complex process. Therefore, the role of public scholarship in policy making requires deft knowledge of the local political landscape.

Public Policy as a Function of Public Scholarship

Despite calls for increasing the role of public scholarship, the current production model of academic research does not translate into policy research suitable for state governance systems. Institutional barriers such as tenure practices and promotion policies motivate faculty members to pursue traditional academic research in peer-reviewed journals rather than in teaching and service (Bridger & Alter, 2006). In this sense, research is produced for other academics rather than to promote community action. In other terms, academic research is often viewed as an act of knowledge generation in isolation, without praxis, or as Keller (1985) criticized it, trees without fruit.

The research activities associated with the tenure process, such as new knowledge, theory crafting, and the advancement of research methods in peer-reviewed scholarly journals, hold significantly more value in the university structure system than the scholarship produced for the public policy realm (Hillman, Tandberg, & Sponsler, 2015). Higher education incentivizes empirical research, and this focus on knowledge production persists primarily in the traditional structuration of the epistemic communities. Faculty are accustomed to frame their research to study ill-defined problems, issues, and situations. However, this approach to producing scholarship does not take into account the practicality of public scholarship and the interaction between faculty and policymakers in using knowledge to shape political discourse. Policy analysis emphasizes the importance of accessible research that is pragmatic and timely and does not develop new theories or knowledge but instead advances a specific policy agenda (Hillman et al., 2015; Weimer & Vining, 2005). In many ways, public policy aligns with the underlying goals of public scholarship. Anderson (2011) defined *public policy* as "a relatively stable, purposive course of action or inaction followed by government in dealing with some problem or matter of concern" (p. 7). Similarly, Ashford (1992) said that a public policy study functions as

> a historical narrative; a portrayal of particular motives and intentions at work in a particular setting, an account of prevailing ethical and moral standards at work in political and social life at some moment in history, and an exercise in defining political and social reality for policy makers and for the public. (pp. 4–5)

A more troubling barrier to faculty involvement in public scholarship is the overwhelming view that rigorous and valuable scholarship is fundamentally a private craft detached from building connections among other scholars and the academic communities to help alleviate public issues and problems (Peters et al., 2003). In this regard, bridging the gap between research and policy making represents a deliberate act of public scholarship, or as Yapa (2006) stated in other terms, public scholarship "does not assume that useful knowledge simply flows outward from the university to the larger community" (p. 73). Public scholarship is more cooperative and collaborative. It meets and responds to the needs of the community rather than the needs of the faculty member or the academy. In this sense, research is not a private craft but a public one.

The advent of public scholarship and policy-relevant research does not ensure it will eventually affect or inform the policymaker or the final policy (Radaelli, 1995). A major function of public scholarship is to apply particular knowledge within public processes to develop solutions to policy issues. Public scholarship can offer short-term and long-term solutions in the policy development process, and it can provide "the interpretive frames for policy-makers" (Radaelli, 1995, p. 164) to understand complex societal problems that are based on objective inquiry and scientific methods of research. In public policy, faculty members contribute by making sense of scholarship, interpreting and synthesizing various sources of data, and shaping policy discourse (Radaelli, 1995).

The Case Study: A White Paper Initiative

Although policy analysis and academic research are driven by different factors, public scholarship demands a movement toward balance between faculty members' dual roles as citizens and experts, allowing scholarly achievement and the public good to exist symbiotically (Bridger & Alter, 2006; Hillman et al., 2015). Contrary to the idea that a faculty member must desert research to participate in public policy, we describe an institutional case study in which faculty managed to be fully engaged in their traditional functions while still participating in the development of public scholarship. We hope our research provides a model institutional opportunity that embraces academics as well as policy making. Our case exemplifies a new type of research intended to bolster faculty efforts to participate in public policy activities. The next section outlines the conceptual framework guiding the analysis of the case study data, followed by the method and context, and presentation of findings.

Conceptual Framework

Knowledge is instrumental to the policy process. In his discussion of knowledge in the policy process, Radaelli (1995) asserted that public policies contribute to the political process by infusing ideas and knowledge that integrate debate into the development and output of policy decisions. Knowledge is dependent on and independent from the political process through which social science and education aid, refine, or evaluate the relevant facts, ideas, and data to inform the actual policy decisions (Radaelli, 1995). Radaelli's (1995) research on the role of knowledge in the public policy process serves as the conceptual framework guiding this chapter.

Three main tenets of Radaelli's (1995) framework are action generation, a policy-shaping community, and policy stream. Radaelli's concept of action generation emphasizes the interconnected roles of knowledge, postsecondary institutions, faculty, students, and policy decisions. In other words, knowledge produced in the university setting has a role in the policy arena that can contribute to the decision-making process and generate significant outcomes. Second, Radaelli emphasized the critical role of a policy-shaping community in which college and university faculty synthesize social science research, data, opinions based on experience, ideas, and concepts into an integrative model of knowledge with utility for state and local entities.

Finally, Radaelli (1995) considers the treatment of knowledge and research as part of the evaluative process in which faculty become part of the policy stream, which signifies how educational issues are selected in the decision-making process. In this regard, the knowledge produced by faculty is constructed outside political systems (e.g., lobbying) and is considered to be independent and objective and adheres to the scientific processes and standards of production. Faculty provide stable decision-making perspectives to the policy arena with their epistemic community approach. From this perspective, academics in universities are experts operating within a network of professionals. A visual representation of the public policy process is shown in Figure 7.1.

The next section describes the unique context of the Nevada legislature and the process that university faculty and senior leadership used to generate data to inform state policy. Our case study showcases a public research institution that established white papers through the traditional function of faculty engaging in research activities. The series of events that culminated in the production of these white papers required the participation of university leaders with political acumen and an understanding of the political process.

Method and Context

Our research team employed a single-site case methodology to investigate policy-relevant scholarship in the state of Nevada. The case study creates "further understanding of a particular problem, issue, or concept in higher education" (Pasque, Khader, & Still, 2017, p. 79), and it is an ideal research methodology to gain a thorough understanding of the the University of Nevada, Las Vegas (UNLV) College of Education white papers developed by faculty, staff, and students for the Nevada legislature. The state of Nevada, its legislature, and the public policy scholarship produced in the

Figure 7.1. Visualization of the public policy process.

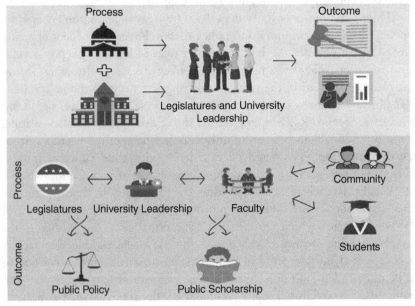

form of white papers are all unique phenomena, and single-site case studies are particularly relevant when there is a unique situation that needs to be examined (Yin, 2003).

Yin (2003) indicates that case studies must be considered within their context, and what makes the state of Nevada particularly unique is that the Nevada constitution sets its legislative sessions biennially, convening "on the first Monday of February following the election of members of the Assembly, unless the Governor of the State or the members of the Legislature shall, in the interim, convene the Legislature by proclamation or petition" (Nev. Const., art. IV, §2, cl.1). Nevada is one of only four states, along with Montana, North Dakota, and Texas, that meets biennially on odd years. Although the alternate year format reduces the budgetary cost of legislative organizations (Snell, 2011), political scientists Keefe and Ogul (2001) argued that the legislatures' increasing role in state government and the growing complexity of problems challenging today's legislatures renders the biennial sessions ineffective in resolving these problems. Furthermore, these biennial sessions hinder the policy-making process, often bottlenecking the number of bills at the end of the session (Keefe & Ogul, 2001). Consequently, this biennial system limits the time in which scholars can produce and supply policy-relevant research to legislatures.

Also unique to the state of Nevada is its fast-growing population. It is home to the fifth largest school district in the nation. Currently, the state of Nevada has a population close to three million people, and most of the residents are concentrated in the south near the city of Las Vegas or in the north near Reno (U.S. Census Bureau, 2017). State appropriations have not kept pace with the growth in the K–12 and postsecondary sectors, which has made Nevada's public educational system severely understaffed and underfunded (Jacquette & Curs, 2015).

This chapter includes data from interviews with 10 authors of white papers as well as input from the key individuals involved in their development and dissemination such as the dean, vice president of government affairs, and additional staff at UNLV. Interviews were audio recorded, transcribed, and reviewed by all of us. Additionally, the research team read all the policy papers, the executive summaries, and short briefs that were prepared for both sessions. The team also attended all meetings pertaining to white paper authors, participated in the mock legislative days at the UNLV College of Education, made presentations at a dean's meeting with faculty and staff and at the Nevada Education Summit, a day-long event for educators. The team took observation notes at these events, and all data were collected and analyzed using an interpretative qualitative approach to try to better understand the meaning of policy making for those involved (Merriam, 2002; Pasque et al., 2017). The next section focuses on synthesizing the conceptual framework and the findings that resulted from the UNLV College of Education's legislative white papers.

Findings

Although formation of public policies is not a traditional charge of U.S. colleges and universities, this case study illustrates a new type of public scholarship in an institutional structure intended to encourage and support social scientists in a College of Education in their efforts to participate in the decision-making process of state policy. Using the conceptual framework (Radaelli, 1995) as a guide, findings on the action generation, policy shaping, and policy stream are discussed next. Our findings illustrate an institutional case study that describes the expert role of faculty and senior leadership in advancing knowledge via public policies to state decision makers.

Action Generation

Institutions of higher education are primarily involved in the production of research. Radaelli (1995) stated that knowledge should have utility and should not be restricted solely to the processes of sharing knowledge within the structures and culture of the academy. Action generation emphasizes the utility of knowledge outside traditional conventions (e.g., academic journals) that has applications in the real-world. The actors (i.e., faculty and institutions' senior leadership) depend on the institutional setting and infrastructure to determine the public policy agenda.

Prior to the past two legislative cycles (2015 and 2017), the dean of the UNLV College of Education, Kim Metcalf, issued a call for white papers on educational topics likely to come before the legislative body for deliberation. In the dean's words, "On the basis of conversations with legislators and community members, agenda items drawn from the meetings of the Educational Legislative Committee, and ideas presented by the Governor and his representatives, there appear to be at least eight issues." Therefore, as one way to raise awareness of these educational issues facing Nevada, Metcalf commissioned a series of nonpartisan white papers to be distributed to state policymakers during two legislative sessions. The white papers were developed and written by faculty and students in the college and were on topics specific to education and the educational needs of the state. Metcalf also made strong efforts to "make personal contact with and develop relationships with individual legislators around the state at all levels" (K. Metcalf, personal communication, June 22, 2016). He solicited information regarding issues, topics, or concepts that legislators were considering, then sent out a call for proposals, identified which papers to invest in, and determined which authors could combine ideas.

Faculty members were selected by Metcalf and given directions to analyze a problematic issue or topic in the realm of education. He then followed up with an e-mail to faculty detailing the purpose and goals of the white papers, requesting that the white papers convey "the science and research associated with the topic in ways that directly and concretely inform policy makers and policy development" (K. Metcalf, personal communication, August 5, 2016). For example, in 2017 the topics included but were not limited to: the teacher pipeline; school funding; high school completion and college transition; career and technical education; and science, technology, engineering, and mathematics education. Past topics also included special education, charter schools, mental health, and common core curriculum. Eight papers were written and presented to the Nevada legislatures in 2015, and 10 papers were submitted during the 2017 legislative cycle. The white papers were one way of addressing local educational issues by putting data and scholarship in front of the legislators.

Each white paper was about 25 pages in length and included an executive summary, an overview of the available literature and research on the topic, a summary of approaches by other states, an evaluation of the effects or impact of the topic, and a set of clear conclusions and implications to inform policy development. Metcalf also emphasized that these papers were to include academic sources but should be written for nonacademic audiences. In an e-mail to the UNLV College of Education faculty, he wrote, "These papers are an important element of our ongoing work to establish the College of Education as the primary source of substantive information to inform education policy, practice, and research" (K. Metcalf, personal communication, June 22, 2016). The authors of the white papers were notified that they may be called to testify before relevant legislative committees or speak to the local media. The College of Education, along with the UNLV vice president of government relations, Luis Valera, held mock legislative days with former state assemblymen and senators to prepare authors for potential appearances before legislative committees. Valera and Metcalf developed mock legislative days to prepare College of Education faculty to appear before the Nevada legislature and discuss their policy papers. Former and current members of the Nevada legislature served as assembly representatives and provided faculty with their perspectives on the types of questions public officials might ask about the policy papers. Metcalf and Valera consistently focused on building relations between the university and the state, as well as translating government affairs for the university community because the language and venues were unfamiliar for the majority of the white paper authors.

Under Radaelli's (1995) framework, public policies use the rigorous scientific and dynamic processes of knowledge to create units of analysis that are intended to apply solutions to problems. In this case, faculty submitted proposals, provided research expertise for specific areas, and applied the research in various public spheres. Many of the white paper authors also included insight from the community and shared their work with students, some of whom cowrote papers with faculty members. The organizational environment of postsecondary institutions provided the venue, values, and reward system to generate research. This type of public scholarship was created by and with university leadership while also providing greater opportunities for faculty, staff, and students' action and analysis in the public policy process.

The idea of faculty members' engagement in the public policy arena was apparent throughout the interviews conducted. The faculty members we interviewed positively affirmed Metcalf's leadership and interest in making this type of public scholarship opportunity a permanent fixture in the College of Education at UNLV. For example, one faculty member we interviewed stated that the dean's goal was to make the university and the College of Education a place where state decision makers can go "where the research is; we are where the expertise is, and I think this [public scholarship] goes a long way toward doing that." Behind the scenes, Metcalf and Valera worked with legislatures as liaisons and leaders for the campus community. Together they relayed information to policymakers, worked to understand motives and intentions, and discovered prevailing ethical and moral standards within political and social dimensions with other actors (Radaelli, 1995).

Policy Shaping
The production and dissemination of knowledge is central to the role of faculty. In community policy shaping, faculty functioned in epistemic disciplinary committees and belonged to a "network of professionals with recognized expertise and competence in a particular domain and an authoritative claim to policy-relevant knowledge within that domain or issue-area" (Haas, 1992, p. 3). The qualitative interviews revealed that faculty who were part of epistemic communities contributed research and expertise in the policy process and aided in the production of public scholarship. Our interviews with authors of policy papers revealed that faculty were central to the formation of public scholarship via the creation of white papers. The participating authors felt their role as public scholars was complementary to their role as academic faculty. For example, one faculty member emphasized the important need to support a diverse democracy not simply through the production of research but the act of disseminating research into public spheres: "[If] we can't convince other people [about our research issues] and what needs to be happening, it's in a vacuum and nobody's going to do anything about it."

The research of Radaelli (1995) indicates that participation in the democracies of discourse and exchange of ideas is central to the policy process. This is analogous to the free market of ideas embedded in the collegiality of higher education in engaging in scholarship and research activities. To further extend this idea, Valera referred to "the symbiotic relationship" that exists between K–12 and higher education and how this opportunity allows the two entities to converge. This process allowed academics to transmit knowledge, construct meaning, and shape understanding of complex societal and educational issues to develop public scholarship. One of the faculty members who was encouraged by the opportunities leadership provided to present research to a legislative audience, said "The college has created different platforms to reach out. . . . These platforms and opportunities provided by the college will be very helpful for us to convey our paper to policymakers." These opportunities for engagement included the Nevada Education Summit, mock legislative days, and legislative visits in the state capital, Carson City. This process upholds the value of faculty research expertise and its contributions to generating change.

The authors of the white papers also revealed how this type of public scholarship demonstrated the potential to affect students and connect them to the policy process. One of them stated,

> The paper indirectly helps the doctoral students in the program to understand the need to recruit and retain teachers of color. So even though the legislatures are the intended audience of the paper, it can inform the work of our doctoral and masters students, and the courses that our undergraduate students are taking.

The opportunity to reach students was also mentioned in the following comment from another author:

> I wish that there would be more opportunities to do [this . . . especially] for our doc students that are at the College of Education . . . because it is different than academic writing. It is great that we have academic writing, but if we are not necessarily giving it to the people who need it most who can actually implement change, then our work isn't really done.

Other faculty emphasized the important roles that graduate students were able to contribute as purveyors of knowledge in the policy arena. Furthermore, faculty recognized that student contributions to these papers will help train and prepare future faculty and practitioners to engage in public scholarship. Graduate students may be socialized so that their future research may contribute to policy processes. This also demonstrates to students that they are essential to generating change and exhibits the cyclical nature of the theoretical framework in connecting to research to create policy-shaping communities and action generation.

A review of interview transcripts also revealed a desire for public scholarship to become a consistent element in the College of Education. Metcalf would especially like to continue the program indefinitely; he emphasized how this strengthens trust in the college and cultivates involvement of all our scholars, students and faculty alike, in public scholarship. He added, "We are influencing policy as a change. We are influencing policy in the state by continually trying to contribute to the conversation in ways that build people's trust in us as honest purveyors of information."

Policy Stream

University faculty and leadership disclosed that their contributions to the public scholarship process informed state policy decision makers and affected various outcomes depending on the topic and its importance to the legislative cycle. According to one faculty member, "The dean did get a number of requests for more copies of the whole book of the papers." Likewise, another stated, "From what I have heard, [my paper] was well received by policymakers." Another faculty member further elaborated on this idea stating, "I know the Nevada Department of Education staff was thrilled—at least that's the feedback that I received from their communication specialist. I heard through the dean that the paper was positively received."

Affirming the role of faculty in participating in the political sphere, one faculty member said, "We have the responsibility and expertise to make an impact on the local community. It is very important. This is a smart initiative to bridge the university, legislators, and the community we serve." Faculty made sense of scholarship, interpreted and synthesized various sources of data, and shaped public policy discourse (Radaelli, 1995). As a result of the program, there is greater visibility of the issues and by extension, greater visibility for the College of Education in the state, local community, and even in the university. For example, when the dean served as a guest on the floor of the Nevada State Assembly during a visit to Carson City, the policymakers publicly mentioned "the UNLV College of Education" multiple times to the entire assembly. Collectively, the faculty agreed that the white paper initiative bridged the gap among scholars and policymakers. As one faculty member said,

> It is a great initiative to connect [the] legislature with higher education and inform and impact policy making through rigorous scholarly research . . . . As researchers, we produce empirical or theoretical articles . . . . It is also important for us to get involved in the state level policy making. This paper

helped me understand how important it is for faculty to be involved in the schools and state level policy.

The goal of the white papers was to inform state policymakers on pertinent education issues in Nevada. In some instances from 2015, the impact was achieved. For example, a faculty member commented, "I do think long-term that it has had an impact, because the city has ultimately used it [his policy paper from 2015] as its framework for school turnaround." Meanwhile, another revealed that since her paper was provided to the legislature in 2015, a commission had been established with people from all over the local school district and the community that specifically focused on her topic of teacher recruitment.

Half the faculty interviewed had written papers for the 2015 legislative session and thus were able to reflect on the impact their papers had. However, three of these faculty members expressed some ambiguity about their papers' impact on the legislative session. As one stated,

> The legislative session led to the single largest increase in K–12 educational funding in Nevada's history. My hope is that my white paper helped to provide support and a rationale based on the research for how the money could be best used.

Although this author's paper was reported to have been well received by the legislature, he was not certain his paper had a direct impact on policy. Another expressed similar uncertainty about the impact of his paper, saying, "The repeal bill never made it out of the Assembly Education Committee, although I am unsure to what degree my paper had an influence on that." Hillman and colleagues (2015) make clear that placing academic research in the hands of policymakers does not guarantee it will be used for policy, a sentiment shared by Valera, who said,

> During the off-session when the legislature is not in session, there is a tremendous amount of curiosity. . . . They are happy to take the information, digest it, and read through it. It is a different dynamic though once the session is up and running. There is a lot of running around during the session where you have a limited amount of time to make decisions on complex issues.

Research may not resonate with policymakers because of their political principles or values, competing sources of information, and whether the results can stand the test of time (Hillman et al., 2015). Furthermore, Hillman and colleagues state, "The art of communicating results can only go so far as a policymaker is willing or able to listen to or utilize those results" (p. 60). Although a number of the authors questioned the impact their papers had on policy, three of the six authors interviewed from 2015 found their papers had some impact at the state level. Regardless of the impact, none of the authors from 2015 opted to participate as policy paper authors in 2017. The main reason cited for nonparticipation after two years was the time element of the process, as significantly more effort was required for a policy paper than a typical academic paper (e.g., meetings with legislators and local commissions, testifying on bills, following up via e-mail, mock legislative sessions, educational presentations, and much more). We hope to follow the 2017 group through 2019 to see if this situation was a trend or an anomaly. Although the 2017 legislative session had not yet concluded as of this writing, many of the 2017 authors have expressed interest in writing papers again.

Conclusion

The purpose of the white papers was to connect nonpartisan educational research with state policymakers to effect positive change for the people of Nevada. Historically, Nevada has exhibited low educational achievements, so the papers have been one avenue to illuminate important information surrounding key educational topics. There is an urgent need to create and adopt state strategies that promote greater educational attainment in Nevada. Knowing that state funds may be allocated differently and new policies may be enacted provides the impetus for greater involvement by education faculty in the legislature. Collectively, the faculty authors from the 2015 and 2017 legislative sessions agreed that the white paper initiative bridged the gap between scholars and policymakers. As one assistant professor said, "It is a great initiative to connect [the] legislature with higher education and inform and impact policy making through rigorous scholarly research." Through this policy program, the academic world was able to transmit knowledge into public policy with the purpose of constructing meaning and shaping understanding of complex societal and educational issues. This sentiment was affirmed by the administrators who were key to the project as well as other policy paper authors. One said, "As researchers we produce empirical or theoretical articles. . . . This paper helped me understand how important it is for faculty to be involved in the schools and state level policy." Because of the policy program, awareness of the topics increased, and by extension, the UNLV College of Education attained greater visibility in the university, local community, and state. There is still much work to be done for education, especially in Nevada, but the legislative policy papers are a step in the right direction.

References

Anderson, J. E. (2011). *Public policymaking: An introduction* (7th ed.). Boston, MA: Cengage Learning.

Ashford, D. (1992). *History and context in comparative public policy.* Pittsburgh, PA: University of Pittsburgh Press.

Boyer, E. (1996). The scholarship of engagement. *Bulletin of the American Academy of Arts and Sciences, 49*(7), 18–33. doi:10.2307/3824459

Bridger, J. C., & Alter, T. R. (2006). The engaged university, community development, and public scholarship. *Journal of Higher Education Outreach and Engagement, 11*, 163–178.

Geiger, R. G. (2015). *The history of American higher education: Learning and culture from the founding to World War II.* Princeton, NJ: Princeton University Press.

Haas, P. M. (1992). Introduction: Epistemic communities and international policy coordination. *International Organization, 46*(1), 1–35.

Hillman, N. W., Tandberg, D. A., & Sponsler, B. A. (2015). Public policy and higher education: Strategies for framing a research agenda. *ASHE Higher Education Report, 41*(2).

Keefe, W. J., & Ogul, M. S. (2001). *American legislative process: Congress and the states* (10th ed.). Upper Saddle River, NJ: Pearson.

Keller, G. (1985). Trees without fruit: The problem with research about higher education. *Change, 17*(1), 7–10.

Jacquette, O., & Curs, B. R. (2015). Creating the out-of-state university: Do public universities increase non-resident freshmen enrollment in response to declining state appropriations? *Research in Higher Education, 56*, 535–565.

Jongbloed, B., Enders, J., & Salerno, C. (2008). Higher education and its communities: Interconnections, interdependencies and a research agenda. *Higher Education, 56*, 303–324.

McLendon, M. K., Hearn, J. C., & Mokher, C. G. (2009). Partisans, professionals, and power: The role of political factors in state higher education funding. *Journal of Higher Education, 80*, 686–713.

McMahon, W. (2009). *Higher learning greater good.* Baltimore, MD: Johns Hopkins University Press.

Merriam, S. B. (2002). *Qualitative research in practice: Examples for discussion and analysis.* San Francisco, CA: Jossey-Bass.

Nev. Const., art. IV, §2, cl.1.

Pasque, P. A., Khader, L. M., & Still, C. (2017). Critical case study as an imperative for organizational activism and institutional change. In P. A. Pasque & V. M. Lechuga (Eds.), *Qualitative inquiry in higher education organization and policy research* (pp. 75–90). London, England: Routledge.

Peters, S. J., Jordan, N. R., Alter, T. R., & Bridger, J. C. (2003). The craft of public scholarship in land-grant education. *Journal of Higher Education Outreach and Engagement, 8*, 75–86.

Radaelli, C. M. (1995). The role of knowledge in the policy process. *Journal of European Public Policy, 2*, 159–183.

Snell, R. (2011). State experiences with annual and biennial budgeting. Retrieved from www.ncsl.org/documents/fiscal/BiennialBudgeting_May2011.pdf

Tandberg, D. A. (2010). Interest groups and governmental institutions: The politics of state funding of public higher education. *Educational Policy, 24*, 735–778.

Tandberg, D. A. (2013). The conditioning role of state higher education governance structures. *Journal of Higher Education, 84*, 506–543.

U.S. Census Bureau. (2017). *QuickFacts: Nevada.* Retrieved from www.census.gov/quickfacts/table/PST045216/32

Weerts, D. J. (2014). State funding and the engaged university: Understanding community engagement and state appropriations for higher education. *Review of Higher Education, 38*, 133–169.

Weerts, D. J. (2015). The public-good variable: Can public engagement boost state support for higher education? *Change, 47*(3), 20–25.

Weimer, D. L., & Vining, A. R. (2005). *Policy analysis: Concepts and practice* (4th ed.). Upper Saddle River, NJ: Prentice Hall

Wharton-Michael, P., Janke, E. M., Karim, R., Syvertsen, A. K., & Wray, L. D. (2006). An explication of public scholarship objectives. *New Directions for Teaching and Learning, 105*, 63–72.

Yapa, L. (2006). Public scholarship in the postmodern university. *New Directions for Teaching and Learning, 105*, 73–83.

Yin, R. K. (2003). *Case study research: Design and methods* (3rd ed.). Thousand Oaks, CA: Sage.

8

INVOLVEMENT IN NATIONAL MOVEMENTS

Working Closely With Students

Amalia Dache-Gerbino

On August 9, 2014, in Ferguson, Missouri, Michael Brown's body lay on Canfield Drive for four and a half hours after he was executed by a police officer. I watched television in horror as I unpacked boxes in my new home in Columbia, just 120 miles up the road. As I began my first year as an assistant professor at the University of Missouri (also commonly known as Mizzou), I was immediately thrust into activism in Ferguson and on my campus in support of Concerned Student 1950 (CS1950) a year later. As I participated in these movements, I simultaneously researched and taught courses from a scholar activist lens or what Harney and Moten (2013) describe as fugitive planning. In this chapter, I illustrate how racial justice faculty activism as fugitive planning, a collective form of knowledge production in service of liberation, contributes to public scholarship.

Although the term *liberation* may be understood as hyperbole, especially within the context of U.S. higher education, Kelley (2002) shares insights on the central role of social movements in American society, and what I argue is a definition of *liberation*, when he wrote,

> In the poetics of struggle, and lived experience, in the utterances of ordinary folk, in the cultural products of social movements, in the reflections of activists, we discover the many different cognitive maps of the future, of the world not yet born. (p. 10)

A world where diverse democracies are cultivated and thrive. A world where the academy and professoriate respond to the most pressing needs of those on the margins.

In the context of racial justice movements, as a participant and researcher, I situate the *public good* (Kezar, 2005) to its rightful status as central rather than peripheral to the purpose and future of higher learning, and I beg the questions, Have U.S. higher education institutions, in their organization and functioning, assisted in the liberation of the marginalized? Have they advanced a diverse democracy? Rhoades and Valadez (1996), argued that they haven't and that although community colleges were supposedly created to democratize higher learning through an open enrollment admissions system, working-class segments of our population became precarious in their worker identities and in their labor. This includes racial and ethnic othered populations, U.S. domestic citizens and global citizens, those with varying mental and physical abilities, and those oppressed by gender and heteronormative systems.

Protests and acts of civil disobedience off and on campus were frequent throughout the evolution of U.S. colleges and universities and served to diversify our society and higher education (Wolf-Wendel, Twombly, Tuttle, & Gaston-Gayles, 2004). However, inquiries of resistance directed toward faculty studying higher education are far less frequent. In our field, topics of resistance typically center on students, with little attention on faculty or our research and teaching. I believe this is because of a misconceived discourse that activism is on the opposite side of the professoriate, as if activism and faculty work were mutually exclusive. Although the professoriate has become more diverse in the past 60 years, it is still predominantly White and male. The supremacy of White maleness still clouds the imagination of many. Activists on the other hand, specifically racial justice activists in the United States, have historically and contemporarily been understood as subjective law breakers and outright criminals during social movements despite a constitutional right to protest for the recognition of their humanity (Taylor, 2016). Typically, racial justice activists become heroes or martyrs posthumously. It is no surprise then that being a scholar engaged in activism seems oxymoronic to those who are not aware of the distorted assumptions that U.S. society places on professorial bodies (read White male), and activist bodies (read non-White, women, or queer).

As U.S. academics, we must free our shackled imaginations, we must imagine a world that has never existed before, where Western binaries of individualism and collectivism, good and evil, and Black and White are dismantled, and where nation, citizen, and migration are reconceptualized. As Nelson Mandela (1994) states in one of his most famous quotes, "a nation should not be judged by how it treats its highest citizens, but its lowest ones" (p. 23). How we create public scholarship must come from organizing and planning alongside and on behalf of the working class, the homeless, the targets of the police state, the marginalized, and the forgotten.

Theoretical Approach

The theoretical framing this chapter employs is anticapitalist and antiracist. Harney and Moten (2013) lay a foundation for a radical higher education agenda. Although they don't explicitly compartmentalize the faculty or administrator role in their text, I focus on faculty and our role in the university in fugitive planning. Within this theoretical framing, I describe fugitive planning as the lens for interpreting my engagement in racial justice activism while researching and teaching and being within the university, yet not of the university.

To not be of the university while being within it is to challenge notions of abstract liberalism (Bonilla-Silva, 2010), which suggests that freedom, liberty, and democracy are universal ideals with which members of U.S. society are endowed regardless of class, race, ethnicity, gender, ability, sexuality, and citizenship status. Although higher education was founded on these ideals of a public common good, a review of history and austerity politics quickly debunks these liberal ideals as American myths (Coates, 2015). Myths set within White supremacist, patriarchal, and capitalist ideologies that challenge whether higher education has yet to achieve its ideal of serving the public good as non-White, nonmale, nonwealthy populations have not historically been embraced by campuses. Public scholarship for the public good therefore means not being of the university and goes beyond the supremacist, patriarchal, and capitalist ideologies to serve and speak for populations that have been underserved and excluded. To not be of the university is also embracing a collective consciousness that resides outside the brick-and-mortar walls of the academy; engaging in radical inquiry, knowledge creation, and sustainment; and allowing a fugitive planner to take the pulse of the local working-class community surrounding the university. For me, this community was the Black working class of St. Louis, which for generations has been the target of the police state, an institution created by U.S. settler colonialism.

Harney and Moten (2013) describe settler colonialism as synonymous with the university in terms of its founding and how it is organized. They state that "the settler, having settled for politics, arms himself in the name of civilization [read liberalism] while critique initiates the self-defense of those of us who see hostility in the civil union of settlement and enclosure" (p. 18). The university is symbolic for civilization, for the production and creation of consumable knowledge that sustains itself only through coercion of the fantasy and myth of liberalism and capital accumulation through policy creation.

The protection of the civilization's land and capital by the police state leaves low-income communities that are predominantly of color in urban areas as targets for not only physical violence (Taylor, 2016) but also symbolic violence (Bourdieu & Passeron, 1990; Kiyama, Harris, & Dache-Gerbino, 2016) and surveillance leading to the execution of Black high school graduates like Michael Brown. The policing system is the military arm of the domestic state and U.S. civilization. Higher education institutions are aiding and abetting these outcomes with their silence and lack of engagement with local communities under fire.

Through its historical production of students who have become the politicians, chief executive officers, college and university presidents, and policymakers, the university is complicit in sustaining the state and its capital. True critique of the settler academy comes from fugitive planners who instead of trying to fix and correct settler colonialism, an illusory system, juxtapose their existence with others who oppose the relics of settler colonialism. I argue in this chapter that my engagement in activism as an assistant professor at the University of Missouri and my teaching and research allow me to create public scholarship in service of liberation from the police state for local Black working-class communities in St. Louis.

I interpret fugitive planning and define its experiments as collective acts of bonding through faculty research and teaching alongside and in service of local populations that continue to be targets of *the state*, which is here defined as the U.S. political-economic system and its institutions. As faculty, fugitive planning is a nexus centered among historical materialist (Harvey, 2005) research, emancipatory teaching (Freire, 1970/2005), and collaborations with and on behalf of local marginalized communities, which include marginalized students on our campuses as well as the residential communities that surround campuses. The research prong of fugitive planning should aim to reveal the state's use and mechanization of power by employing methodologies and methods that interrogate domination and oppression centrally. Theoretical approaches in service of liberation should similarly be employed. Teaching as fugitive planning follows the same line of inquiry, where approaching traditional higher education topics or content (organization and governance, college access, curriculum, and finance) are framed from transformative lenses in service of liberation. Solely doing research and teaching does not constitute fugitive planning. A collective consciousness and collaboration with local communities is tantamount to this form of activism.

Fugitive planning attempts to illustrate the contradictions of settler colonial relics such as de facto forms of segregation in public schooling, regressive property taxation of the poor for municipal profit, and new forms of Jim Crow through mass incarceration (Alexander, 2010). Such relics contribute to discourses of college accessibility for those viewed as potential college students or those viewed as criminal (Dache-Gerbino & White, 2016). How higher education scholarship should resist instead of serve the mechanisms of settler colonialism is part of a historical materialist inquiry (Harvey, 2005) of fugitive planning that may help us reimagine higher education and the possibility of one day living in a diverse democracy and pluralistic society.

Fugitive Planning Toward Public Scholarship

Having looked for politics in order to avoid it, we move next to each other, so we can be beside ourselves (Harney & Moten, 2013, p. 19).

The collective consciousness and collaborative component of fugitive planners with and on behalf of local communities are central in how I have conducted research in Ferguson. In the fall of 2014, while attending Mizzou's new faculty orientation, I met my coprincipal investigator and my collaborative fugitive planner for the project Teaching From the Margins: Mapping Ferguson's Community Cultural Wealth as Public Education (Dache-Gerbino & Mislan, 2015). This project was an attempt to combine my interest in the publics of higher education and my coplanner's interest in media activism. The project grew out of our engagement in Ferguson activism, and as we walked alongside community members fighting for justice for Mike Brown, we began thinking of how we could research this historical moment.

Cristina Mislan, a new assistant professor in the journalism school, worked in the area of critical media studies. She studied the history of the Black press in Cuba, and I studied urban college access from a postcolonial lens. We used similar theories in understanding our different units of analysis. These overlaps allowed a collective activism to emerge in our scholarly interests our first year and in beginning our research project in Ferguson. We quickly came to realize that the training we received in our PhD programs prior to this moment of collective consciousness did not prepare us for how to engage and study community activism concurrently. Before we researched, we engaged and "move[d] next to each other" and with others "so we could be beside ourselves" (Harney & Moten, 2013, p. 19), a communal self in solidarity with Ferguson activists and their and our liberation.

Mislan and I attended our first protest together in mid-October 2014 in Ferguson, a suburb of St. Louis with a 67% African American population. When driving to and through Ferguson for the first time, I was surprised by what I was seeing in front of me and what I had seen on the mainstream news. How the media misrepresented Ferguson and Ferguson activists as people burning down their community shocked me to my core because I understood the root of this rhetoric. Here was a local community mourning the loss of recently graduated 18-year-old Mike Brown, coupled with the trauma of seeing his body lie on the street pavement in the scalding August Missouri sun for four and a half hours.

Going to Mike Brown's *ofrenda* (shrine) and witnessing the communal outpouring at the site of his death was reminiscent of the *ofrendas* I had gone to as a high school student in Rochester, New York, when high school classmates were killed by gun violence. The *ofrenda* was at Canfield apartments, which looked like a suburban housing complex that could have been anywhere in U.S. suburbia. How race and class were concentrated in the suburbs of North County looked different from what I was familiar with growing up in Rochester and what is popularly known in discourses of urban public housing as the projects. Although the infamous failure of an urban public housing development in St Louis—Pruitt-Igoe (1954–1972)—depicted what popular discourse and media referred to as ghettos or inner-city slums, Ferguson was definitely not in this category. The uneven geographic development of Ferguson was more insidious than Pruitt-Igoe; the Ferguson municipal court system, Ferguson policing, and employment segregation were tools for Black residential exploitation. One of its main streets, West Florissant, runs perpendicular to Canfield and contains rows of commercial businesses, mostly national chains like McDonald's, Walmart, Quik Trips, and so on. These commercial plazas were common in Ferguson and are neoliberal sites of capital accumulation (Harvey, 2005).

We left the *ofrenda* and headed toward the office of Hands Up United, an organization created after the killing of Michael Brown and inspired by the Black Panther Party. We drove up from Columbia, Missouri, early Saturday morning to drop off some radical books for the Books and Breakfast program at Hands Up United. There we learned about a protest taking place at the Walmart on West Florissant, and we wanted to take part. The Walmart protest brought attention to the killing of John Crawford at a Walmart in Beavercreek, Ohio, for playing with a toy gun that Walmart sold. In addition, residents were protesting how Walmart exploited the local Black working-class community in their employment practices.

This first action at Walmart lasted several hours. We made our first Black Lives Matter signs and sang many protest songs while walking with St. Louis community members as young as 5 and as old as senior citizens. There were more than 100 protestors out that morning, and by midafternoon there were even more. People came from all over the country.

Creating Public Scholarship

The media coverage and gaps in our field's literature pushed us to design an activist-centered research study. After months of protest and activism, we began putting together a plan for funding and laying out the goals of the project. Our first goal was to explore how Ferguson and St. Louis community voices were teaching from the margins, providing insight into the resistance of activists in St. Louis as they struggled for political, social, economic, and educational inclusion. Our second goal was to explore how this activist community was embedded within local geographic and college-going discourses of exclusion. We designed our research as a mixed-methods ethnography collecting four types of data: geographic, interviews, digital media, and archival data related to the Michael Brown shooting. The digital media and archival data consisted of documents available through Washington University in St. Louis's (2015) digital collection called Documenting Ferguson, consisting of materials provided by members of the St. Louis public who were involved in the aftermath of Michael Brown's death. The collection contains more than 700 sources and archives. The geographic data consisted of the U.S. Census Bureau's American Community Survey (www .census.gov/programs-surveys/acs) data that we mapped across the geography of St. Louis County and the city to understand how domination and resistance were spatialized. Finally, we conducted 19 interviews of activists. We were also in the field for about 15 months, attending actions as well as the funeral of a Ferguson activist. We drove to St. Louis from Columbia about once a month, and we stayed overnight several times to avoid having to drive 240 miles in a single day.

Because we were engaged in actions prior to starting our research project, we had some familiarity with the St. Louis landscape. Our original research plan was to make contact with community organizations that were activist-oriented. After contacting organizations via e-mail and telephone, we received only one response, and that person become our first research participant. After our first participant interview, we changed our interview protocol's focus on Ferguson and expanded it to St. Louis because we learned that many activists were from across the county and did not reside in Ferguson. We also learned after our first interview that connecting with other activists took time, and we had to build trusting relationships with each participant so we could connect with others. Snowball sampling was the primary method of contacting and recruiting participants. It took several months to connect with other activists, but after four or five months, we made instrumental connections that led us to meet with activists who were central in the movement. Each participant interview was unique, and after a few interviews we realized we needed to let the questions emerge from conversing with activists and not from the protocol. Informally, our participants were teaching us how to conduct research on their community by sharing strategies of organizing in Ferguson, which are community and activist-centered endeavors. From a geographic lens, they taught us that Ferguson activism was happening strategically in areas of the county that were centers of government and local economies. Hence, we began expanding our interview questions to include not only topics of race but also topics related to the local economy and municipal politics. We learned that transparency in organizing was instrumental for many of our participants in building community and in working together toward change. For example, most participants wanted to know what we would do with our data or how the data would be used. We informed them that we first wanted to publish a community report highlighting their voices and our major findings before publishing in academic outlets. Many of our participants helped us decide that we should not publish our report with a single agency but rather an outlet that wasn't bound by one organization.

In creating public scholarship through fugitive planning, making the community report a central project outcome was informed by my previous research experience cowriting a community report for a Latina and Latino agency in Rochester on Latina and Latino student transitions, successes, and barriers. In the Ferguson community report, we planned on detailing the study's purpose, research design, results, and implications. In conjunction, a subsequent outcome was to write a second cross-disciplinary university report that would provide implications for institutional change with a focus on local activism and campus-community partnerships. Since arriving at Mizzou, it became evident that campus activism and student activism were closely related to community activism in Ferguson. Our focus on creating a report first for the St. Louis community and second for the University of Missouri was grounded in assisting local activists in bringing municipal policy changes to the St. Louis area, particularly related to police reform and the local criminal justice system. Furthermore, our institutional report aimed at revealing and challenging criminalizing college accessibility discourses that contributed to the deaths of Black students, such as Michael Brown, and residents. Several Missouri college campuses engaged in racial justice activism post-Ferguson, and only a few campuses were committed to change. Besides the report from the Ferguson Commission (created by former governor Jay Nixon) and the investigation of the Ferguson police department by the U.S. Department of Justice (2015), there were no local activist-centered reports that highlighted the intellectual merits of community activism in Ferguson and St. Louis. We are confident that our community and university reports, once completed, will respond to such needs and serve as an example of public scholarship cultivated through fugitive planning.

As fugitive planners we were constantly moving; we felt as if we were constantly traveling back and forth to Ferguson physically and emotionally, sometimes not knowing how to be from the university while not being of the university in Ferguson. Meeting with research participants at their homes, in co-ops, at halfway houses, in coffee shops, and at libraries, we never felt like university researchers but rather like members of a community. The lives of many of our participants were precarious, some awaiting trial because of false police accusations and others awaiting jail time because of criminal records as youths before engaging in activism.

The Ferguson uprising lasted two years because it was slippery, because it didn't have a leader or leaders. It couldn't be lead, contained, or categorized. After more than a year of moving in and out of ethnographic research in St. Louis, we have come to realize that in its chaos was its success. On the streets of Ferguson, we witnessed the outpouring of community resistance. We engaged in protest chants inspired by Assata Shakur's (1987) famous quote, "It is our duty to fight for our freedom. It is our duty to win. We must love each other and support each other. We have nothing to lose but our chains" (p. 52). We were handed food and water from strangers driving by in cars who knew we were hungry because we were outside, together moving as fugitive planners. In between watching the police harass demonstrators and witnessing protestors being chased and arrested, we all planned. In between writing the Jail Support phone number in permanent marker on our forearms in case we were arrested and couldn't bring our belongings, we planned. We planned against Ferguson Police Department policymakers such as Darren Wilson, the epitome of the policy enforcer using his fears of Blackness, to correct, fix, and pull the trigger on an unarmed teenager who community members to this day argue had his hands in the air when executed.

There were protests and actions happening almost every day across St. Louis county and the city from 2014 through 2016. The Concerned Student 1950 (CS1950) protests at Mizzou followed Ferguson in a sequential pattern and grew out of previous student and community activism stemming from the precipitating killing of Michael Brown. However, it was a little over a year from the time of Brown's death to CS1950's first action at the Mizzou homecoming parade in the fall of 2015. Engaging in the publics of higher education is a conversation of recreating a system of higher learning that disassociates itself from the legacy of slavery and colonial capitalism to build a U.S. academy that is liberatory and truly democratic for all people. At Mizzou I used teaching as a central tool to engage students on topics of the police state and racial justice resistance in Missouri, topics rarely discussed in higher education programs or curricula yet critical in creating a diverse and just democracy.

Fugitive Planning in Teaching and Supporting Campus Activism

> Distinguish between the desire to correct and the desire to plan with others. (Harney & Moten, 2013, p. 82)

This comment from Harney and Moten (2013) conveys how as Western academics we are trained to fix and resolve the problems of the world by creating implications and policies that are corrective in nature, that are aimed at fixing people, communities, and their families without a mechanism for how to create a different world with them, a world that doesn't orbit capitalism and Western hegemony and that hasn't existed in the history of the West but has existed in the subaltern. Teaching can also be a form of resistance, especially when teaching with the aim of transgression (hooks, 1994).

While engaging in actions in Ferguson during my first semester at Mizzou, I allowed the figurative voices of Ferguson community members to penetrate my pedagogy and course content. I engaged in an emancipatory pedagogy (Freire, 1970/2005) grounded in raising students' levels of political consciousness. In the fall of 2014, I taught a course called Overview of Higher Education. During the week when I discussed the role of faculty in higher education, I was inclined to display an image of Mislan and myself while we were in Ferguson that semester, with my first protest sign displaying in large black permanent marker the words BLACK LIVES MATTER. Discussing resistance to state-sanctioned violence with students in this course was coupled with content ranging from external campus communities to the legacy of slavery in the Ivy League. Students asked questions related to college accessibility for these residents and how we could do more as a campus. They expressed frustration that the Mizzou administration had not been vocal about Ferguson or how it could assist in working with this community and current Mizzou students who resided in St. Louis.

I didn't know then that a student in this course, Jonathan Butler (JB), would later be one of the students in the CS1950 social movement. During that academic year, I taught two students from CS1950 within the year leading up to the fall 2015 uprising. Maxwell Little was the second student, and he and JB were in my Race, Ethnicity, and Gender in Higher Education course in the fall of 2015, before and during the uprising. Being engaged in activism in Ferguson and on-campus activism while teaching and creating lesson plans in my courses that overlapped activism and resistance is a prong of fugitive planning. In essence, classroom sites became spaces of planning and communal learning in service of the Ferguson and St. Louis community—the public. Although my role in teaching some of the CS1950 members was not central in their organizing, how they built on the foundations of previous organizations, such as the Legion of Black Collegians and others, illustrates fugitive planning at the student level. Black resistance to White institutional norms and culture was evident since the first Black students entered Mizzou's campus in 1950 (and is why CS1950 named themselves to reflect this history).

In Conclusion: Hunters, Wolves, and Fugitives

> We say, rightly, if our critical eyes are sharp enough, that it's evil and uncool to have a place in the sun in the dirty thinness of the atmosphere; that house the sheriff was building is in the heart of a fallout zone. And if our eyes carry sharpness farther out we trail the police so we can put them on trial. (Harney & Moten, 2013, p. 18)

Engaging in faculty activism and public scholarship is an iterative process that is organic to being a fugitive planner. Teaching University of Missouri students, current and future racial justice activists, while walking alongside them is a necessary component of fugitive planning. Concurrently, by creating a research project that has allowed my colleagues and me to understand modern policing and educational institutions as places in the sun that are shaped and maintained by the relics of history and regressive capitalist policies, we see it as our duty to protest injustice unapologetically. The house in the sun and the house the sheriff built are crimes; they are crimes against humanity and criminal acts that deserve attention.

In the field of higher education, we have learned that racism is rarely discussed as a major factor in topics of access, retention, and degree attainment (Harper, 2012). Exploring urbanization (Dache-Gerbino, 2016), suburban sprawl, and criminalization (Dache-Gerbino & White, 2016) as factors contributing to accessibility to urban residential local colleges is also a rare area of inquiry in higher education. Harper, Patton, and Wooden (2009) contend that researchers and policymakers must be aware of the educational barriers producing racial disparities in American higher education, highlighting the need for new policy efforts to solve persistent racialized problems. Policy making should address the root of White supremacist capitalism deployed in communities like Ferguson.

Ultimately, we must create public scholarship through fugitive planning until marginalized people and communities are as much a part of the political and economic life of our country as dominant groups controlling capital and shaping hegemony. When the inhumanity of a racially marginalized people is no longer reflected in educational outcomes, then liberation is on the horizon. In conclusion, Dead Prez (2000), in the introductory track to their album *Let's Get Free,* paint a picture of what I find is a metaphor for the current role of U.S. higher education embodying the role of hunter with Black, Brown, indigenous communities, and students taking the role of wolves. As professors within the U.S. academy we can no longer be metaphorical hunters and we can no longer allow the drive for capital accumulation to shift our research and our scholarship away serving the needs of Black, Brown, and indigenous communities—the public. Academic capitalism (Slaughter & Rhoades, 2004) can no longer be accepted as business as usual; *our silence is violence,* as echoed in protest chants, and resistance includes us. We cannot continue to allow the public good (Kezar, 2005) to became anachronistic, a stone statue of a past world that once was, when millions of people living in the United States continue to be put to death, figuratively and literally. As a fugitive planner creating public scholarship, I use the resources of the hunter (the university) in a way that reveals to the wolf the hunter's allegiance to other hunters (the police state and the corporate state). Through research and teaching in service of liberation for local Black working-class communities, I gather the resources of the hunter and use them to tell a narrative centered on the public—the protestors, radicals, and storytellers, the wolves.

References

Alexander, M. (2010). *The new Jim Crow: Mass incarceration in the age of colorblindness.* New York, NY: The New Press.

Bonilla-Silva, E. (2010). *Racism without racists: Color-blind racism & racial inequality in contemporary America.* Plymouth, UK: Rowman & Littlefield.

Bourdieu, P., & Passeron, J. C. (1990). *Reproduction in education, society and culture* (2nd ed.). Thousand Oaks, CA: Sage.

Coates, T. (2015). *Between the world and me.* New York, NY: Random House.

Dache-Gerbino, A. (2016). College desert and oasis: A critical geographic analysis of local college access. *Journal of Diversity in Higher Education.* Advance online publication. Retrieved from dx.doi.org/10.1037/dhe0000050

Dache-Gerbino, A., & Mislan, C. (2015). *Teaching from the margins: Mapping Ferguson's community cultural wealth as public education.* Columbia: University of Missouri Richard Wallace Grant.

Dache-Gerbino, A., & White, J. (2016). College students or criminals? A postcolonial geographic analysis of the social field of whiteness at an urban community college branch campus and suburban main campus. *Community College Review, 44,* 49–69.

Dead Prez. (2000). Wolves. On *Let's get free* [CD]. New York, NY: Loud Records.

Freire, P. (2005). *Pedagogy of the oppressed* (M. B. Ramos, Trans.). New York, NY: Continuum. (Original work published 1970)

Harney, S., & Moten, F. (2013). *The undercommons: Fugitive planning and Black study.* New York: NY: Minor Compositions.

Harper, S. R. (2012). Race without racism: How higher education researchers minimize racist institutional norms. *Review of Higher Education, 36,* 9–29.

Harper, S. R., Patton, L. D., & Wooden, O. S. (2009). Access and equity for African-American students in higher education: A critical race historical analysis of policy efforts. *Journal of Higher Education, 80,* 389–414.

Harvey, D. (2005). *A brief history of neoliberalism.* Oxford, UK: Oxford University Press.

Hooks, B. (1994). *Outlaw culture: Resisting representations.* New York, NY: Routledge.

Kelley, R. D. G. (2002). *Freedom dreams: The Black radical imagination.* Boston, MA: Beacon Press.

Kezar, A. J. (2005). Challenges for higher education in serving the public good. In A. J. Kezar, T. Chambers, & J. C. Burkhardt (Eds.), *Higher eduction for the public good: Emerging voices from a national movement* (pp. 23–42). San Francisco, CA: Jossey-Bass.

Kiyama, J. M., Harris, D. M., & Dache-Gerbino, A. (2016). Fighting for respeto: Latinas' stories of violence and resistance shaping educational opportunities. *Teachers College Record, 118*(12), 1–50.

Mandela, N. (1994). *Long walk to freedom.* New York, NY: Back Bay Books.

Rhoades, R. A., & Valadez, J. R. (1996). *Democracy, multiculturalism, and the community college: A critical perspective.* New York, NY: Routledge.

Shakur, A. (1987). *Assata: An autobiography.* Chicago, IL: Lawrence Hill.

Slaughter, S., & Rhoades, G. (2004). *Academic capitalism and the new economy: Market, state, and higher education.* Baltimore, MD: Johns Hopkins University Press.

Taylor, K. Y. (2016). *From #BlacklivesMatter to Black liberation.* Chicago, IL: Haymarket Books.

U.S. Department of Justice. (2015). *Investigation of the Ferguson police department.* Retrieved from www.justice.gov/sites/default/files/opa/press-releases/attachments/2015/03/04/ferguson_police_department_report.pdf

Washington University in St. Louis. (2015). *Documenting Ferguson.* Retrieved from digital.wustl.edu/ferguson

Wolf-Wendel, L. E., Twombly, S. B., Tuttle, K. N., Ward, K., & Gaston-Gayles, J. L. (Eds.). (2004). *Reflecting back, looking forward: Civil rights and student affairs.* Washington, DC: National Association of Student Personnel Administrators.

9

WHERE SCHOLARSHIP AND PRACTICE MEET

Perspectives From Cooperative Extension

Casey D. Mull, Jenna B. Daniel, and Jenny Jordan

I believe that education, of which Extension is an essential part, is basic in stimu-
lating individual initiative, self-determination, and leadership; that these are the
keys to democracy and that people when given facts they understand, will act not
only in their self-interest but also in the interest of society. (Townson, 2014)

A public service organization in operation for more than 100 years, the Cooperative Extension System in partnership with the National Institute of Food and Agriculture has helped individuals throughout the United States improve their daily lives. This chapter explores the public scholarship of cooperative extension and the mutual impact of this learning on our college university systems and our communities. Although public scholarship and engagement is a fledgling art in some university settings, it has been a cornerstone of the land-grant mission of higher education institutions and local faculty from its early history through today's evolving program. Through a historical journey, we explore the commitment to identifying a public need, involving the public in research, and sharing those results. Throughout the chapter, we use cooperative extension and extension interchangeably. Extension has responded to a changing clientele and created transformation in investigation and practice. As others in higher education look to evolving needs, engaging communities, and translating results, cooperative extension serves not only to bring lessons from the past from bringing community members into the design and dissemination of research but also implications for the future.

History of Cooperative Extension

Throughout the history of the United States, three pieces of legislation, enacted between 1862 and 1914, set the stage for the creation of the Cooperative Extension System. These are integral to extension's role in supporting research for the public good and its foundational role in public scholarship.

The Morrill Acts

The Morrill Acts of 1862 and 1890 embody the foundational tenets of higher education, reaching beyond the pillars of the academy to the needs of its constituency. Rather than create institutions of higher learning, the Morrill Acts brought to the forefront equality, public welfare, and community needs in the structure of higher education. In creating the acts, Justin Morrill was able to illustrate his belief that the kind of education offered at institutions of higher learning during the time did not meet the practical demands of a growing and industrializing nation. The Morrill Act (1862) elevated the role of scholarship, public good, and the engagement of communities to higher education in the United States.

Abraham Lincoln signed the Morrill Act (1862) designating federal land to each state for the establishment of a public institution of higher education. The Morrill Act sought to provide university access to individuals who had previously lacked the ability to enroll. From inception, these land-grant colleges provided working-class individuals with a practical education through subjects like agriculture, military tactics, home economics, and the mechanical arts at a time when higher education was available only to the advantaged and elite. The establishment of land-grant colleges gave individuals from a common life (Taylor, 1981) the opportunity to access the knowledge historically held only by those who matriculated in liberal arts education. This congressional act sought to reach those previously disenfranchised from higher education in a meaningful, accessible manner, modeling the idea that education can be for all, an idea that is essential to public engagement today.

The second Morrill Act (1890) provided additional endowments for the establishment of 17 land-grant universities providing educational access to racial and ethnic underrepresented populations. A third wave of funding in the Improving America's Schools Act (1994) supported the inclusion of Native American–serving institutions, commonly referred to as 1994 institutions. These expansions underscore the importance of serving those disconnected from higher education by establishing resources in the community. Currently, more than 100 land-grant colleges and universities exist.

One land-grant university is housed in each state and territory in the United States, with multiple states in the South and West having two or more land-grant institutions.

The Hatch Act

Another act fundamental to the establishment of the Cooperative Extension System was the Hatch Act of 1887 (Moore, 1988). This legislation created experiment stations and provided an opportunity for research stations operated by land-grant institutions across states and territories. This early stage of moving researchers away from campuses into communities and localizing the research furthered the concept of elevating communities' involvement with higher education. Most important, neither the knowledge of the institution nor the knowledge of the research center is kept isolated but rather is shared with campus-based faculty and disseminated to the surrounding community.

The Smith-Lever Act

In September 1913 the Agricultural Extension Bill was introduced by Ashbury Lever of South Carolina and Hoke Smith of Georgia. The bill proposed an extension system that would authorize "the appointment of two farm demonstration agents in each of the nation's 2,850 rural counties" (Grant, 1986, pp. 111–112). The bill passed in 1914, creating what is now known as the Cooperative Extension System. Throughout the land-grant universities, extension is not only an entity but also an idea. The Cooperative Extension System is a large public-private partnership made up of distinct entities, departments, and units in each level of government reaching each community with the resources of the land-grant institution and connecting each land-grant with end users of research. Ultimately, the Smith-Lever Act institutionalized a system for public scholarship based on the Morrill and Hatch Acts.

As the overarching organization that carries out the public service component of the tripartite mission of the land-grant universities (teaching, research, and service) by "taking the university to the people" (Rasmussen, 1989, p. vii), the charge of public service in higher education was a function of the government through the Cooperative Extension System.

Shortly after its establishment during World War I, cooperative extension's largest successes occurred and remain noteworthy today. The Cooperative Extension System aided in increased yield of many crops, improved processes of agricultural production through the network of knowledge it provided, and improved the preservation of perishable items through canning and other techniques (National Institute of Food and Agriculture, 2017). As a direct result of the Cooperative Extension System, fewer farmers can produce more food today than ever before for a growing population.

Currently, the Cooperative Extension System employs more than 17,000 professionals, most of whom are embedded in the communities they serve; manages tens of thousands of volunteers; and operates in the majority of counties and parishes in the United States. As a "publicly funded, non-formal education system that links the teaching and research resource and activities of the U.S. Department of Agriculture" (Zacharakis, 2008, p. 14), the Cooperative Extension System focuses on providing practical education to assist all people in solving any problems they encounter in their lives from financial literacy to local food systems, and positive youth development.

As a three-tiered organization, the Cooperative Extension System operates on levels similar to the funding it receives: national, state, and local. These levels of operation allow the Cooperative Extension System to provide direct public service to communities across the country, and in turn the communities provide the cooperative extension at the state and national levels with information related to current trends and issues. This two-way transmission of knowledge and needs up and down the organization remains today as the integral process that keeps the Cooperative Extension System relevant, necessary, and active in communities across the country.

In its role as a public service entity and an organization that involves communities, the Cooperative Extension System remains foundational to the discussion surrounding public scholarship. As those in public scholarship evolve and work to better define its role in higher education by acknowledging its close connection to a diverse democracy, equity, and social justice (see chapter 1), we look first to the origin of these notions in the theoretical tenets of adult education. The line we draw in connecting the Cooperative Extension System, public scholarship, and adult education shows that people, not institutions or organizations, and their needs remain the common denominator in the history and the future of this conversation.

Embedded in the legislation that created the Cooperative Extension System, the idea that the boundaries of the university should be the limits of the state and available to all who inhabit those boundaries (McDowell, 2001) gave voice and purpose to the notion of public service and community engagement. More than a century later, and largely because of organizations such as the Kellogg Commission on the Future of State and Land-Grant Universities and the Carnegie Foundation for the Advancement of Teaching, the idea of public service has broadened, and the concept of community engagement in the university setting has "emerged as a major priority" (Weerts & Sandmann, 2010, p. 702). Intertwined in the Cooperative Extension System, community engagement calls for "engagement in the form of service-learning, outreach, and university-community partnerships" (Kellogg Commission, 2001, p. 17) and "describes collaboration between institutions of higher education and their larger communities (local, regional/ state, national, global) for the mutually beneficial exchange of knowledge and resources in a context of partnership and reciprocity" (New England Resource Center for Higher Education, 2017). Community engagement and public service have roots in the Cooperative Extension System through its work to meet the needs of individuals across communities to provide better, safer, and more meaningful lives for its constituents.

Engaging Adults in Cooperative Extension

Recognized as one of the largest adult education organizations in the United States (Franz & Townson, 2008), the Cooperative Extension System serves adults across the nation with diverse needs, life experiences, and educational levels. When President Woodrow Wilson signed the Smith-Lever Act (1914), "he called it 'one of the most significant and far-reaching measures for the education of adults ever adopted by the government'" (Rasmussen, 1989, p. vii). Committed to lifelong learning, the Cooperative Extension System uses theoretical perspectives central to adult education to provide programs and services throughout the nation.

Developed as voluntary, community-based education that operates on a short-term basis (Merriam, Caffarella, & Baumgartner, 2007), programmatic efforts of the Cooperative Extension System are typically "organized, systematic, and programmatic education activity, external to formal education frameworks and providing target subgroups with selected types of learning" (Romi & Schmida, 2009, p. 259). Extension programs and services comfortably fit within these specifications. The Cooperative Extension System programming "has always embodied adult education's teaching-learning process, where the goal is not to tell people what to do but to teach them how to solve their problems" (Zacharakis, 2008, p. 15). This teaching-learning process should echo the larger discussion of how public scholarship provides the opportunity for two-way engagement between institutions of higher education and the communities served. As with public scholarship, the Cooperative Extension System and its work in public service and community engagement creates the opportunity for this two-way engagement.

Public Scholarship in Extension Today

The program continues to connect land-grant institutions with the people of the state through research trials, education, and experiences. Some individuals critique cooperative extension as being only a one-way service, rather than two-way engagement. However, the notion of two-way engagement is a critical component to public scholarship where stakeholders play a role in creation, dissemination, and application. The county faculty and staff members live and work among the people they serve and span the boundaries of local needs and issues to connect the resources and research of the land-grant institutions. Local and state extension faculty engage the general public with limited access to research and resources through the creation, dissemination, and application of information and then, in turn, sharing that information throughout the community, collecting additional information, and returning it to the institution to inform additional research.

Extension stories exemplify the nature of public scholarship, the impact of empowering communities through institutional research, and the change that occurs with a two-way engagement model. In the Cooperative Extension System, local faculty serve as public scholars who bridge discipline-based faculty and practitioners, assisting in engaging people in scholarly work. The role of the individual is the key component and unit of cooperative extension's role in public scholarship. County agents or field staff, whom we refer to as a county or local faculty, serve as the connector between the university and stakeholders; they are essential in aiding local constituents' understanding of and access to the information at the institution level. County faculty members' skills, competencies, and trust in the community serve as a catalyst for effective public scholarship.

At the University of Georgia (UGA), cooperative extension faculty members facilitate public scholarship in three program areas: agriculture and natural resources, family and consumer sciences, and 4-H youth development. Although other state extension systems may have additional or different nomenclature for their areas, these three exemplify a cross-section of extension programming. Some states use dedicated faculty focused on community and economic development, for example, as a fourth program area of extension. At UGA other dedicated public service units focus on this area, and therefore it is not a part of extension programming. It is important to note that these units at UGA grew from UGA extension. In our institution, many other units and departments may also engage in public service work, although they are not part of the Cooperative Extension System. Many of these organizations also grew from the extension model and replicated the two-way engagement idea of public scholarship.

In cooperative extension's agricultural program area, the connection to local farmers with real-world issues enables researchers at universities to explore not only the scientific impacts but also the sociological ones. Engagement in learning provides communities with otherwise limited access the means to access information and the voice to propel changes and needs. Cooperative extension was instrumental in changes in cotton production because of the boll weevil through eradication and using early-maturing cotton varieties (Haney, Lewis, & Lambert, 2012), and county extension agents were crucial in the development of blueberry production in southeast Georgia. Georgia produces more blueberries than any other state, and the fruit has a $335 million economic impact on the state (Angle, 2015; Wolf & Stubbs, 2014). External stakeholders, including commodity groups, policy groups, foundations, and practitioner audiences, are involved at multiple steps of this growth and impact. The following example of the growth and development of blueberries as the most important fruit crop in Georgia illustrates involving the public at each stage of research and learning.

According to the UGA Blueberry Blog, blueberries became an essential crop following the decrease in timber prices in the 1990s and the end of the tobacco quota program (Sial, 2013). The existing relationship of the county agent in Bacon County with local farmers after the fall in timber prices and the loss of tobacco quotas created the opportunity to explore other viable profitable commodities. The local agent, working with state specialists in fruit production, discovered that the low cost of land, growing conditions along riverbeds, and the optimal climate in southeast Georgia would make blueberries the perfect replacement for the declining crops. The local county agent located farmers growing timber and tobacco who were interested in new research related to crop production and set up research plots on their properties. The local farmers tested cultivars on these plots to determine whether they could be grown successfully in the local climate.

The county agent working with the farmers faced new challenges in changing from timber to blueberries. A stand of timber is not affected by frost, and there is no need for watering systems and fans. The challenge of moving to blueberry production can include costs such as overhead irrigation (more than $400,000) and orchard fans (more than $210,000; Sial, 2013). By working with extension faculty at the state and county level, researchers provided resources such as demonstrations of overhead irrigation and orchard fans, economic forecasts, and other best practices in fruit production through the county agent. Some of this information would otherwise not be available to or understood by the community, which was growing tobacco or timber. In connecting a local land owner with a blueberry researcher at the university, the county agent cultivated a relationship that changed the economy of the region. The small farmers who allowed plots for blueberry research on their land accepted the risk and challenges of change and eventually a new product.

Through this creation of public knowledge (i.e., how to grow blueberries in southeast Georgia), the successful farmer becomes a form of peer review. One farmer's success leads to the distribution and application of new crops and techniques among other farmers, transmitted through word of mouth, local media, and other community sources such as professional groups, advocacy organizations, and associations. The dissemination of this new information also occurs through the county agent who conducts demonstration days for farmers, rather than the faculty members, to share their successes. Dissemination continues through other local production and commodity group meetings locally or regionally. Credibility is harnessed because a local citizen interacts with the community, and the university continues to build a network and research program through others that further expands its ability to discover new knowledge in new contexts.

Although this example of the impact of the extension took place on several farms over several years, it is indicative of the extension model, that is, university connections creating shared change in a community. The results of decades of work by campus-based faculty working with faculty residing and working with and among agricultural producers equipped Georgia farmers to make a change in commodity production. Blueberry acreage in 1955 was "essentially zero" (Scherm & Krewer, 2003, p. 84). According to Scherm and Krewer (2003), the following elements influenced the growth of blueberries as a crop in Georgia: (a) establishment of a breeding program that released new cultivars; (b) blueberry and marketing cooperatives; (c) mechanical harvesters purchased through the Model Cities program, an economic development program for economically disadvantaged communities; and (d) a second round of a blueberry variety in the mid-1990s because it could be harvested early. At each level of growth, creation and dissemination of knowledge were taking place with the institution and the producers.

Pest issues on blueberry farms offer a present-day example of the role of cooperative extension support and public scholarship in blueberry cultivation. Blueberry replant disease significantly affects southern highbush varieties. A plant parasite known as the ring nematode appeared in more than half the blueberry farms in southeastern Georgia in 2010 and 2012 (Noe, 2016). This problem surfaced organically when local community farmers delivered evidence of parasites to the county agent for identification. Agents working with entomology specialists reported mounting concern. As a result, campus-based entomology and fruit production specialists and county-based agents collaborated with producers to install randomized research plots "to evaluate combinations of pre-plant nematicide application in combination with plastic mulches" (Noe, 2016, para. 3). Taking the research from the university, the local agent recruited growers to host research plots on local farms for two long-term nematode research trials. As directed by the researcher, the trials examined different management strategies for controlling nematodes. The blueberry producers addressed the researchers' concerns and challenges relative to different strategies, and the local agent supported and guided the process. Although this shows public service and research in action, the local agent described the public scholarship side of the experience in the following:

> The results of these trials have been shared at meetings and allowed growers to see the benefits of treating for nematodes before replanting a field. Not only can I discuss the benefits of using soil fumigants in a replant blueberry field, but there is also a local research trial to take growers to for them to see for themselves the different treatments. Over 15 local growers have visited the research site representing over 2,250 acres of blueberries. As a result of this research, blueberry nematode samples have increased 10%, and over 400 acres of blueberries have been replanted using soil fumigants. (Curry, 2016)

Using the soil fumigant potentially prevented $2.5 million in fruit losses for the blueberry growers (Curry, 2016). The impact provided additional opportunities for study as the information funneled back to the university to support additional research studies, journal articles, new knowledge, and understanding. Although the blueberry farmers' experiences are limited to the blueberry, the role public scholarship has played in integrated pest management (IPM) is more widespread and demonstrates the transdisciplinary role of extension work. IPM affects most Americans each day, but few Americans know or understand its importance. Kogan (1998) defines *IPM* as

> a decision support system for the selection and use of pest control tactics, singularly or harmoniously coordinated into a management strategy, based on cost/benefit analyses that take into account the interests of and impacts on producers, society, and the environment. (p. 249)

In simpler phrasing, IPM takes into consideration different and often conflicting influences to determine the best course of action to provide food and fibers to society.

IPM's role grew tremendously in the final decades of the twentieth century, in part because of cooperative extension. Chemical advances in agriculture resulted in fertilizers, pesticides, and insecticides to assist in feeding and clothing an explosive population worldwide. IPM's significance extends beyond the impact on the farmer or producer in its ability to protect agricultural investments. The impact of pesticides and people's scrutiny of the chemicals in food, fibers, and the environment provide a social context beyond the simple education of growers and correct applications. Because of the cultural aspects of IPM and decision-making, county agents use aspects of the social sciences including sociology, psychology, and adult education topics of experiential and transformational learning. Without adjusting their belief systems, growers may use only one type of pest control, perhaps one that has far-reaching impacts for other producers, consumers, and society. For change to take place, an approach of involving those affected in the creation and dissemination of knowledge is crucial. Using participatory research in this realm is vital as growers have localized knowledge in adapting pest management to local crops and conditions and have shown an interest in IPM experimentation (Grieshop, Zalom, & Miyao, 1988; Norton, Rajotte, & Gapud, 1999).

The uniqueness of cooperative extension is, in part, attributed to grassroots involvement in local communities and empowerment of individuals through education and community-based problem-solving (Archer et al., 2007). These examples of blueberries and IPM are just two of many on the needs of communities, innovations of research, and the collaboration of the university and the people to meet local challenges and affect future learning. Blueberries and IPM exemplify the work of collaborative efforts to create scholarship in the public domain. Although the research at the university level created solutions, the change to communities occurred once that research and learning were supported, integrated, and formed at a community level. Through a partnership with the publics served, university researchers develop processes and procedures that change methods and ways of being. Publics, not usually connected to the research or knowledge, connect with the resources and information needed for change. The resulting changes are shared publicly with communities and publicly with other scholarly entities. Through these process and partnerships, extension exemplifies the role of public scholarship.

Implications for Higher Education as a Whole

The concept of integrating teaching, research, service, and thus public scholarship is deeply rooted in the practice of land-grant institutions and their mission of developing, disseminating, and applying knowledge to create an enlightened and productive citizenry. For more than 100 years, cooperative extension has connected communities in every corner of every state with institutions of higher education through this mission. This organization that began and thrived as an educational support unit for rural America is still meeting the needs of communities. The question remains: What can colleges and universities learn from the examples described in this chapter to promote faculty engagement in public scholarship?

The idea that knowledge is learned in communities rather than given to those communities is illustrated in the growth of the extension model. Extension faculty are part of the community, often living and always working with the community and learning beside the community. This model effectively creates a knowledge base that not only is new information but also practical and relevant to the community and the institution. The extension model of anticipating and responding to critical and emerging issues; establishing partnerships; involving the public in planning, implementation, and evaluation; and using the university's and the client's expertise to facilitate change is easily replicable by other colleges, units, and faculty in supporting authentic engagement in higher education. The key is to seek excellence in each area of the model. Regardless of the content or context, the university and the citizenry will grow, learn, and explore through a careful blending of community engagement with teaching and research. Effective public scholarship projects often colocate university faculty and staff in the community; these boundary spanners effectively navigate university and community by building individual and organizational trust (Mull, 2016; Weerts & Sandmann, 2010)

Extension is a systematic and consistent approach to community involvement. Although faculty in many university systems place students in the community for service-learning and engagement or network with community members to develop research partners, these activities can appear individually motivated and episodic. At its core, extension links the land-grant mission of a university to the people with an established, long-term presence and grassroots involvement of the local communities (Archer et al., 2007). As an institutionalized component of public scholarship, the Cooperative Extension System is readily available for the community at any point in time, not necessarily when university scheduling permits. This linkage is visible in the most basic approach of educating adults in the areas most pressing for their needs at a specific time and extends to the work done in the blueberry fields discussed earlier. Extension extends the borders of the land-grant institution to the people, and, in turn, the people extend their learning beyond their community boundary to the land-grant.

Although the content is critical to the university partner, the context is as important to the communities where extension is present. Extension uniquely empowers the citizenry through education and community-based problem-solving (Archer et al., 2007). An important distinction from other service-learning activities or community engagement is that extension seeks to engage people and work beyond a simple idea of becoming problem solvers and thinkers. Colbeck and Michael (2006) said, "Public scholarship enables faculty, students, and community members to work together to define real-world problems in all their complexity and then to cooperate with the process of addressing those problems" (p. 17).

As we have seen in the case of blueberry cultivation with extension, communities are a part of the research, application, and results achieved by higher education faculty. In working with the public to establish research questions, scientists and scholars see the potential and emerging trends as well as those identified by the work of the university. Communities widen potential data sources and test the procedures themselves, not just the application and results. As described in extension's history, educators and scientists look more broadly and perhaps discover trends or issues not considered in the laboratory environment when the community is involved in all phases (Cohen & Yapa, 2003). This combination of the social sciences and involving the community lifts up issues and challenges natural scientists may not discover on their own.

As other units and faculty in higher education seek to replicate the ideals of cooperative extension, it is important to note the role of the extension educator as a community member. Creating a close relationship and collaborative partnership requires giving up turf and developing trust. Although it may not be possible for every public scholarship initiative to place university employees in local communities, it is critical to establish the understanding of and commitment to the community that comes from being a resident. The Extension Professionals' Creed states in part, "the greatest university is the home" and that clientele have "their right to make their own plans and arrive at their own decisions" (Townson, 2014, para. 4). Cooperative extension serves as the connector and the catalyst for sharing knowledge between academic and practitioner. Because collaboration requires enhancing capacity by working together for a common purpose, information is exchanged, ideas are altered, and resources are shared (Himmelman, 2001). The more closely connected university and community partners are, the more efficiently collaboration occurs, as illustrated by the success of extension programs.

Extension is committed to new and evolving technologies. From the use of trains to deliver faculty to rural areas such as George Washington Carver's Jesup Wagons and the demonstration farms of Seaman Knapp, extension has made use of the technologies of the day and those of the future to bring to all communities knowledge from their universities. Extension, however, has taken this a step further today in "lowering the barriers to adoption of research-based information by innovation in communication and program delivery" (Henning, Buchholz, Steele, & Ramaswamy, 2014). For institutions to connect with publics, there must be an emphasis on and a willingness to adopt new and evolving methods of interaction. Cooperative extension today uses eXtension.org, an online portal to connect with land-grant universities, where community and university can engage in a virtual world, learning from one another, sharing challenges, and discovering answers. For public scholarship to be open, all communities must be connected. Technology has created a world that is more connected than ever, taking the idea of bringing a university and the people to a more open and inclusive level. No longer are those geographically close to faculty the only ones able to learn. Creation of a public knowledge involves leveraging the strengths of technology to globally connect the community to the university and the university to the community.

The Extension Professionals' Creed (Townson, 2014) underscores the faculty member's role of taking his or her sense of wonder, exploration, and leadership to create a stronger, self-determined democratic society. Through the passage of legislation to create education for the people, a unit of service has crafted more than a century of public scholarship. Consider any portion of extension history, such as fighting the boll weevil, introducing blueberries as an alternative crop, adding robotics to 4-H programming, or moving money management tasks to online applications, and the theme remains the same: Extension is a problem-solving resource for local issues (Henning et al., 2014). Rasmussen (1989) said that throughout history, extension has solved contemporary challenges with resource-based solutions in a local context and with innovative education across all ages and segments of life. And through all this, extension offers higher education a model for building with communities a knowledge base that exemplifies public scholarship and community engagement.

References

Archer, T., Warner, P., Miller, W., Clark, C., James, S., Cummings, S., & Adams, U. (2007). Excellence in extension: Two products for definition and measurement. *Journal of Extension, 45*(1). Retrieved from joe.org/joe/2007february/tt1.php

Angle, J. S. (2015). *2015 ag snapshots: A brief focus on Georgia's agricultural industry.* Retrieved from caes2.caes.uga.edu/center/caed/pubs/agsnapshots/documents/AGsnaphots.spreads_2015.pdf

Cohen, J., & Yapa, L. (2003). Introduction. In J. Cohen, L. Yapa, J. Cohen, & L. Yapa (Eds.), *A blueprint for public scholarship at Penn State* (pp. 5–8). University Park: Pennsylvania State University.

Colbeck, C., & Michael, P. (2006). The public scholarship: Reintegrating Boyer's four domains. *New Directions for Institutional Research, 129*, 7–18.

Curry, D. (2016). Helping blueberry growers with replant disorder. Retrieved from apps.caes.uga.edu/impactstatements/index.cfm?referenceInterface=IMPACT_STATEMENT&subInterface=detail_main&PK_ID=7239

Franz, N. K., & Townson, L. (2008). The nature of complex organizations: The case of cooperative extension. *New Directions for Evaluation, 120*, 5–14.

Grant, P. A., Jr. (1986). Senator Hoke Smith, southern congressman, and agricultural education, 1914–1917. *Agricultural History, 60*, 111–122.

Grieshop, J. I., Zalom, F. G., & Miyao, G. (1988). Adoption and diffusion of integrated pest management innovations in agriculture. *Bulletin of the Entomological Society of America, 34*(2), 72–79.

Haney, P. B., Lewis, W. J., & Lambert, W. R. (2012). *Cotton production and the boll weevil in Georgia: History, cost of control, and benefits of eradication.* Athens: Georgia Agricultural Experiment Stations.

Henning, J., Buchholz, D., Steele, D., & Ramaswamy, S. (2014). Milestones and the future of cooperative extension. *Journal of Extension, 52*(6). Retrieved from www.joe.org/joe/2014december/comm1.php

Himmelman, A. (2001). On coalitions and the transformation of power relations: Collaborative betterment and collaborative empowerment. *American Journal of Community Psychology, 29*, 277–284.

Kellogg Commission on the Future of State Land-Grant Universities. (2001). *Returning to our roots: Executive summaries of the Kellogg Commission on the future of state and land-grant universities.* Retrieved from www.aplu.org/library/returning-to-our-roots-kellogg-commission-on-the-future-of-state-and-land-grant-universities-executive-summaries-of-the-reports-of-the-kellogg-commission-on-the-future-of-state-and-land-grant-universities-2000/file

Kogan, M. (1998). Integrated pest management: Historical perspectives and contemporary developments. *Annual Review of Entomology, 43*, 243–270.

McDowell, G. R. (2001). *Land-grant universities and extension into the 21st century: Renegotiating or abandoning a social contract.* Ames: Iowa State University Press.

Merriam, S. B., Caffarella, R. S., & Baumgartner, L. M. (2007). *Learning in adulthood: A comprehensive guide* (3rd ed.). San Francisco, CA: Jossey-Bass.

Moore, G. E. (1988). The involvement of experiment stations in secondary agricultural education, 1887–1917. *Agricultural History, 62*, 164–176.

Mull, C. D. (2016). A dissertation of boundary-spanning actors within community engagement. *Journal of Higher Education Outreach and Engagement, 20*, 157–162.

National Institute of Food and Agriculture. (2017). *Extension.* Retrieved from nifa.usda.gov/extension_

New England Resource Center for Higher Education. (2017). *Carnegie community engagement classification.* Retrieved from nerche.org/index.php?option=com_content&view=article&id=341:carnegie-foundation-community-engagement-classification&catid=914:carnegie-foundation-classification&Itemid=618

Noe, J. (2016). *Minimizing crop losses due to blueberry replant disease.* Retrieved from apps.caes.uga.edu/impactstatements/index.cfm?referenceInterface=IMPACT_STATEMENT&subInterface=detail_main&PK_ID=7680

Norton, G. W., Rajotte, E. G., & Gapud, V. (1999). Participatory research in integrated pest management: Lessons from the IPM CRSP. *Agriculture and Human Values, 16,* 431–439.

Rasmussen, W. D. (1989). *Taking the university to the people: Seventy-five years of cooperative extension.* Ames: Iowa State University Press.

Romi, S., & Schmida, M. (2009). Non-formal education: A major educational force in the postmodern era. *Cambridge Journal of Education, 39,* 257–273.

Scherm, H., & Krewer, G. (2003). Blueberry production in Georgia: Historical overview and recent trends. *Small Fruits Review, 2*(4), 83–91.

Sial, A. (2013). Georgia blueberries [Web log]. Retrieved from blog.caes.uga.edu/blueberry/2013/10/georgia-the-blueberry-state

Taylor, J. F. A. (1981). *The public commission of the university: The role of the community of scholars and industrial, urban, and corporate society.* New York, NY: New York University Press.

Townson, L. (2014, July 2). Extension professionals' creed. [Web log]. Retrieved from extension.unh.edu/articles/Extension-Professionals-Creed

Weerts, D. J., & Sandmann, L. R. (2010). Community engagement and boundary-spanning roles at research universities. *Journal of Higher Education, 81,* 702–727.

Wolfe, K., & Stubbs, K. (2014). *2013 farm gate value report.* Athens, GA: University of Georgia Center for Agribusiness & Economic Development.

Zacharakis, J. (2008). Extension and community: The practice of popular and progressive education. *New Directions for Adult and Continuing Education, 117,* 13–23.

USING SOCIAL MEDIA AS PUBLIC SCHOLARSHIP

Constance Iloh

Academics have been late adopters of social media compared to professionals in other fields; however, given vast contemporary societal inequities, their role in engaging the public is more critical than ever (Lipsett, 2010). Although much of the current discourse on academics and social media engagement revolves around practical uses, far less discussion has been devoted to the role of social media in dismantling the structures that limit the reach of public scholarship. I argue that the use of social media among academics goes well beyond its practical importance because it facilitates the democratization of knowledge and uniquely supports underrepresented scholars. In presenting these arguments, I offer new conceptual perspectives regarding social media and public scholarship that center social media as a critical space for the engaged academic as well as addressing serious challenges for society (Espinoza Vasquez & Caicedo Bastidas, 2015).

This chapter begins with a discussion on public scholarship within the academy. I then define *social media* and describe its current state and usage among academics. In the final section, I argue how social media use by academics democratizes knowledge and supports the advancement of racially minoritized academics.

Public Scholarship

In public scholarship, it is not assumed that useful knowledge simply flows outward from the university to the larger community (Yapa, 2006); new knowledge is created through its application in the field and therefore benefits the teaching and research mission of the university (Yapa, 2006). Although similar to common conceptions of service-learning or civic engagement, public scholarship is neither supplemental to primary teaching or research responsibilities, nor can it be accomplished by simply adding community service and reflection components to the courses faculty teach (Colbeck & Weaver, 2008). Public scholarship reframes academic work as an inseparable whole in which teaching, research, and service components are teased apart only to see how each informs and enriches the others, and faculty members use the integrated whole of their work to address societal needs (Colbeck & Wharton-Michael 2006; Kellogg Commission on the Future of State and Land-Grant Universities, 2000).

There are many reasons for considering public scholarship as legitimate work for faculty and students (Ramaley, 2009). At one level, it offers a way for scholars to integrate their scholarly interests into their personal experiences and motivations (Ramaley, 2009). On another level, important developments in academic work and various disciplines, such as sociology and education, have at least indirectly stemmed from social movements with *emancipatory* and *public interests* that have fueled a new or reconfigured social analysis (Bhattacharyya & Murji, 2013). Powerful integration of this kind by academics provides students and society with a powerful view of an engaged mind at work and even an example of passionate engagement.

Social Media

The Internet has profoundly changed the human experience. We use the Web to find information, buy and sell products, watch television shows, find partners, search for entertainment, and participate in political spheres (Gil de Zúñiga, Puig, & Rojas, 2009; Park, Kee, & Valenzuela, 2009). People once went online because of the anonymity it offered (McKenna & Bargh, 2000) and now more often use the Internet to socialize with people they know and to expand their circle of friends (Jones & Fox, 2009). Through the Internet, a number of Web technologies emerged, and social media networks are making waves in regard to information sharing and communication (Mingle & Adams, 2015). Among the vast variety of online tools that are available for communication, social networking sites have become the most modern and attractive tools for connecting people throughout the world (Aghazamani, 2010).

Social media is a term used to describe a range of online applications that enable and specifically encourage interactive communication among users (White, 2013). Millions of people around the world use social media to ask questions, network, learn, and share their interests. The social media ethos is all about engagement, participation, and relationship building (White, 2013). Every platform encourages its users to take part by commenting on what they see and by getting involved in conversations with others. In addition to having conversations and giving their opinions, visitors to social media sites also like to share information (Hampton et al., 2014). This can have a powerful amplification effect (known as *going viral*) with articles, videos, or images shared among thousands or even millions of people.

For the purposes of this chapter, *social media* is defined as Web-based services that allow individuals to (a) construct a public or semipublic profile within a bounded system, (b) create a list of other users with whom they share a connection, and (c) view and traverse their list of connections and those made by others within the system (Boyd & Ellison, 2007). The nature and nomenclature of these connections may vary from site to site. Social network sites are unique not because they allow individuals to meet strangers, but rather because they enable users to cultivate and make visible their social networks (Rushby & Surry, 2016; Tiryakioglu & Erzurum, 2010). This can result in connections between individuals that would not otherwise be made. However, that is often not the goal, and these meetings are frequently between latent ties (Haythornthwaite, 2005) that share some offline connection. On many of the large social media sites, participants are not necessarily networking or trying to meet new people; instead, they are primarily communicating with people who are already a part of their extended social network (Boyd & Ellison, 2007).

Social Media in Research and the Academic Space

Social media can be used at all points of the research cycle, from identifying research opportunities to disseminating research results. According to the results of a large international survey conducted by Rowlands, Nicholas, Russell, Canty, and Watkinson (2011), the most popular tools allow collaborative writing, conferencing, and scheduling and meeting. Although Nicholas, Williams, Rowlands, and Jamali (2010) were surprised at the absence of social media sources in their study on the scholarly behavior of researchers in the United Kingdom, a similar study conducted in the United States reported a notable trend in the use of collaborative technology for sharing information with colleagues and students (Niu et al., 2010). Social media may allow informal communication that is similar, or in some cases superior, to traditional channels of informal communication for dissemination and collaboration. Because social media is intended to support collaborative creation and dissemination of knowledge, it is not surprising that scholars have explored their use for academic purposes and that a number of social media services specifically targeting the academic community (blogs; online comments on journal articles; social bookmarking sites; wikis; websites to post slides, text, or videos; etc.) have emerged in the past few years.

Despite the worldwide growth of social media for personal use, educators and academics have been slow to use social media technologies for academic practice (Guy, 2012). Thus, only a minority of scholars have taken up the use of social media tools and platforms as a regular part of their professional work (Lupton, 2014). This number appears to be slowly growing as moves toward making research data and publications and teaching materials available outside the academy, and for academics to interact with the wider public, have become more dominant in higher education (Lupton, 2014; Rumbley et al., 2014).

The published literature regarding faculty use of social media for academic practice cites cyber security, cyberbullying, and faculty workloads for the lack of social media use and innovative practice (Jabeur, Tamine, & Boughanem, 2010). When used by faculty as a supplemental tool, social media activities were informal, open, and self-regulated (Adema, 2013; Chen & Bryer, 2012). Similar to students, faculty are using social media technologies for personal communication, information sharing, and professional connections (Tiryakioglu & Erzurum, 2010). LinkedIn was the most used site for professional purposes other than teaching, followed by blogs and wikis, Facebook, podcasts, and Twitter (Seaman & Tinti-Kane, 2013).

Social Media as a Public Forum

The term *public forum* is often associated with the concept of a designated space within a community where individuals can gather to discuss topics, exchange information, and develop interpersonal relationships with other members (Gruzd & Goertzen, 2013). Today social media has become a unique, expansive, and attractive public forum as it usually does not cost the user much or anything at all to participate and is relatively fast to use (Lidsky, 2011). Throughout history, however, gathering points were established in central and physical locations such as public squares (Gruzd & Goertzen, 2013). Because of closer interconnections by way of the virtual realm, many individuals and groups rely on social media such as blogs, microblogs, social networking sites, and the like to group and connect in various online communities. In the following sections, I describe through the literature and personal example how social media democratizes knowledge and offers a unique platform for racially minoritized scholars (Donelan, 2016).

Social Media and Democratizing Knowledge

Expansion of the World Wide Web and newer technologies has improved the ways science is communicated (Kumar & Mishra, 2015). Rather than being dependent on the end user searching for or pulling relevant knowledge from the literature base, social media instead pushes relevant knowledge directly to the end user via blogs and sites such as Facebook and Twitter (Allen, Stanton, Di Pietro, & Moseley, 2013). Further, studies have indicated the potential of social networking sites in providing an informal network for sharing academic knowledge and resources and allowing peer-to-peer learning (Forkosh-Baruch & Hershkovitz, 2012; Madhusudhan, 2012; Veletsianos & Kimmons, 2013), as well as sharing information about practical issues in their practice (Veletsianos & Kimmons, 2013) and identifying problems with research design (Mandavilli, 2011). Moreover, the use of social media, even for passive consumers, allows academics to follow others in their field who are interested in similar issues.

Social media is more accessible to many people than traditional academic publications. The rapid rise in popularity of social media sites such as Facebook and Twitter has positioned them as critical tools that can aid dissemination (Allen et al., 2013). The advent of social media and peer-to-peer technologies offer the possibility of driving the full democratization of news and information, undercutting the agendas of spaces that thrive from unequal access to information. As a result, social scientists can use social media to get the word out about important research findings. In addition, social media can spread ideas to other social scientists leading to increased citations (Sawyer, 2011).

In particular, social media offers great potential for sharing and disseminating academic scholarship far more widely and rapidly than ever before, while at the same time allowing greater transformation of the scholarship. Since the rise of the Internet in the early 1990s, the world's networked population has grown from the low millions to the low billions (Shirkey, 2011). Over the same period, social media have become a fact of life for civil society worldwide, involving many actors—regular citizens, activists, nongovernmental organizations, telecommunications firms, software providers, and governments (Shirkey, 2011). As the communications landscape gets denser, more complex, and more participatory, the networked population is gaining greater access to information, more opportunities to engage in public speech, and an enhanced ability to undertake collective action by way of social media.

Social media has been critical in my ability to disseminate research to broad audiences. As a scholar, I often use Twitter, Facebook, LinkedIn, and Instagram to share my insights and research, taking different approaches on each platform. I usually share my research most frequently and consistently on Twitter to take advantage of its microblogging culture and ethos (Gregg, 2006). This usually results in a sizable number of retweets, shares, and replies, which creates more demand and exposure for my other content. When presenting my research and giving keynote lectures, I always include my social media handles. This way those present can share insights in the social media sphere and expose new work to their networks too. When I began inviting people to do this years ago, I would have an enormous amount of people requesting copies of papers or links to my published research. Because of the high amount of engagement and requests for my research, I decided to create a professional website and also an Academia.edu page where people can access my published work and stay abreast of my projects.

Social media is an essential means to share information on hot topics and quickly evolving conversations that my research is part of. Much of the dialogue on areas I explore (e.g., underserved student populations, for-profit higher education, community colleges, and college access) develops and changes quickly in the public sphere while taking much longer in traditional academic publications. I regularly connect my work to ongoing social media conversations by posting my research article links on multiple platforms, occasionally blogging, serving as a guest expert on Twitter chats, participating in live-streamed panels and keynote lectures, and inviting people to live tweet or share forthcoming or published work on social media. Thus, I have been able to engage in conversations with reporters, practitioners, and the public about my work while expanding the readership beyond that of any specific academic journal.

One such example is the wide circulation of one of my most recent articles, "Exploring the For-Profit Experience: An Ethnography of a For-Profit College" (Iloh, 2016). This publication was shared on multiple social media platforms, including Twitter and Facebook, and quickly captured interest from university leaders, politicians, policymakers, practitioners, students, and scholars. It was especially important that this article appeared on social media because much of the for-profit college debate occurs outside academia. In 2017, I found out the article was the second most-read article in the journal for the entire year of 2016. I even shared insights from this study and a few others at an invited keynote lecture with NBC Universal, Telemundo, and the Idea Center. Social media provided increased visibility, which ultimately created more avenues to share my research with diverse stakeholders.

Although I argue that social media democratizes information, I would be remiss to overlook that within the social media domain some information is likely to have greater reach than others. On social media platforms, viewers tend to favor and engage in fast thinking. Therefore, content accompanied by images that use simpler vocabulary makes us more likely to use and share it (Berger & Milkman, 2011). Further, highly emotional content such as stories evoking awe, amusement, anger, and anxiety tends to be shared more often (Berger & Milkman, 2011). My social media posts of text accompanied with images, a short but powerful narrative, or a concise and interesting data point get the most traction and circulation.

Social Media and Support for Racially Minoritized Scholars

I also argue that social media builds community and highlights the expertise of minoritized scholars in ways typical academic spaces do not. The literature concerning non-White people (and women) in academia is replete with examples of their marginalization, isolation, and compartmentalization (Stanley, 2006; Turner, 2002; Turner, González, & Wood, 2011). It delineates a clear pattern of institutional and interpersonal oppression in the academy as underrepresented faculty try to fit into an environment steeped in White male privilege (Cobb-Roberts, 2011).

Racially minoritized scholars and women tend to be disproportionally exposed to exclusionary practices, negative and gossipy commentary, harassment, censure, and even loss of employment as a result of their social media involvement or other professional activities. In addition to the factors influencing all faculty, faculty of color are subjected to racist ideologies and racially discriminatory behaviors. Particular challenges and barriers negatively influence faculty of color including (a) low numbers of minorities in the professoriate and on campus, (b) barriers to tenure and promotion, (c) feelings of otherness, and (d) experiences of racial and ethnic bias (Astin, Antonio, Cress, & Astin, 1997; Jayumkar, Howard, Allen, & Han, 2009; Turner, 2000).

Because managing and developing an intellectual identity is essential for researchers, social media sites are helping them with this task in ways that might level the playing field for scholars often given less attention for their scholarly contributions because of racism in the academy (Barbour & Marshall, 2012). Researchers are increasingly showcasing their expertise and achievements through multiple online profiles (Bukvova, 2011; Stewart, 2008). Social media also facilitates the diffusion of researchers' work (Bullinger, Neyer, Rass, & Moeslein, 2010), which is especially important for scholars whose work may not be circulated as much by their institution and intellectual community. Kelly (2013) adds that social media maximizes the public awareness of one's research output, thus increasing chances of document downloads.

Social media also provides an intellectual and professional community that is often not available for scholars of color, particularly those with limited social capital and formal connections. The ivory tower can often be a lonely place for faculty of color. Social injustices run deep and are entrenched in academia (Ford & Mason, 2013). Faculty of color, more specifically Black and Hispanic faculty, often lament about the Black and Brown tax that frequently takes its toll personally and professionally, and pushes them out of the academy (Ford & Mason, 2013). One of the major advantages of social media tools, which has been reported many times in the research, is the creation of community. Veletsianos (2013) suggests that social media sites can be places where scholars congregate to share their work, ideas, and experiences. The ability of finding relevant communities of scientists and the ability to disseminate findings to a broader audience contribute to researchers' enrollment in social media sites (Kelly & Delasalle, 2012) and perhaps even more so for underrepresented scholars.

As a person of color, woman, and assistant professor, social media has been a critical tool for using my expertise and building supportive networks in ways the academy traditionally does not. I would be remiss to overlook the enhanced exposure my work has received in this space, which is not always granted to minoritized groups in conventional ways. Through sharing my research on social media such as Twitter, Facebook, and Instagram, groups committed to educational equity and excellence for underserved communities have reached out to me. For example, I caught the attention of representatives from the White House Initiative for Educational Excellence for African Americans who invited me to serve as a guest expert for several education discussions. During many of these dialogues, my data-driven insights were given a heightened platform, and the organization regularly shared my research or asked me to share links and resources. This organization is just one of many that has taken an interest in my work, and it has been instrumental in connecting me to broader audiences. More recently, National Public Radio honored me as a Source of the Week and shared my research, which is another instance of an organization finding me on social media and elevating my voice as an authority in the field.

Social media has been critical in allowing me to cultivate identities central to my commitment and ethos as a scholar. In addition to being Black, a woman, a millennial, and having a host of other important identities, I also consider myself a digital scholar. As an academic with a particular interest in equity and education, access to information is just as important as the access I explore in higher education. Through social media, I have been able to explore the many possibilities for a scholar committed to developing his or her signature in digital spaces and advancing knowledge contributions through platforms with sizable audiences. Social media provides me with the freedom to emphasize parts of my identity I also wish to celebrate and develop as my career advances.

Consistent with the research mentioned earlier, social media space has allowed me to extend my community of colleagues and supporters. I recognize that community is important for anyone in the academy but especially for those who often might deal with isolation and marginalization because of one or more identities, in addition to intersection of their identities. I have connected with like-minded colleagues, mentors, thinkers, leaders, and consumers of research just through connecting over shared interests and shared identities on social media (Gruzd, Staves, & Wilk, 2012). I even cultivated a relationship with two mentors after they heard about my work through social media, and from there we have been conversing extensively on and offline.

Through regular posts on Facebook, LinkedIn, Instagram, and Twitter, I am able to keep my community of colleagues, mentors, family, and friends abreast of my publications, speaking engagements, and other professional opportunities and milestones. This phenomenal network shares a commitment to celebrate and support me especially because of what I represent in the academy. Through them, my posts are often shared or retweeted with others, bringing more followers or supporters to my pages that I did not anticipate.

One example took place on the LinkedIn social networking site regarding a post announcing my Forbes's 30 Under 30 honor and an article celebrating me as the first Black tenure-track professor in the history of my school of education. As people in my network shared and circulated these posts, soon each received more than 7,000 likes and hundreds of comments. I still receive e-mails from people I have never met from as far as South Africa sharing how inspirational it is to see someone who looks like me making strides in the academy and the power of my research in changing narratives. This virtual encouragement, camaraderie, and exposure is priceless and continually reminds me that I am embedded in a community that is supportive and excited for each new achievement and contribution to research.

As with many social spheres, social media can also be a hostile place for women and scholars of color who are more likely to be subject to trolling and scrutiny for their remarks. Although social media may in fact elevate the scholarly presence of those most underrepresented in the academy, it comes at the risk of increased harassment for these groups just the same (Ovadia, 2013). For these reasons, the advantages of social media must be put in context, as it can place already vulnerable scholars in academe under a microscope.

Conclusion

Most discussion of social media among scholars has been concerned with who, what, and how much. Although these conversations have advanced our understanding of social media in academic practice, the potential of social

media for advancing critical public scholarship has received little consideration. Although this conversation is just the beginning of a timely and broad
discussion, this chapter is deliberate in positioning social media as essential
to the academic enterprise and public scholarship in particular. As we move
further into a time of political unrest and turmoil, the role of social media
will only become more significant.

References

Adema, J. (2013). Practice what you preach: Engaging in humanities research
through critical praxis. *International Journal of Cultural Studies, 16,* 491–505

Aghazamani, A. (2010). How do university students spend their time on Facebook?
An exploratory study. *Journal of American Science, 6,* 730–735.

Allen, H. G., Stanton, T. R., Di Pietro, F., & Moseley, G. L. (2013). Social media
release increases dissemination of original articles in the clinical pain sciences.
PLoS ONE, 8(7), 1–6.

Astin, H. S., Antonio, A. L., Cress, C. M., & Astin, A. W. (1997). *Race and ethnicity in the American professorate, 1995–1996.* Los Angeles, CA: Higher Education
Research Institute.

Barbour, K., & Marshall, D. (2012). The academic online: Constructing persona
through the World Wide Web. *First Monday, 17*(9). Retrieved from http://
dx.doi.org/10.5210/fm.v0i0.3969

Berger J. & Milkman, K. L. (2011). Arousal increases social transmission of information. *Psychological Science, 22,* 891–893. doi:10.1177/0956797611413294

Bhattacharyya G. & Murji K. (2013). Introduction: race critical public scholarship.
Journal of Ethnic and Racial Studies, 36(9), 1359–1373.

Boyd, D. M., & Ellison, N. B. (2007). *Social network sites: Definition, history, and
scholarship. Journal of Computer-Mediated Communication, 13*(1), 210–230.

Bukvova, H. (2011). Scientists online: A framework for the analysis of Internet profiles. *First Monday, 16*(10). Retrieved from firstmonday.org/article/
view/3584/3065#author

Bullinger, A. C., Neyer, A. K., Rass, M., & Moeslein, K. M. (2010). Community-based
innovation contests: Where competition meets cooperation. *Creativity and Innovation Management, 19*(3), 290–303. doi:10.1111/j.1467-8691.2010.00565.x

Chen, B., & Bryer, T. (2012). Investigating instructional strategies for using social
media in formal and informal learning. *International Review of Research in Open
and Distance Learning, 13,* 87–100.

Cobb-Roberts, D. (2011–2012). Betwixt safety and shielding in the academy:
Confronting institutional gendered racism—again. *Negro Educational Review,
62–63*(1/4), 89–113.

Colbeck, C. L., & Weaver, P. W. (2008). Faculty engagement in public scholarship:
A motivation systems theory perspective. *Journal of Higher Education Engagement
and Outreach, 12*(2), 7–32.

Colbeck, C. L., & Wharton-Michael, P. (2006). Individual and organizational influences on faculty members' engagement in public scholarship. *New Directions for Teaching and Learning, 105*, 17–26.

Donelan, H. (2016). Social media for professional development and networking opportunities in academia. *Journal of Further and Higher Education, 40*, 706–729.

Espinoza Vasquez, F. K., & Caicedo Bastidas, C. E. (2015). Academic social networking sites: A comparative analysis of their services and tools. Retrieved from www.ideals.illinois.edu/bitstream/handle/2142/73715/380_ready.pdf

Ford, D. P., & Mason, R. M. (2013*). A multilevel perspective of tensions between knowledge management and social media, 1/2*, 7–33. Retrieved from dx.doi.org/1 0.1080/10919392.2013.748604

Forkosh-Baruch, A., & Hershkovitz, A. (2012). A case study of Israeli higher-education institutes sharing scholarly information with the community via social networks. *The Internet and Higher Education, 15*(1), 58–68.

Gil de Zúñiga, H., Puig, E., & Rojas, H. (2009). Weblogs traditional sources online and political participation: An assessment of how the Internet is changing the political environment. *New Media & Society, 11*, 553–574.

Gregg, M. (2006) Feeling ordinary: Blogging as conversational scholarship. *Continuum, 20*, 147–160.

Gruzd, A., & Goertzen M. (2013). *Wired academia: Why social science scholars are using social media.* Retrieved from doi.ieeecomputersociety.org/10.1109/ HICSS.2013.614

Gruzd, A., Staves, K., & Wilk, A. (2012). Connected scholars: Examining the role of social media in research practices of faculty using the UTAUT model. *Computers in Human Behavior, 28*, 2340–2350.

Guy, R. (2012). The use of social media for academic practice: A review of literature. *Kentucky Journal of Higher Education Policy and Practice 1*(2).

Hampton, K., Rainie, L., Lu, W., Dwyer, M., Shin, I., & Purcell, K. (2014). *Social media and the "spiral of silence."* Retrieved from www.pewinternet.org/ 2014/08/26/social-media-and-the-spiral-of-silence

Haythornthwaite, C. (2005). Social networks and Internet connectivity effects. *Information, Communication & Society, 8*, 125–147.

Iloh, C. (2016). Exploring the for-profit experience: An ethnography of a for-profit college. *American Educational Research Journal, 53*, 427–455.

Jabeur, L. B., Tamine, L., & Boughanem, M. (2010, April). *A social model for literature access: Towards a weighted social network of authors.* Paper presented at the International Conference on Adaptivity, Personalization and Fusion of Heterogeneous Information, Paris, France.

Jayumkar, U. M., Howard, T. C., Allen, W. R., & Han, J. C. (2009). Racial privilege in the professoriate: An exploration of campus climate, retention, and satisfaction. *Journal of Higher Education, 80*, 538–563.

Jones, S., & Fox, S. (2009*). Generations online in 2009. Pew Internet and American Life Project.* Retrieved from www.pewinternet.org/2009/01/28/generations-online-in-2009

Kellogg Commission on the Future of State and Land-Grant Universities. (2000). *Renewing the covenant: Learning, discovery, and engagement in a new age and a different world.* Retrieved from http://www.aplu.org/library/renewing-the-covenant-learning-discovery-and-engagement-in-a-new-age-and-different-world/file

Kelly, B. (2013, June) *Using social media to enhance your research activities.* Paper presented at the Social Media in Social Research Conference, London, England.

Kelly, B., & Delasalle, J. (2012, July). *Can LinkedIn and academia.edu enhance access to open repositories?* Paper presented at the International Conference on Open Repositories, Edinburgh, Scotland.

Kumar, N., & Misra, S. (2015). An intelligent approach for building a secure decentralized public key infrastructure in VANET. *Journal of Computer and System Sciences, 81,* 1042–1058.

Lidsky, L. B. (2011). *Incendiary speech and social media.* Retrieved from heinonline.org/HOL/Page?handle=hein.journals/text44&div=10&g_sent=1&collection=journals

Lipsett, A. (2010, December 7). Academics encouraged to share work with the public. *The Guardian.* Retrieved from www.theguardian.com/education/2010/dec/07/academics-public-engagement-comedy

Lupton, D. (2014). *"Feeling better connected": Academics' use of social media.* Bruce, Australian Capital Territory, Australia: News and Media Research Centre, University of Canberra.

Madhusudhan, M. (2012). Use of social networking sites by research scholars of the University of Delhi: A study. *International Information & Library Review, 44,* 100–113.

Mandavilli, A. (2011). Peer review: Trial by Twitter. *Nature News, 469,* 286–287.

McKenna, K., & Bargh, J. A. (2000). Plan 9 from cyberspace: The implications of the Internet for personality and social psychology. *Personal, Social Psychology Bulletin, 4,* 57–75.

Mingle, J., & Adams, M. (2015). Social media network participation and academic performance in senior high schools in Ghana. *Library Philosophy and Practice (e-journal),* 1–51.

Nicholas, D., Williams, P., Rowlands, I. & Jamali, H.R. (2010). Researchers' ejournal use and information seeking behavior. *Journal of Information Science, 36,* 494–516.

Niu X., Hemminger, B., Lown, C., Adams, S., Brown, C., Level, A.,... Cataldo, T. (2010). National study of information seeking behavior of academic researchers in the United States. *Journal of the American Society for Information Science and Technology, 61,* 869–890.

Ovadia, S. (2013). When social media meets scholarly publishing. *Behavioral & Social Sciences Librarian, 32,* 194–198.

Park, N., Kee, K. F., & Valenzuela, S. (2009). Being immersed in social networking environment: Facebook groups, uses and gratifications, and social outcomes. *Cyber Psychology & Behavior, 12,* 729–733.

Ramaley, J. A. (2009). Community-engaged scholarship in higher education: An expanding experience. *Metropolitan Universities Journal, 20*, 139–153.

Rowlands, I., Nicholas, D., Russell, B., Canty, N., & Watkinson, A. (2011). Social media use in the research workflow. *Learned Publishing, 24*, 183–195.

Rumbley, L., Altbach, P., Stanfield, D., Shimmi, Y., de Gayardon, A., & Chan, R. (2014). *Higher education: A worldwide inventory of research centers, academic programs, and journals and publications* (3rd ed.). Bonn, Germany: Lemmens Media.

Rushby, N. & Surry, D. (2016). *Mapping the field and terminology.* San Francisco, CA: Wiley.

Sawyer, S. (2011). *The impact of new social media on intercultural adaptation.* Retrieved from digitalcommons.uri.edu/cgi/viewcontent.cgi?article=1230&context=srhonorsprog

Seaman, J., & Tinti-Kane, H. (2013). *Social media for teaching and learning.* Retrieved from www.onlinelearningsurvey.com/reports/social-media-for-teaching-and-learning-2013-report.pdf

Shirkey, C. (2011). *The political power of social media: Technology, the public sphere, and political change.* Retrieved from www.foreignaffairs.com/articles/2010-12-20/political-power-social-media

Stanley, C. A. (2006). Coloring the academic landscape: Faculty of color breaking the silence in predominantly White colleges and universities. *American Educational Research Journal, 43*, 701–736.

Stewart, C. (2008). Alternative frames of participation: The East-Timor newsgroup. *International Journal of Electronic Business, 6*, 631–650.

Tiryakioglu, F., & Erzurum, A. (2010). Use of social networks as an educational tool. *Contemporary Educational Technology, 2*, 135–150.

Turner, C. S. V. (2000). New faces, new knowledge: As women and minorities join the faculty, they bring intellectual diversity in pedagogy and in scholarship. *Academe, 86*(5), 34–37.

Turner, C. S. V. (2002). Women of color in academe: Living with multiple marginality. *Journal of Higher Education, 73*, 74–93.

Turner, C. S. V., González, J. C., & Wood, J. L. (2011). Faculty of color in academe: What 20 years of literature tell us. In S. R. Harper, & J. F. L. Jackson (Eds.), *Introduction to American higher education* (pp. 41–73). New York, NY: Routledge.

Veletsianos, G. (2013). Open practices and identity: Evidence from researchers and educators' social media participation. *British Journal of Educational Technology, 44*, 639–651.

Veletsianos, G., & Kimmons, R. (2013). Scholars and faculty members' lived experiences in online social networks. *The Internet and Higher Education, 16*, 43–50.

White, C. (2013). *Using social media to engage, listen and learn.* Retrieved from www.networks.nhs.uk/nhs-networks/smart-guides/documents/Using%20social%20media%20to%20engage-%20listen%20and%20learn.pdf

Yapa, L. (2006). Public scholarship in the postmodern university. *New Directions for Teaching and Learning* 105, 73–83. doi:10.1002/tl.226

11

ART AND THE ACADEMY

How Arts-Based Research Can
Support Public Scholarship

Yianna Drivalas and Adrianna Kezar

Picture a graduate school classroom that has nothing spectacular or fancy about it, even though the university's endowment would have you assume otherwise. The tables are arranged in a U shape. Ten first-year doctoral students sit around the U, laptops bright with the blank pages of Google docs. A professor enters the room of a qualitative research course, taking time settling in. The previous week the professor described the importance of considering artistic methods for communicating research data and gave students an assignment about using their data to try to create poems. Students continue their conversations, until the professor speaks.

> Professor: Good morning! (Morning greetings and responses from students.) Hope you all are rested from the weekend. If you haven't yet, please take out a sample of your data. Today I want you to focus on voice, think about how the participants of your studies have lent their voices to your work in exchange for the opportunity your research provides them. Consider circles—how the exchange of information and experience informs your project, and how your project moves those voices forward and provides a new platform for them.
>
> Student: Shouldn't voice also include how *we* interpret and present the data?
>
> Professor: Yes, good—talk more about that.
>
> Student: I just mean as we're writing our poems, our voice, as the author, matters. There's still a filter there; my participants' words are going through the filter of me. So even when I am quoting my data word for word in phrases, I'm still cutting, arranging, and adding my voice in the construction. I'm bringing in observation data that maybe the participants

I'm quoting in each stanza weren't at those spaces and places, but themati-
cally, data are supporting what the participants' voices are saying, or at least
they should be, and I—we—need to be careful of that in our writing.

Professor: Absolutely, yes, that's a big part of what is going on here.
Or what should be, rather. That ties in to audience too, right? Who will be
engaging with your poems, why will they be engaging, what is your goal,
what is their goal, and so on. It is good you are thinking about members of
the community and potential policymakers. Good, I'm glad you brought
that up. Okay so in 15 minutes, I'll ask a couple of you to read from your
work, even just a line or two. Think about voice, but don't overthink, and
how does that voice reach your audience? We'll reconvene in 15.

This opening vignette shows a faculty member involving students in
more artistic approaches to collecting and communicating research that are
often a central part of arts-based research (ABR). The faculty member in
the vignette is encouraging students to grapple with, interpret, and share
research findings through art—in this case storytelling through research-
based poems. These sorts of encounters with ABR are limited in most social
science graduate programs and most doctoral programs generally. Yet, there
is a creative element to understanding and identifying problems and solutions, and exploration of the human experience can often be more fully
understood or expressed through artistic means. Through the Aristotelian
mimesis lens, or art imitating life, researchers can create works through
artistic processes with deliveries that are artistic in nature. This opening
vignette highlights just one example of how graduate students, scholars,
and other interested parties can use artistic expression as a method of analyzing data and as a way to communicate public scholarship with audiences
in a different, creative, and more accessible way that speaks to the human
experience.

Public scholarship, as described and defined in the first chapter of this
volume, elevates the obligation of the responsible education researcher to
make a meaningful impact on policy and practice by directly involving the
communities the research is conducted for and about. This conceptualization of public scholarship is rooted in social justice in that it recognizes the
immediate need for research findings to be communicated to the publics
where they can be rendered most useful. It also means that public scholars
must recognize their own shortcomings and positionalities and gracefully
depend on community subjects to take part in the creation and sharing of
knowledge. ABR naturally lends itself to both sides of public scholarship,
helping engage communities in the creation of research and providing a
mode or outlet for research that is more comprehensible to the communities
that are the beneficiaries for such research (e.g., artistic expression).

Applying ABR is an important consideration for higher education researchers invested in public scholarship. The field has various stakeholder communities and therefore multiple audiences for research work, many of which can be meaningfully reached and can become involved through artistic approaches. Using art to convey important messages and demonstrate urgency is useful because it doesn't necessarily require a degree or special training to interpret and understand. A major tenet of public scholarship is ensuring that research findings are presented to the appropriate audiences; art expects an audience to interact with it. Researchers can cater to tone, presentation, and other aspects of the work according to specific audience groups, just as they would consider those same elements for academic journal submissions. For these reasons, we believe that ABR is an underused research approach in higher education and has the possibility of creating not only important work but also work that involves and serves the communities it is meant to serve.

In this chapter, we briefly define and provide a historical context for *ABR* in education, offer examples of ABR in higher education that create opportunities in public scholarship and that communicates its products, and offer recommendations for ways to begin to become involved in ABR as a higher education public scholar.

On Arts-Based Research

ABR is an interdisciplinary qualitative research methodology that uses artistic modes of expression to collect data and disseminate research findings (Eisner, 2017; Liamputtong & Rumbold, 2008; O'Donoghue, 2009). Although ABR is situated in the qualitative research tradition, it is unique among such modes of inquiry because of its dependence on artistic expression (Cahnmann-Taylor & Siegesmund, 2008). Researchers who are artists and artists who are researchers use ABR, and for the purposes of this chapter, we use *artist* and *researcher* interchangeably.

Methodological rigor and integrity are imperative to creating studies with trustworthy findings (Barone, 1995). ABR studies can still take on the form of traditional projects, such as ethnographies or case studies, and can still take advantage of traditional modes of data collection, such as interviews and focus groups. However, ABR work can also include some form of artistry in data collection. For instance, researchers may ask participants to describe a setting or occasion through a drawing or poem as a way to add texture to interview or document data, or as the sole means of collecting information regarding a topic, event, or experience (Barone & Eisner,

1997). ABR does not assume that one form of data collection is superior to another, but it does privilege artistic vehicles. The forms of data collection and expression vary and include poetry, photography, documentary, theater, painting and sculpture, to name a few (Knowles & Cole, 2008). Often, ABR researchers choose to have participants use artistic modes of data collection that may be more culturally relevant or appropriate to the community or phenomenon under investigation (Barone & Eisner, 1997). This consideration is in line with public scholarship because it takes into account participants as the keepers of knowledge and experience, and working with them is helpful in ensuring that the findings are reflective of their knowledge.

ABR also gives researchers the opportunity to move beyond traditional modes of dissemination (Knowles & Cole, 2008). Barone (2000) argues that the significant contribution of ABR's varied, artistic modes of dissemination is the potential they pose for challenging traditional beliefs and values. For example, the traditional social scientist expects to produce publishable journal articles as evidence of completing research studies. This is, as we know, what is rewarded by the academy as illustrated by tenure and promotion criteria. This also makes the act of producing an artistic rendering of research findings challenging in itself. However, the artistic mode of dissemination also creates the opportunity to challenge tradition by appealing to the senses in a way that more common modes of dissemination do not. Watching actors physically embody the heavy anxiety students experience in college will petition the emotions of an audience differently than if that same audience read an account of such episodes in a traditional journal article. This is not to say that journal articles are incapable of emotional appeal, or that researchers are not able to adequately capture the lived experiences of individuals and communities in two dimensions. Rather, we argue that by using ABR in public scholarship, the unique elements of ABR that Barone (2008) describes offer added benefits while creating a unique opportunity to engage with audiences and stakeholders. ABR studies offer audiences and researchers and participants a rich way to access experiential knowledge (Liamputting & Rumbold, 2008; Rolling, 2010) because of the equitable participation in the research process by researchers and participants.

Although ABR is relatively unexplored in higher education, the methodology has existed for decades in other education fields, specifically art and K–12 education research (Barone, 2008; Eisner, 2017). Such studies include explorations of teacher preservice training (Dixon & Senior, 2009), school leadership (Riddle & Cleaver, 2013), adults who work in early childhood education (Knight, 2011), and how elementary school students deal with stereotypes (Hadjitheodoulou-Loizidou, Fokaidou, & Papamarkou, 2012).

ABR in Higher Education

Higher education research has been slower to adopt ABR than other fields of educational research. Of the many artistic options for data collection and dissemination, higher education researchers most often use theater or dramatic performance. In this section, we first introduce theater performance from an arts-based perspective and then provide examples in higher education that use this mode for public scholarship.

According to Denzin (2003), we inhabit a performance-based, dramaturgical culture in which culture itself becomes a dramatic performance. Socialization and norms ensure that populations and spaces, including our institutions of higher education, perform and present values or norms according to expectation. Gender expectations, for instance, can dictate much of how women fare during their college tenure. Graduate students learn to perform according to the norms of their departments and schools by emulating faculty and more senior students, assuming that this mirroring practice will lead to rewards like future faculty employment. We perform in job interviews, when meeting strangers, and sometimes even with close family and friends. This is not meant to convey negativity on socialized performance; rather, this serves as a platform to introduce theater performance as a less foreign and less threatening engagement.

Staged plays are uniquely positioned to evoke emotion and response from audiences. Messages can be didactic and fablelike, or subtle and embedded. Although not all potential beneficiaries of your research findings may consider themselves fans of the theater, the accessibility of this mode of communication alone is worth the attempt. Much theater follows a traditional narrative structure, with stories that arc similarly to audiences' favorite television shows and films. But staged performances create an immediacy and intimacy different from prerecorded media; audiences witness real, three-dimensional humans depict pain, discomfort, joy, and success right in front of them. There is no screen to shield reality, because reality is the performance before you. For many higher education scholars, the realness and importance of student experience are what we hope to bring to light. Plays and theater can also be an approach to collecting data. For example, studies have used enactments of situations to elicit data, such as understanding differences by gender of audience members in interpreting behavior and communication while they watch a violent and conflictual encounter. But next we showcase theater as a means to communicate findings from research.

College Orientation Skit

The first example of arts-based public scholarship in the higher education context is related to a college orientation skit meant to convey information about students' initial college experiences and to bring parents and students into a conversation about the encounters acted out in the skit. Many who have attended a college orientation in the past decade have probably been exposed to something like the following:

Enter orientation leaders (OLs), in matching uniforms, on the makeshift wings of the makeshift stage in the student union courtyard. Microphones are placed at downstage left (DSL) and right. First OL, a White woman, moves in front of microphone DSL.

First OL (Mimes opening a letter and reading): We are happy to share with you your roommate assignment for the 2016–2017 academic year. You will be placed at Kelly House. Your roommate will be Katie McCormack. Please find your roommate's contact information here.

As First OL finishes her lines and beings to mouth words, as if reading more of the letter, Second OL (a Black woman) moves in front of microphone down stage right (DSR).

Second OL (Mimes opening a letter and reading): We are happy to share with you your roommate assignment for the 2016–2017 academic year. You will be placed at Kelly House. Your roommate will be Esmerelda Aguilar. Please find your roommate's contact information here. (She mouths as if continuing to read.)

First OL: Katie! Katie is my new roommate! I bet we'll have a ton in common. Should I call her? Text her? E-mail her? Do they—(looks at letter)—nope, no Instagram account name listed.

Second OL: Esmerelda sounds great. I wonder where she's from?

This is a retelling of a skit presented at Yianna Drivalas's undergraduate orientation in the summer of 2005. The skit went on to address the assumptions each woman had made based on the name of her future roommate, cultural, racial, and so forth. The OLs took part in storytelling using a skit, taking the role of incoming students to share common issues students may face and have to deal with on matriculating to college, all the while keeping the attention of the audience of students (and their guardians) who are matriculating to college in real life.

Drivalas remembers little from her orientation, but this skit has stuck with her for a few reasons. First, she did not expect to see any sort of staging of collegiate life on arriving at school. The quality of the script or the acting didn't matter—and she of course doesn't remember the words line for line—but the sentiment and goal stayed with her over the years. Second, the

OLs invited the small group of students, including Drivalas, and the parents in the audience to discuss what they thought had happened in that skit. The OL posed questions, offered challenges, and said that the content for this skit and the handful of others they presented were all based on research conducted by different departments on campus. The skit performed by the OLs was informed by data from the housing department at her alma mater. The OLs said it was important to them and the university orientation leadership to offer accurate (albeit interpreted) depictions based on real data to illustrate their expectations of what it meant to join the university community.

This example from Drivalas's experience reflects the principles of ABR and why it is so important. The performance was derived from two types of data—research about bias and stereotyping and institutional data about student subgroups. Many groups collaborated to develop the performance such as education, sociology, and psychology researchers and students and administrators on campus who provided feedback. It puts the research in the hands of stakeholders and links research directly to the audience in engaging ways. Taking part in this kind of arts-based public scholarship provides the opportunity to involve relevant audiences in creative ways in research that was collected from similar stakeholders and publics. In this case, two important stakeholder communities were reached: students (current, the performers, and the incoming students) and their parents. By supporting the skit with targeted development materials for both groups (e.g., questions to discuss between parent and child before the school year formally begins, first-week residence hall events including orientation programs such as this skit), higher education public scholars also create opportunities for generating further data and further research that supports their larger agendas.

Theater Players

The next example from the University of Michigan's Center for Research on Learning and Teaching (CRLT) uses theater to educate faculty, graduate students, and administration staff. The CRLT Players create "theatrical representations of a range of issues common in academic life," generally focusing on aspects of institutional climate (CRLT, 2016). Members of the Michigan community can hire the players to support professional development efforts, such as preparing graduate students and faculty for managing conflict in the classroom. Some of their skits have been directed at students as well, similar to the orientation skit described earlier. Topics include responding to student climate concerns, how to clearly negotiate personal and professional boundaries graduate students face in managing diverse roles, the roles of department chairs in faculty mentoring, climate in classrooms, critical differences in identity as students study course content and interpret instructors' methods, identifying students' mental health challenges, common tensions that emerge between adviser and advisee in graduate education, demonstrating the ways students with disabilities manage the classroom, department exchanges about whether a junior colleague should be awarded tenure, and difficulties that can emerge in scientific lab settings. The players have also developed dozens of customized plays based on the needs of campuses across the country to solve problems and bring research to address issues. The players also offer consultations, including sessions for individuals or teams seeking to create educational scripts such as those the players perform. They also use the same approach to develop workshops where audiences may be more involved in role-playing and by serving as actors to address a research-based topic (e.g., how to create change on college campuses, deal with difficult people on campus, or responsibly evaluate colleagues).

All the sketches the players perform are created after extensive research, including reviewing the relevant literature and interviewing appropriate stakeholders. Research in this case includes formal literature reviews, keeping up with new work in the content areas the plays address, and speaking with experts in the field. Once the plays are constructed, the players check the quality of their sketches by screening them through focus groups and the CRLT Faculty Advisory Board before bringing them to the public (http://www.crlt.umich.edu/crltplayers/faqs). For audience members, the players' sketches are "more effective than formal presentations and facilitate the "kind[s] of conversation[s] about classroom dynamics that . . . couldn't have taken place otherwise" (CRLT, 2016).

Faculty public scholars can insert themselves into this work and become part of staging research findings through construction of the play script and quality checks once a full script and performance have been derived to see that it aligns with research of the plays. For instance, if faculty members were hesitant to engage in an arts-based project on their own, this would be a way to familiarize themselves with theater approaches that is already established in a professional organization and still provide the research findings that inform the work of the CRLT Players or similar groups. Attending previews of showings or working with a center (or arts and theater department) at one's own home campus to begin an initiative such as this can alleviate some of the jitters that may come with embarking on this type of work for the first time. As public scholars, faculty are obligated to involve and support the communities their work (and therefore their reputations) is based on and that benefit from their work.

Cornell Theater Troupe

The last example is Cornell's Theater Troupe and its work with the National Science Foundation's ADVANCE Program. As faculty members and administrators on college campuses tackled the challenge of helping more women and people of color to be hired and succeed as faculty members in science, technology, engineering, and mathematics (STEM), they soon turned to ABR as an approach to advance their efforts. Dozens of college campuses have received grants aimed at increasing hiring and improving the success of woman and people of color as faculty in STEM. One of the core challenges campus leaders face is the need to help faculty and administrators identify and understand implicit bias that prevents them from hiring and promoting women and faculty of color. Decades of research illustrates that when faculty members review résumés, they tend to rate White males more favorably than women and candidates of color. This bias continues in interviews with candidates where impressions of them are developed. Moreover, implicit bias affects women's success in the way their materials are reviewed for promotion and tenure, the opportunities they are given, student evaluations of their teaching, and the ways their work is received.

Leaders of ADVANCE Program grants recognized that distributing journal articles on implicit bias has not been successful in addressing bias among faculty and department chairs. To address this complex problem, and armed with research from psychology about implicit bias, the ADVANCE Project at Cornell teams up with the theater department to develop skits that model hiring situations, search committees, tenure and promotion committees, and interactions among faculty and department chairs. The skit or performances result from faculty in psychology and theater working with faculty and administrators, combining faculty research expertise with administrators and faculty examples from practice. Many of the skits go further, requiring role-playing by inviting audience members (e.g., department chairs, faculty) to join the cast in trying out their skills in moderating a meeting where implicit bias is taking place and how they can work to mitigate the bias. All the skits put on by the Cornell Theater Troupe, like in the CRLT example, are based on research and developed in collaboration with faculty researchers in the social sciences.

The program has been evaluated, and results demonstrate that the skits appear to shape the perspectives of faculty and department chairs who participate by helping them to think about situations outside their own experience and see the situation from other people's perspectives and also through the lens of research. Based on its success, the theater troupe has been asked to come to various other campuses across the country to help address implicit bias that prevents women and faculty of color from being hired and being successful in STEM disciplines. This form of arts-based public scholarship involves stakeholders in research products through theater to meaningfully address issues on bias that affect research stakeholders (e.g., higher education faculty, staff, students, and administrators), which traditional modes of research have failed to do so. Again, this illustrates the compelling role the public scholar must play in advancing the public good by involving stakeholder communities in research conducted about, with, and alongside those communities.

Conclusion

This chapter describes several examples of engaging in public scholarship and the dissemination of research-based information through artistic expression, in this case theatrical-based arts and production. We chose these examples for two reasons. First, options are limited as those in higher education have only recently begun to adopt ABR. Second, these examples are meant to showcase accessible and relatively simple work that does not require significant resources. *Theater* and *script* and *playwriting* can be intimidating words that invite images of grand productions, but as these examples show, this does not have to be the case. Depending on their roles and experiences, the actors can also contribute to script writing. Putting on a production like this takes time and attention, like any worthy research endeavor, but it should be quicker and easier with each subsequent use of this approach.

Writing a successful play is not done haphazardly or without proper preparation. However, with practice and guidance from better-equipped community members (e.g., the theater department on campus), playwriting should not be beyond the scope of dissemination possibilities for scholars. As illustrated in the examples in this chapter, sharing research through theater is a useful and appropriate way to engage in public scholarship. By using community-based practices and allowing participant voices to quite literally take center stage, diverse stakeholder audiences are given an opportunity to engage with the research in meaningful, practical ways. ABR invites the publics we serve in higher education to participate in topics guided and informed by scholarship. Some of the examples we present here also have a reciprocal element to them, a bidirectional flavor in which scholars' research is shared through artistic means and through involving stakeholders, and those experiences and the products of that engagement can also be assessed and researched to determine their effects on the stakeholders involved.

To conclude this chapter, we present a list of recommendations for higher education public scholars as they consider how to begin participating in ABR work.

1. Use the resources provided by the American Educational Research Association (AERA). If you are reading this chapter, you are most likely a member of AERA, which has an arts-based special-interest group called Arts-Based Educational Research (abersig.com). Join its mailing list, attend its presentations at the annual meeting, and see what projects are already happening that align with your line of inquiry and research agenda.

2. Expose yourself to more art. Many folks somewhere along the line have been told that they aren't creative or artistic; this builds a false belief and prevents people from engaging in creative endeavors. Does it mean that if we visit the Louvre we'll automatically have so much faith in ourselves that we can recreate the Mona Lisa? No, but using art in small but meaningful ways can have an impact. Commit to reading a book of poetry and go through a few pages each night before bed. (National Public Radio's program *All Things Considered* aired a discussion of accessible and timely poetry). Visit your local library and check out various 10-minute-play volumes. We recommend *Facing Our Truth: 10-Minute Plays on Trayvon, Race and Privilege* (www.samuelfrench.com/p/58272/facing-our-truth-ten-minute-plays-on-trayvon-race-and-privilege) and *The Bully Plays* (www.dramaticpublishing.com/the-bully-plays), each highly relevant to education scholars. The more you familiarize yourself with works that aren't by Keats, Whitman, Shakespeare, or O'Neil, the more you'll realize how much art by real, everyday people is available, and the more you may feel you are able to meaningfully engage in ABR through your own public scholarship.

3. Contact your local arts departments. If your institution has a music, film, theater, creative writing, or dance program, check their websites for events that may align with your work. Ask for recommendations of community groups that use arts-based messaging. It could be the beginning of an important partnership that greatly supports everyone's work while reaching relevant audiences and communicating important research you want to put into the hands of those it most affects.

4. Reexamine your own work. What messages do you have to send practitioners, policymakers, and other constituents? How have you been successful in doing so? How could you improve that success rate? Do you have specific studies or reports that may lend themselves more easily to ABR work? Think about the many modes of possible artistic expression

such as documentaries, media, poetry, and painting and sculpture. Remember, you can disseminate your findings in more than one way; arts-based public scholarship can be conducted on its own, or it can complement the other forms of dissemination and communication of findings you regularly use (e.g., journals).

Humans are creative, curious beings. We enter the research sphere to answer questions, and we often must do so in novel ways. Few problems in education can be solved without creativity, and even fewer can be solved without the support and involvement of the various communities our institutions aim to serve.

References

Barone, T. (1995). The purposes of arts-based educational research. *International Journal of Educational Research, 23*, 169–180.

Barone, T. (2000). *Aesthetics, politics, and educational inquiry: Essays and examples.* New York, NY: Peter Lang.

Barone, T. (2008). How arts-based research can change minds. In M. Cahnmann-Taylor & R. Siegesmund (Eds.). *Arts-based research in education: Foundations for practice* (pp. 34–56). New York, NY: Routledge.

Barone, T., & Eisner, E. (1997). Arts-based educational research. *Complementary Methods for Research in Education, 2*, 75–116.

Cahnmann-Taylor, M., & Siegesmund, R. (2008). The tensions of arts-based research in education reconsidered: The promise for practice. In M.Cahnmann Taylor & R. Siegesmund (Eds.), *Arts-based research in education: Foundations for practice* (pp. 231–246). New York, NY: Routledge.

Center for Research on Learning and Teaching. (2016). *About the players.* Retrieved from www.crlt.umich.edu/crltplayers/about-players

Denzin, N. K. (2003). *Performance ethnography: Critical pedagogy and the politics of culture.* Thousand Oaks, CA: Sage.

Dixon, M., & Senior, K. (2009). Traversing theory and transgressing academic discourses: Arts-based research in teacher education. *International Journal of Education & the Arts, 10*(24), 1–22.

Eisner, E. W. (2017). *The enlightened eye: Qualitative inquiry and the enhancement of educational practice.* New York, NY: Teachers College Press.

Hadjitheodoulou-Loizidou, P., Fokaidou, M., & Papamarkou, S. (2012). My house of value: School intervention programme investigating aspects of self-knowing, knowing of the other, identity, diversity and interaction. *Education 3–13, 40*, 532–546.

Knight, S. (2011). *Risk & adventure in early years outdoor play: Learning from forest schools.* Thousand Oaks, CA: Sage.

Knowles, J. G., & Cole, A. L. (2008). *Handbook of the arts in qualitative research: Perspectives, methodologies, examples, and issues.* Thousand Oaks, CA: Sage.

Liamputtong, P., & Rumbold, J. (2008). *Knowing differently: Arts-based and collaborative research methods.* Hauppauge, NY: Nova.

O'Donoghue, D. (2009). Are we asking the wrong questions in arts-based research? *Studies in Art Education, 50,* 352–368.

Pamatmat, A., O'Brien, D., Morisseau, D., Mansour, M., Miller, W., Gardley, M., . . . Flores, Q. *Facing our truth: 10-minute plays on Trayvon, race, and privilege* and *the bully plays.* Retrieved from www.samuelfrench.com/p/58272/facing-our-truth-ten-minute-plays-on-trayvon-race-and-privilege

Riddle, S., & Cleaver, D. (2013). One school principal's journey from the mainstream to the alternative. *International Journal of Leadership in Education, 16,* 367–378.

Rolling, J. H., Jr. (2010). A paradigm analysis of arts-based research and implications for education. *Studies in Art Education, 51,* 102–114.

PART THREE

ENCOURAGING AND LEARNING PUBLIC SCHOLARSHIP

12

REENVISIONING GRADUATE AND EARLY CAREER SOCIALIZATION TO ENCOURAGE PUBLIC SCHOLARSHIP

Michael Lanford and William G. Tierney

Milton Babbitt (1958/1998), a widely respected professor of music composition at Princeton University, wrote a commentary for the popular magazine *High Fidelity* provocatively titled "Who Cares If You Listen?" Babbitt argued that the music composed by his colleagues at other colleges and universities had attained the same level of erudition and theoretical sophistication as advanced scholarship in mathematics, philosophy, or physics. Hence, he praised the "unprecedented divergence between contemporary serious music and its listeners" (p. 1306). Because there was little hope of the layperson being able to decipher work of such complexity, Babbitt concluded that other composers interested in creating "complex, difficult, and problematical" music "would do [themselves] and [their] music an immediate and eventual service by total, resolute, and voluntary withdrawal from [the] public world to one of private performance" (p. 1310).

Throughout the twentieth century, other artists and intellectuals extolled the separation of difficult art from the tastes and aesthetic values of the general public (McClary, 1989). In some instances, they even questioned the value of any work that was appreciated by a broad audience. Arnold Schoenberg (1975), an avant-garde composer most famous for the development of pantonality through the mathematical manipulation of various tonal patterns, wrote,

As soon as the war was over . . . my works were played everywhere and acclaimed in such a manner that I started to doubt the value of my music....
If previously my music had been difficult to understand on account of the peculiarities of my ideas and the way in which I expressed them, how could it happen that now, all of a sudden, everybody could follow my ideas and like them? Either the music or the audience was worthless. (p. 51)

To many reading this passage, it may seem patently absurd that an artist like Schoenberg would openly question the value of his own work simply because it achieved broad appeal. And yet, much of academia seems comfortable with the notion that scholarship published in scholarly journals and university press monographs is beyond the reach of the general public. Some may even feel their work is bound to be misunderstood or unfairly neglected because of a nescient audience's lack of sophistication. Given enough time, the belief goes, truly groundbreaking scholarship will eventually be discovered for the revelatory insights it can provide about society, scientific inquiry, or the human condition.

Although we recognize the necessity for methodological rigor, theoretical advancement, and peer critique in academic discourse, we also believe that an ability to communicate one's research to the general public is essential in today's higher education environment. The justification for our position is based on the following primary developments: (a) an increased demand by various stakeholders for public accountability in higher education and (b) the potential for empirically sound research to be disregarded by the public because of a perceived lack of researcher credibility. Before any of these developments can be addressed, however, we believe that graduate-level training needs to be reenvisioned so that the next generation of scholars can engage with the public.

By grounding our discussion in sociocultural theories on writing, we consider how graduate programs can encourage students to participate in public scholarship. Central to this discussion is the premise, as articulated by Tardy (2005), that "expert writers . . . see texts rhetorically, existing within social activity, created for and by real people" (p. 327). By applying a sociocultural lens, we consider how exposing graduate students to diverse writing assignments and genres can instill a sensitivity to the appropriate modes of discourse for different social communities. Through the institutionalization of peer review and feedback from individuals who reside outside academia, we argue that students can learn how to shape their writing to match the expectations of different audiences. As a final matter, we discuss how students can use technology to communicate findings, as well as their implications, to the general public.

Two Developments Necessitating Public Engagement

Increased Public Accountability

In recent years a plethora of articles, books, and assorted commentaries have argued that American higher education lacks a strong accountability regime, resulting in poor student retention and completion statistics, degrees that are unsuitable for the demands of a twenty-first-century workforce, and questionable research agendas that have a minimal impact on society (Carey, 2015; Deming & Figlio, 2016; Hicks, 2012; Leef, 2016). At the heart of this conversation is a breakdown in trust among higher education institutions, the market, and society (Tierney, 2006; Trow, 1996). From a market-oriented perspective, the demand for accountability can be linked with neoliberal values that advocate for limited-term faculty contracts, institutional efficiency, and a notional view of the student as a consumer who deserves a certain level of service in exchange for tuition payments (Ranson, 2003; Tight, 2013). Because taxpayers subsidize higher education, a market-oriented perspective also maintains that research should have a sufficient economic impact to justify public investment. As state funding for colleges and universities continues to decline, higher education institutions across the country are compelled to develop innovative programs to help students attain degrees in greater numbers (Tierney & Lanford, 2016). They are also obligated to view research and other university activities with an entrepreneurial mindset, rather than as socially oriented ventures where initial inefficiencies are rationalized by an activity's eventual positive impact on society (Slaughter & Rhoades, 2004).

Nevertheless, criticism of higher education abounds from a socially oriented perspective as well. Observers of higher education have criticized the lack of relevance that much contemporary university research seems to have for society (Hess & LoGerfo, 2006). In particular, the arts and humanities have come under fire for propagating research that is considered either exceptionally limited in its purview or so esoteric it is incomprehensible outside the miniscule scholarly communities that critique and publish such work (Hazelkorn, 2014; Holm, Jarrick, & Scott, 2015).

Although we understand these concerns, we do not believe they are caused by profligate spending, a lack of concern for student welfare, or a widespread problem with self-serving research agendas. Calls for public accountability in higher education are hardly a new phenomenon (Heller, 2001), nor are they exclusive to the United States (Huisman & Currie, 2004; Rhoades & Sporn, 2002). We contend that one of the primary barriers to understanding and trust concerns the inability of the higher education community to effectively communicate the efficacy of its programs, values, and research to politicians, journalists, and other important public constituencies. Limerick (1993) memorably lamented this gulf in communication and understanding between politicians and the professoriate in the following:

> In Colorado, as in most states, the legislators are convinced that the university is neglecting students and wasting state resources on pointless research. Under those circumstances, the miserable writing habits of professors pose a direct and concrete danger to higher education. Rather than going to the state legislature, proudly presenting stacks of the faculty's compelling and engaging publications, you end up hoping that the lawmakers stay out of the library and stay away, especially, from the periodical room, with its piles of academic journals. The habits of academic writers lend powerful support to the impression that research is a waste of the writers' time and of the public's money. (p. 201)

Since then, Limerick's periodical room has been largely supplanted by an array of academic databases, yet her critique of academic journals and other scholarly publishing outlets remains valid. Writing for one's scholarly peers is, of course, essential for peer review and the development of disciplinary knowledge. However, writing in publicly accessible genres is equally vital so that one can communicate the importance of research to a broad array of constituencies, especially as higher education fights for continued resources and financial support from increasingly skeptical external stakeholders.

The Predicament of Researcher Credibility

University scholars working in scientific disciplines have long advocated for public engagement. In recent years, there has been a specific call for undergraduate and graduate training in communicating research to the general public (Brownell, Price, & Steinman, 2013). In fact, the label *civic scientist* has been adopted by many scientists who have taken it upon themselves to conduct groundbreaking research while communicating their findings and expertise to the general public (Greenwood & Riordan, 2001; Langenberg, 1991). Justifications for devoting time to such civic duty include the recruitment of students into the sciences, the possibility that greater engagement can lead to increased funding and activities that promote an appreciation for scientific inquiry, and discovery among the populace.

This promotion of civic science has been successful in fostering positive attitudes among scientists about the importance of public engagement. A survey by the Pew Research Center showed that nearly 87% of surveyed American scientists agreed with the notion that they should be active in public policy debates concerning science and technology (Rainie, Funk, &

Anderson, 2015). Some individuals, such as theoretical physicist Michio Kaku, have in fact been successful at attracting broad audiences through television and radio appearances while explaining complex scientific and theoretical phenomena. In the realm of the arts and humanities, scholar performers who feel comfortable with various forms of media, like pianist Jeremy Denk, have also successfully contextualized the importance of their society's cultural heritage through written contributions to newspapers, magazines, and blogs.

Nonetheless, an additional Pew Research Center (2015) study showed that scientists and the general public frequently hold vastly divergent views on a range of science-related topics, from the safety of genetically modified foods to the importance of childhood vaccines. Possibly nowhere is the gulf between the researcher and the public citizen more apparent than on the issue of climate change. Among major scientific organizations, a strong consensus has emerged that climate change is negatively transforming the environment and severely affecting social and economic systems. However, the general public is unsure whether debate is ongoing in the scientific community (Knox, 2016; Leiserowitz, Maibach, Roser-Renouf, Feinberg, & Rosenthal, 2016). A number of factors have contributed to this disparity in attitudes and beliefs, including citizens' political inclinations, economic rationalizations, and the conflation of climate change with other environmental phenomena (Somerville & Hassol, 2011). Perhaps most distressing, though, is the fact that scientific data on climate change has rarely been communicated in an effective and consistent manner (Brownell et al., 2013). As a result, public perceptions of professional researchers' trustworthiness are quite low especially among those who are already inclined to be skeptical of climate change (Funk & Kennedy, 2016).

Research has consistently shown that "readers are persuaded not only by what is said, but also by how it is said" (Tardy, 2005, p. 327; also see Geisler, 1994; McNabb, 2001). Hence, we believe that scholars who communicate their empirical findings and their analyses in an engaging style, with clarity and an understanding of their intended audience's expectations, can make the value and significance of their work apparent. Most important, they can establish credibility and trust with their intended audience. The perils of confirmation bias are well known, and we are not claiming that unanimity on any given topic can be achieved simply through convincing rhetoric. A lack of credibility should nevertheless concern everyone in the academy. Only when credibility is established can researchers influence public opinion on important topics like climate change, have an impact on policy, and foment change.

To be sure, individuals like Michio Kaku and Jeremy Denk who have the gift of communicating complex concepts in a rhetorically effective manner are rare. However, the ability to communicate to varied audiences is not a natural ability. Like learning a musical instrument, writing is a skill that is developed through repeated practice, feedback, and continuous experimentation grounded in accrued expertise. Furthermore, in an increasingly multicultural and globalized environment, it is an essential skill, lest one's work become limited in its impact by a narrowly conceived audience and purpose. The remainder of this chapter, then, is a call for greater engagement with writing theory so that graduate students' abilities as communicators can be developed. In what follows, we first briefly depict the development of writing theory in the twentieth century. Then we focus on the two most prominent contemporary theories on writing. After describing the influence of the cognitive process framework on writing theory, we use a sociocultural framework to conceptualize what a rhetorically effective curriculum for graduate students might encompass.

Theories on Writing

For much of the mid-twentieth century, research on composition was dominated by an expressive view of writing that was largely derived from nineteenth century German philosophy but with intellectual precursors that can be traced to ancient Greece. This expressive view celebrated Romantic concepts of integrity, spontaneity, and originality (Elbow, 1973; Faigley, 1986). According to early theorists, integrity concerned an author's sincerity in believing an argument, expressing opinions in a credible manner, and supporting ideas with persuasively formulated rhetoric (Stewart, 1969). Spontaneity celebrated the advantage of composing a text without a final goal in mind; theorists argued that the writing process is initially marked by false starts, imperfectly formed thoughts, and roadblocks that eventually coalesce into a polished essay. Therefore, exposure of these fragmentary ideas could lead to insights about the compositional process and the mechanisms of the imagination. Finally, the value of originality in writing was recognized through the virtue of *self-actualization*. From this theoretical position, writing has the potential to benefit students as a creative activity that encourages personal understanding and an exploration of the subconscious (Rohman, 1965).

Although each of these individual concepts are alluring in their depiction of the writing process, they are also limited in their theoretical purview and pose formidable problems for a rigorous study of writing instruction. Integrity all but ignores the significance of society and culture in regulating an author's belief systems and setting the standards an author's integrity should be judged by (Giroux, 1983). An emphasis on spontaneity may be helpful for authors encountering writer's block (and, in fact, teachers to this day encourage free writing in the classroom to help students get started with writing assignments). However, it does not helpfully address the role of planning, organization, and revision in the writing process (Rose, 1985). Accordingly, a theory of writing founded on originality can lead to tautologies because people who are psychologically more self-actualized would also conceivably be better writers.

Cognitive Process Theory

In the latter half of the twentieth century, two theoretical perspectives achieved distinction with researchers who wished to investigate writing in a systematic fashion: the cognitive process and sociocultural frameworks. The cognitive process perspective emphasizes the analysis of individual decisions that generate an artifact of writing (Flower & Haynes, 1981). When graduate-level faculty address writing-related concerns with their students, much of their feedback (consciously or unconsciously) approaches a topic from a cognitive process perspective, which means that writing is portrayed as a solitary activity in which students endeavor to organize their thoughts and express their ideas through acceptable academic prose (Cooper, 1986). If a student produces a document that receives positive feedback, it is assumed that he or she cognitively organized distinct writing processes (e.g., researching, planning, and revising) in a systematic fashion (Kellogg, 2008). It is also assumed that the student successfully met the grammar- and vocabulary-related expectations of the assignment. If students struggle to meet the expectations of their professors, they are often tasked with understanding the conventions of writing in their chosen disciplines through emulation, further reading in the discipline, and additional trial and error.

This training is reinforced by the use of rubrics that help writers understand the expectations of the instructor, establish priorities, and self-assess their work as they progress through different drafts (Jonsson & Svingby, 2007). In fact, rubrics have enjoyed considerable popularity in recent years because they distill writing into specific characteristics that can be presumably taught and assessed, and they also arguably shield the instructor from accusations of excessive subjectivity in grading. After composing multiple research papers, graduate students are effectively trained in a single form of written expression. Through this process, they also internalize the recognized data presentation, citation style, paper formatting practices, and frequently employed jargon of their fields.

Sociocultural Theory

Although graduate training has been described here using a cognitive framework, it could also be depicted in sociocultural terms. The sociocultural perspective is an implicit critique of cognitive process theory in that it argues that writing is not a solitary process that is largely the product of the writer's ability to organize and articulate thoughts. Instead, a writer's decisions are mediated by the writer's immediate environment in addition to the social interactions, cultural expectations, and historical contexts that contribute to a writer's development (Vygotsky, 1934/1986).

Central to sociocultural theory is the concept of *discourse communities*. Gee (2015) defines *discourses* as "ways of behaving, interacting, valuing, thinking, believing, speaking, and (often) reading and writing that are accepted as instantiations of particular identities by specific groups" (p. 4). Thus, a discourse community is a group of individuals who share a set of values and assumptions, as well as preferred methods for communicating their ideas (Swales, 1990). From a sociocultural perspective, then, writing is deeply informed by the writer's initiation and continued exposure to these discourse communities.

As argued by Ivanič (1998), educational institutions privilege specific forms of writing that may not be appreciated or understood in other social domains. Doctoral course work, in particular, is designed to acculturate students into disciplinary practices of research and rhetoric, develop critical and discriminatory skills that can lead to cogent peer review, and ultimately produce future faculty members for colleges and universities (Donald, 2002; Kuteeva & Airey, 2014). As discussed previously, this acculturation typically comes about almost exclusively through the assignment of research papers. The intention of these papers, and similar genres of high-stakes writing, is to help students achieve an understanding of complex discipline-specific concepts and the expression of these ideas in the native language (Elbow, 1997; Hyland, 2004).

Implications of Sociocultural Theory for Graduate Training

A sociocultural perspective, however, reveals that such training may be too narrowly conceived if a graduate student is to be effective in communicating with other discourse communities (Lee & Anderson, 2009). For example, Burawoy (2004) has convincingly argued that pathologies of "self-referentiality, servility, dogmatism, and faddishness" (p. 1607) prevent sociologists with different research agendas from communicating and interacting with each other effectively. Even scientists and social scientists who feel that public engagement is a necessary component of their scholarly life might be unaware of the self-referential or even faddish way they express their ideas. Although much of the research they conduct has tangible benefits for society, scientists are sometimes in a position of *servility*, beholden to the pressures of grant funding and academic capitalism (Slaughter & Rhoades, 2000).

Even worse, they might approach public engagement by taking a dogmatic stance, presuming that their job is to inform or enlighten, rather than to stimulate dialogue. Leshner (2003) has noted that "one traditional response of the scientific community to what it views as a lack of appreciation or misinterpretation by the public has been to mount so-called public understanding or education campaigns designed to 'enlighten' the populace" (p. 977). Such campaigns can come across as tone-deaf, alienating the audience before opportunities for dialogue can be forged (Bennett & Jennings, 2011).

Although sociocultural theory is the most widely accepted paradigm for contemporary research on writing, the insights that could be gained from a sociocultural approach have had a limited influence on writing pedagogy and practice at the graduate level (Prior, 2006). Sociocultural theory does not assume that a single approach to writing is ideal for effective communication to all audiences. Instead, it acknowledges that multiple literacy practices exist, and it encourages students to identify the intended target discourse community for their writing (Rose, 1989). Students are also encouraged to consider exigence—why an author is engaging in discourse—as well as contextual factors relating to the setting where discourse takes place. These considerations are considered fundamentally important if a student is to achieve an advanced level of academic literacy (Tardy, 2005).

When students target a journal for publication, closely read articles that have been already accepted, take notes on the preferred vocabulary and length for individual sections, and revise their article submissions accordingly, they are already thinking on an advanced rhetorical level. The goal, then, is to apply this advanced level of academic literacy to other genres, audiences, and purposes. Many advisers have achieved success by honing their craft in one genre, that is, scholarly writing for one's peers through academic journals or academic press monographs. A narrow focus on this form of discourse has been acceptable as long as colleges and universities solely incentivized scholarly publication. As we have discussed, though, the dynamics of higher education are changing, and a researcher's credibility is essential for communicating the value of research to politicians and policymakers while meeting increased public demands for accountability. For these reasons, we now reenvision graduate socialization in writing to encourage public scholarship.

Reenvisioning Graduate Socialization

Writing Assignments in Different Genres

The incorporation of a sociocultural perspective begins with the institutionalization of writing assignments in different genres. For several years, Mike Rose at the University of California, Los Angeles has led a two-course workshop on writing for graduate students (Rose, 2010; Rose & McClafferty, 2001). The first course focuses on scholarly writing, and the second course asks students to transform their scholarly research into two different genres: a 700- to 800-word newspaper opinion piece and a 1,500- to 2,000-word magazine article. Through such assignments, students not only develop an awareness of their own writing style and biases but also learn to recognize that evidence marshaled in support of an author's arguments needs to be recognized as valid by their intended audience. The shortened word length of these two assignments gives students an appreciation for concise language and the value of multiple revisions. Moreover, as Rose (2010) asserts, students develop a keen eye for rhetorical effect, noticing "the commonalities in language, the accessible vocabulary, the lack of jargon (or the judicious use of it), the frequent use of colloquial speech—always for rhetorical effect" (p. 288). An understanding of these rhetorical devices is key to constructing accessible and persuasive prose that can draw attention to one's scholarly research.

Peer Review

According to Starke-Meyerring (2011), students' writing experiences frequently "involve a considerable rupture in their sense of themselves as writers, as well as friction, tension, identity struggles, loss of self-confidence, and anxiety" (p. 91). Hence, many graduate students choose to hide from the very review processes and critiques that could help them move past similar crises of confidence or even full-blown writer's block. Research studies show that face-to-face feedback by regular critiques from peers and professors alike not only helps graduate students learn the techniques and strategies of academic writing but also prepares them for discourses in other domains (Caffarella & Barnett, 2000; Paré, 2011; Sallee, Hallett, & Tierney, 2011). The experience of peer review also gives students an invaluable opportunity for self-reflection by reading the work of their peers and reconsidering the criteria they instinctively employ to evaluate an effective piece of writing.

Therefore, we propose that regular peer review sessions should be incorporated into graduate curricula. In conjunction with writing assignments in multiple genres, peer review can stimulate the kind of writing-related discussion and experimentation necessary to consider how research can be effectively communicated to different discourse communities. Peer review also prepares graduate students for their eventual role as teachers, where time is precious and feedback needs to be limited to the higher order revisions a student needs to focus on.

Feedback From Individuals Outside Academia

Feedback from individuals outside the university campus is just as essential as peer review. Many professors can rely on prior work experiences to provide constructive feedback from the standpoint of a policymaker or a newspaper editor. However, the writing standards and expectations for different writing genres can be as mutable as technological developments in the twenty-first century. Thus, it is incumbent on individuals who are contemporary representatives of different discourse communities to provide feedback to doctoral students.

Directors of different graduate programs can—and should—strategically determine the types of outlets that are the most important to engage in public scholarship. For instance, a professor in a graduate program in higher education might ask a newspaper journalist, a policy analyst, or the editor of a popular education-related blog to evaluate student samples of public scholarship. Rose (2010) persuasively argues that

> if academics limit themselves through their specialized language, editors are limited as well by their own definitions of a newsworthy story and can overreact to the mere hint of scholarship, rejecting anything that, as one editor told me, "looks like a study." (p. 286)

As demonstrated in this comment, the discussion engendered by such an exchange can be illuminating for both sides.

We should note that this is not to say that graduate student writing is deficient in one way or another. Instead, the goal is to acclimate students to the multifarious ways their writing can be read and interpreted by constituencies outside the academy. This exposure will benefit them as they interact with different discourse communities and are compelled to respond and rethink their preconceptions about writing in the future.

Involvement With Technology and New Avenues for Dissemination

Additionally, in today's technological age, students should be experienced in contributing to different social media platforms, especially before they face the demands of a faculty position. The experience of regularly contributing to a blog, for example, can instill the virtues of discipline and time management. Both of us contributed for several years to a blog titled 21st Century Scholar (21stcenturyscholar.org), developing exploratory ideas that would have likely remained in the realm of imagination. Later, a few of those blog posts were expanded into full-length scholarly monographs and articles, an experience that demonstrates the reciprocal nature of writing for academe and for the public.

Students enter graduate school with writing experiences that are unique to their cultural, educational, and linguistic backgrounds. Thus, we deliberately avoid prescribing when students should contribute to blog posts, when peer review sessions should occur, and when writing projects in different genres should be assigned. These types of decisions are best made by the individuals who are in a position to assess a program's goals, the faculty's strengths and weaknesses, and students' needs. The important thing to remember is that a sociocultural approach to writing needs to be infused throughout the curriculum, not merely in a single class session or an assignment or two. Without such a commitment, it is unlikely that students will receive the kind of training that will serve as adequate preparation for public scholarship.

Conclusion

In this chapter, we argue that any reenvisioning of graduate and early career socialization should incorporate the necessity of writing for public audiences. However, it is only fair to acknowledge that the manner in which we have conceptualized socialization is not without its limitations and potential downsides. Such an agenda may seem complex to implement in a program that already has competing priorities. Some professors may feel uncomfortable assigning different genres of writing in which they have limited experience. The entire endeavor may be viewed as a distraction from the professional training that is central to graduate study and, potentially, the career paths of students. Furthermore, we acknowledge that not all research is going to have broad relevance to the general public, not all research is going to be understood perfectly by its intended audience, and not every researcher has the time or inclination to become proficient with technology and multiple discourses.

And yet, we also contend that the potential benefits far outweigh these downsides. Because academic research requires extensive knowledge of a given field and is therefore natively complex in its conceptualization, we too often write with a miniscule audience in mind, even perhaps for the two or three reviewers who will ultimately judge the extent of our scholarly contribution to a journal. By placing writing at the forefront of the curriculum, communication and public engagement is prioritized. Furthermore, professors will recognize that their writing can improve through engagement with multiple discourses. Instead of viewing the task of writing as a distraction from the tasks of data collection and analysis, it should be viewed as an essential means of communicating one's findings, procuring funding, and publicly demonstrating the need for university-led research in the twenty-first century.

As stated by Limerick (1993), "Colleges and universities are filled with knowledgeable, thoughtful people who have been effectively silenced by an awful writing style, a style with its flaws concealed behind a smokescreen of sophistication and professionalism" (p. 206). We hope that the next generation of scholarship will not be silenced by its inability to communicate and engage with the general public. Through different publication outlets, such as newspapers, magazines, and social media websites, we believe that public scholarship can be effectively disseminated and consumed, thus strengthening the compact between higher education and society.

References

Babbitt, M. (1998). Who cares if you listen? In O. Strunk (Ed.), *Source readings in music history* (pp. 1305–1310). New York, NY: Norton. Reprinted from *High Fidelity, 8*(2), 38–40, 126–127.

Bennett, D. J., & Jennings, R. C. (2011). (Eds.). *Successful science communication: Telling it like it is.* New York, NY: Cambridge University Press.

Brownell, S. E., Price, J. V., & Steinman, L. (2013). Science communication to the general public: Why we need to teach undergraduate and graduate students this skill as part of their formal scientific training. *Journal of Undergraduate Neuroscience Education, 12*(1), E6–E10.

Burawoy, M. (2004). Public sociologies: Contradictions, dilemmas, and possibilities. *Social Forces, 82,* 1603–1618.

Caffarella, R. S., & Barnett, B. G. (2000). Teaching doctoral students to become scholarly writers: The importance of giving and receiving critiques. *Studies in Higher Education, 25*(1), 39–52.

Carey, K. (2015). *The end of college: Creating the future of learning and the university of everywhere.* New York, NY: Riverhead Books.

Cooper, M. M. (1986). The ecology of writing. *College English, 48,* 364–375.

Deming, D. J., & Figlio, D. (2016). Accountability in U.S. education: Applying lessons from K–12 experience to higher education. *Journal of Economic Perspectives, 30*(3), 33–56.

Donald, J. G. (2002). *Learning to think: Disciplinary perspectives.* San Francisco, CA: Jossey-Bass.

Elbow, P. (1973). *Writing without teachers.* New York, NY: Oxford University Press.

Elbow, P. (1997). High stakes and low stakes in assigning and responding to writing. *New Directions for Teaching and Learning, 60,* 5–13.

Faigley, L. (1986). Competing theories of process: A critique and a proposal. *College English, 48,* 527–542.

Flower, L., & Hayes, J. R. (1981). A cognitive process theory of writing. *College Composition and Communication, 32*, 365–387.

Funk, G., & Kennedy, B. (2016). *The politics of climate.* Washington, DC: Pew Research Center.

Gee, J. P. (2015). *Social linguistics and literacies: Ideology in discourses* (1st ed.). London, England: Routledge.

Geisler, C. (1994). *Academic literacy and the nature of expertise: Reading, writing, and knowing in academic philosophy.* Hillsdale, NJ: Erlbaum.

Giroux, H. A. (1983). Theories of reproduction and resistance in the new sociology of education: A critical analysis. *Harvard Educational Review, 53*, 257–293.

Greenwood, M. R. C., & Riordan, D. G. (2001). Civic scientist/civic duty. *Science Communication, 23*(1), 28–40.

Hazelkorn, E. (2014). *Making an impact: New directions for arts and humanities research.* Retrieved from arrow.dit.ie/cgi/viewcontent.cgi?article=1053&context=cserart

Heller, D. E. (2001). Introduction: The changing dynamics of affordability, access, and accountability in public higher education. In D. E. Heller (Ed.), *The states and public higher education policy: Affordability, access, and accountability* (pp. 1–10). Baltimore, MD: Johns Hopkins University Press.

Hess, F. M., & LoGerfo, L. (2006, May 8). Chicanas from outer space: Educational research is an education! *National Review.* Retrieved from www.nationalreview .com/article/217519/chicanas-outer-space-frederick-m-hess-laura-logerfo

Hicks, D. (2012). Performance-based university research funding systems. *Research Policy, 41*, 251–261.

Holm, P., Jarrick, A., & Scott, D. (2015). *Humanities world report 2015.* New York, NY: Palgrave Macmillan.

Huisman, J., & Currie, J. (2004). Accountability in higher education: Bridge over troubled water? *Higher Education, 48*, 529–551.

Hyland, K. (2004). *Disciplinary discourses: Social interactions in academic writing.* Ann Arbor: University of Michigan Press.

Ivanič, R. (1998). *Writing and identity: The discoursal construction of identity in academic writing.* Philadelphia, PA: John Benjamins.

Jonsson, A., & Svingby, G. (2007). The use of scoring rubrics: Reliability, validity, and educational consequences. *Educational Research Review, 2*, 130–144.

Kellogg, R. T. (2008). Training writing skills: A cognitive developmental perspective. *Journal of Writing Research, 1*(1), 1–26.

Knox, C. C. (2016). The human race as geological agents: Communicating climate change science. *Public Administration Review, 76*, 974–977.

Kuteeva, M., & Airey, J. (2014). Disciplinary differences in the use of English in higher education: Reflections on recent language policy developments. *Higher Education, 67*, 533–549.

Langenberg, D. N. (1991). Science, slogans, and civic duty. *Science, 252*, 361–363.

Lee, J. S., & Anderson, K. T. (2009). Negotiating linguistic and cultural identities: Theorizing and constructing opportunities and risks in education. *Review of Research in Education, 33*, 181–211.

Leef, G. (2016). Will we, at last, do something about accreditation? Retrieved from www.popecenter.org/2016/11/will-last-something-accreditation

Leiserowitz, A., Maibach, E., Roser-Renouf, C., Feinberg, G., & Rosenthal, S. (2016). *Climate change in the American mind: March 2016.* New Haven, CT: Yale Program on Climate Change Communication.

Leshner, A. I. (2003). Public engagement with science. *Science, 299*, 977.

Limerick, P. N. (1993, October 31). Dancing with professors: The trouble with academic prose. *New York Times Book Review, 3*, 23–24.

McClary, S. (1989). Terminal prestige: The case of avant-garde music composition. *Cultural Critique, 12*, 57–81.

McNabb, R. (2001). Making the gesture: Graduate student submissions and the expectations of journal referees. *Composition Studies, 29*(1), 9–26.

Paré, A. (2011). Speaking of writing: Supervisory feedback and the dissertation. In L. McAlpine, & C. Amundsen (Eds.), *Doctoral education: Research-based strategies for doctoral students, AGE supervisors and administrators,* (pp. 59–74). New York, NY: Springer.

Pew Research Center. (2015). *Major gaps between the public, scientists on key issues.* Retrieved from www.pewinternet.org/interactives/public-scientists-opinion-gap

Prior, P. (2006). A sociocultural theory of writing. In C. A. MacArthur, S. Graham, & J. Fitzgerald (Eds.), *Handbook of writing research,* (pp. 54–66). New York, NY: Guilford Press.

Rainie, L., Funk, G., & Anderson, M. (2015). *How scientists engage the public.* Washington, DC: Pew Research Center.

Ranson, S. (2003). Public accountability in the age of neo-liberal governance. *Journal of Education Policy, 18*, 459–480.

Rhoades, G., & Sporn, B. (2002). Quality assurance in Europe and the U.S.: Professional and political economic framing of higher education policy. *Higher Education, 43*, 355–390.

Rohman, D. G. (1965). Pre-writing: The stage of discovery in the writing process. *College English, 16*, 106–112.

Rose, M. (1985). The language of exclusion: Writing instruction at the university. *College English, 47*, 341–359.

Rose, M. (1989). *Lives on the boundary: The struggles and achievements of America's underprepared.* New York, NY: Free Press.

Rose, M. (2010). Writing for the public. *College English, 72*, 284–292.

Rose, M., & McClafferty, K. A. (2001). A call for the teaching of writing in graduate education. *Educational Researcher, 30*(2), 27–33.

Sallee, M., Hallett, R., & Tierney, W. G. (2011). Teaching writing in graduate school. *College Teaching, 59*(2), 66–72.

Schoenberg, A. (1975). How one becomes lonely. In L. Stein (Ed.), *Style and idea: Selected writings of Arnold Schoenberg* (pp. 30–53). Berkeley: University of California Press.

Slaughter, S., & Rhoades, G. (2000). The neo-liberal university. *New Labor Forum, 6*, 73–79.

Slaughter, S., & Rhoades, G. (2004). *Academic capitalism and the new economy: Markets, state, and higher education.* Baltimore, MD: Johns Hopkins University Press.

Somerville, R. C., & Hassol, S. J. (2011). Communicating the science of climate change. *Physics Today, 64*(10), 48–53.

Starke-Meyerring, D. (2011). The paradox of writing in doctoral education: Student experiences. In L. McAlpine & C. Amundsen (Eds.), *Doctoral education: Research-based strategies for doctoral students, supervisors and administrators* (pp. 75–95). Dordrecht, The Netherlands: Springer.

Stewart, D. (1969). Prose with integrity: A primary objective. *College Composition and Communication, 20*, 223–227.

Swales, J. (1990). The concept of discourse community. In J. Swales (Ed.), *Genre analysis: English in academic and research settings* (pp. 21–32). New York, NY: Cambridge University Press.

Tardy, C. M. (2005). "It's like a story": Rhetorical knowledge development in advanced academic literacy. *Journal of English for Academic Purposes, 4*, 325–338.

Tierney, W. G. (2006). *Trust and the public good: Examining the cultural conditions of academic work.* New York, NY: Peter Lang.

Tierney, W. G., & Lanford, M. (2016). Conceptualizing innovation in higher education. *Higher Education: Handbook of Theory and Practice, 31*, 1–40.

Tight, M. (2013). Students: Customers, clients, or pawns? *Higher Education Policy, 26*, 291–307.

Trow, M. (1996). Trust, markets, and accountability in higher education: A comparative perspective. *Higher Education Policy, 9*, 309–324.

Vygotsky, L. S. (1986). *Thought and language.* A. Kozulin (Ed.). Boston, MA: MIT Press. (Original work published 1934).

13

MODELING, MENTORING, AND PEDAGOGY

Cultivating Public Scholars

Angela Clark-Taylor, Molly Sarubbi, Judy Marquez Kiyama, and Stephanie J. Waterman

The Public Good is an aspiration, a vision and destination of a "better state" that we can know in common that we cannot know alone. (Chambers & Gopaul, 2008, p. 61)

In choosing to begin with this epigraph we hope to take a larger philosophical approach, which is "that universities, like other social institutions and even individuals, ought to serve interests that include but move beyond narrow self-serving concerns" (Shapiro, 2005, p. 1). By invoking *non nobis solum* (not for ourselves alone), we point to our shared belief that our scholarship should serve the public good. Specifically, in this chapter we use the term *community-engaged scholars* as our work is deeply rooted in the responsibilities we have to the communities to which we belong that have nurtured and supported our personal and professional growth. As community-engaged scholars, we resist the notion that community-engaged scholarship is anti-intellectual or antitheoretical, as well as the idea that traditional research is best and unbiased. We believe we are responsible to be actors in the public sphere. The aim of our scholarship is to have an impact on practice and policy for higher education to end injustice by raising our awareness of other ways of knowing and mutual engagement in our communities and with research participants.

In a time of unprecedented commodification of higher education as a private good, community-engaged scholarship is important to sustaining the public good mission. As Kezar (2005) notes, one of the most substantial ways the public good has been reinvigorated in higher education is through the community engagement movement, which is inextricably linked to public scholarship. Defined by the reciprocal collaboration between academics and individuals outside the academy for the mutually beneficial exchange of knowledge and resources in a context of partnership and reciprocity (New England Resource Center for Higher Education, n.d.), *community-engaged* scholarship becomes the conduit for change for the public good.

Although students are coming to graduate programs with interest and experience in community-engaged scholarship, there may be few opportunities in graduate programs for students to further develop the skills integral to this work (O'Meara & Jaeger, 2007). How can faculty prepare their students to contribute to higher education's mission to work for the public good through their scholarship? Despite inevitable differences across graduate programs, O'Meara (2006) describes general socialization experiences that help shape student scholar identities. Community engagement provides a platform for knowledge acquisition, investment, and involvement across the graduate student experience (Austin & McDaniels, 2006) and further develops the academic experience (Bloomgarden & O'Meara, 2007). These "windows of opportunity" (O'Meara, 2006, p. 30) in graduate education, such as orientation, curriculum, and content application, reinforce socialization and exist across various disciplines.

In this chapter we discuss how the public good is reinforced through intentionally training and socializing graduate students to practice community-engaged scholarship. Chambers (2005) notes that the public good in higher education should include collaboration among community partners, practitioners, scholars, and students. Specifically, we discuss how embedding these types of relationships and engagement opportunities creates a holistic graduate experience and is integral to cultivating students' identities as scholars and the underlying philosophy of community-engaged scholarship. In this chapter we seek to provide guidance to graduate preparation programs, students, and faculty on how to cultivate space to foster these important student-faculty relationships.

A Dialogue on Cultivating Community-Engaged Scholars

Drawing on our diverse experiences and our student-faculty-adviser relationships, we describe, through reflective conversations, how community-engaged scholars are cultivated through modeling, mentoring, and inclusive pedagogy. As the conversations in this chapter illustrate, this narrative approach was important for us to reconstruct our personal stories and share our authentic experiences. Our intent is to produce a richer text to assist students and faculty in cultivating relationships to train community-engaged scholars.

A Narrative Approach

Narratives allow individuals to construct themselves as actors in their own lives (Clandinin & Connelly, 2006). Narrating or storytelling is intertwined in the human experience, having helped to build lives and communities.

Narration has served to record, construct, and reconstruct personal stories (Mertova & Webster, 2012) and is "embedded within historical, structural, and ideological contexts, social discourses, and power relations" (Pitre, Kushner, Raine, & Hegadoren, 2013, p. 118). Riessman (2008) notes that "stories can have effects beyond their meanings for individual storytellers, creating possibilities for social identities, group belonging, and collective action" (p. 54). Narrative approaches resist the idea of bracketing the researcher and instead asks researchers to remain present within their work and explicit about their voice and interpretation. This approach is well suited to highlight the collaborative nature of the authors' relationships and document the reflective conversational approach that situates the context of this chapter.

Feminist Standpoint

In addition, we take a feminist approach (Collins, 1990; Harding, 1987) to enable us to make sense of our shared experiences and embrace and learn from each other's differences. When we seek to use only a removed academic voice, we silence a piece of ourselves that expands our ways of knowing and being. Exploring our mentoring relationships as community-engaged scholars assists us in interrogating that relationship, enabling us to deepen our practice and share these practices with the reader. Using feminism standpoint theory here guides our approach to investigating our experience as a narrative. Feminist standpoint theory is centered on positioning women as the knowers and experts on their own experience (Collins, 1990; Harding, 1987). In addition, this theory acknowledges the shared and the different and intersecting experiences and identities of women. For us this includes the differentiating identities of women of color, queer women, and differently abled women while simultaneously sharing educational and professional experiences as first-generation college students and former student affairs professionals.

Cultivating Community-Engaged Scholars

The tenets of public scholarship, reciprocity, shared knowledges, equity, and responsibility can often transcend barriers between differing identities and communities (Yapa, 2009). As our individual and collective experiences show, public scholarship is inextricably linked to our unique identities and strengthened by the significance of race, gender, sexuality, class, as well as other axes of difference and community perspectives. We embraced the similarities of our shared identities or experiences, but we also used our

divergent experiences to strengthen and understand the practices and scholarship of the group. The valuing of diverse knowledges and lived experiences
allowed each individual to express and cultivate his or her own identity as a
community-engaged scholar.

Molly is a policy researcher at the Education Commission of the United
States and a doctoral candidate in higher education at the University of
Denver. As a foster care alumna, first-generation college student, White
woman, Molly's graduate student and professional experiences have been
deeply shaped by her identities. She is committed to community engagement
opportunities in partnership with marginalized groups and social justice
imperatives. As such, her work centers on issues related to equity, oppression,
class, race, and gender, and argues for advocacy through research, policy, and
practice.

Angela is an assistant professor in the Department of Leadership and
Higher Education at the University of Redlands. She identifies as a first-
generation, cisgender, queer, White woman navigating academia with an
immune-mediated disease. Angela grew up in a working-class and extended
family household with her mother, grandparents, and uncle in New York.
Her family instilled in her at an early age the value of placing community
needs over the individual. Angela also considers herself to be a product of
campus- and community-based initiatives that support the development
of individuals with minoritized identities of sexuality and gender (Vaccaro,
Russell, & Koob, 2015). Angela works in partnership with students, staff,
faculty, and community members to support the continued development of
services for and deeper understandings of individuals with minoritized identities of sexuality and gender in higher education through her scholarship on
leadership development, feminist university-community engagement, and
qualitative community-based pedagogies and methodologies.

Stephanie, Onondaga, Turtle Clan, is an associate professor at the Ontario
Institute for Studies in Education at the University of Toronto. She identifies
home as the Onondaga Nation where she lived for most of her life. Before
moving to Toronto, Canada, Stephanie was a faculty member at the Warner
Graduate School. She acknowledges that she is a guest of the Mississauga of
the Credit River, that the territory where she works is subject to the Dish
with One Spoon Wampum covenant between the Haudenosaunee and
Anishnaabek peoples of this area, as well as the Huron-Wendat, Petun, and
other First Peoples. She is a cisgendered female faculty member in student
affairs, a mother, grandmother, auntie, and sister. She is in this profession
to educate those who work with indigenous students and those who teach
student and academic affairs personnel about indigenous students and the
settler colonialism that still drives policy today. The purpose of her efforts is

to promote better, more fulfilling, college experiences for indigenous, racialized, and minoritized students. Her goal is to reach the personnel who work face-to-face with students, the faculty who teach them, and those who may influence policy, so that all students thrive in higher education. Her commitment to acknowledging indigenous land and people before her conference presentations is an example of how she brings awareness of indigenous issues to the forefront.

Judy, an associate professor in the higher education department at the University of Denver, is a Mexican American woman and a first-generation college student from a working-class background. Judy centers issues of race and ethnicity, class, urbanicity, gender, and income in her scholarship and in doing so, demonstrates her own engaged and activist identities. She works with local communities in an effort to address systemic social and education issues as she is grounded in the belief that, collectively, community networks can be powerful forces of change when advancing an equity agenda.

In spring of 2011 Angela and Molly met at the University of Rochester in Judy's course titled Service-Learning, Higher Education & the Public Good. They were at once captivated by higher education as a discipline, finally being able to name their desire to serve the public good and the opportunity to learn alongside community-engaged faculty. This commitment was further developed as they began their doctoral program together and enrolled in Stephanie's course, History of Higher Education.

Through shared course work and over the course of their graduate education, they developed a mentoring relationship with Judy and Stephanie, as well as a peer mentoring relationship with each other. Their relationships have spanned time and distance. Judy remained connected as a mentor as she moved on to accept a new role at the University of Denver, whereas Stephanie created Diva Docs, a peer mentoring group she led with most of the women graduate students at the University of Rochester. Formal and informal mentoring relationships continued to support the cultivation of each student's scholarly identity. Although Molly went on to join Judy at the University of Denver, and Stephanie moved to the University of Toronto, they all remained in contact, and Judy and Stephanie remained important mentors for Molly and Angela. Judy serves as Molly's dissertation adviser and was an external committee member on Angela's dissertation, and Stephanie served as Angela's dissertation adviser and remains a valued mentor to Molly.

Modeling, Mentoring, and Pedagogy

In the reflective conversations that follow, we discuss our approach to community-engaged scholarship. We share our work and three narratives that illustrate the importance of modeling, mentoring, and pedagogy in cultivating community-engaged scholars. We describe how we have grappled with and attempted to portray how our values, pedagogies, and research paradigms have evolved into community-engaged scholarship.

Modeling: Representations of Community-Engaged Scholars

It is important for graduate students to see community-engaged scholars at work. During our conversations we came to realize that all of us were drawn to the scholarship of higher education, whether knowingly or coincidentally, because of the work it allowed us to do. We saw the type of scholar we wanted to be modeled for us in others' work and were encouraged to make a space within higher education for our work as well. Today, Judy and Stephanie model the tenets of community engagement across their research, teaching, and service. Angela noted, "I chose higher education to be a scholar activist and to do community-engaged research. I chose it because I felt like I could be engaged in real change so that I could be of service to my communities." Molly expressed feeling similarly and explicitly noted the value that seeing a model of experienced scholars can bring to your work. Molly stated, "I felt like I found a field that cared about the same things I cared about. It modeled an approach I was already doing and gave me the language, technique, and mindfulness to do it better. It's important to cultivate that in doctoral students." This representation could be seen in the faculty experiences as well.

Stephanie and Judy also talked about their feelings of being drawn to the opportunity for community-engaged scholarship in higher education. Stephanie noted, "It wasn't the study of higher education that drove me to the field. It is this space where I could do what I wanted to do and make a difference." Judy seconded this, stating,

> Yes, I believe that is the space higher education provides us. We approach our research from different ontologies and paradigms. My expectation is that folks address their research paradigms in their dissertation work as I'm aware that not all scholarship will be community-based research, nor should it be. I appreciate that in this academic space we can have these differences and debates, and as long as I can keep doing the work that I am doing I'm going to keep pushing forward.

For many faculty, and as signified in Judy's and Stephanie's narratives, community-engaged work is not just a professional lens or passion but a personally rooted responsibility and commitment to one's own communities. Community-engaged work is intertwined with peoples' identities and inevitably in each facet of their professional work. Faculty who are engaged with the community embrace the commitments and the barriers of doing this important work.

Community engagement necessitates the development of a deeply involved and reciprocal relationship between researchers and communities (Bloomgarden & O'Meara, 2007). Establishing a good rapport with community partners, assigning service-learning sites, and providing ongoing service to students often comes in addition to the traditional expectations of faculty. This type of embedded public scholarship is often absent or less incentivized in faculty reward structures (Bloomgarden & O'Meara, 2007; Saltmarsh & Wooding, 2016). As institutions feel the pressure for prestige, coupled with decreased funding and larger enrollment numbers, tenure and promotion are conflated by the value placed on external funding and publications (Saltmarsh & Wooding, 2016). Decreased funding across institutions, particularly regional and community-based institutions known for rich community engagement, has undermined institutional support for this type of work (Saltmarsh & Wooding, 2016). As a result, community-engaged faculty must balance their public scholarship with the often already heavy load of teaching, research, and service roles (Bloomgarden & O'Meara, 2007; Saltmarsh & Wooding, 2016). Yet the importance and influence of this work on graduate student development, as illustrated by Angela and Molly's experiences, makes a strong case for the reinforcement of this work across all levels and institution types. Leadership should take tangible steps by encouraging, supporting, and rewarding the efforts and commitments of community-engaged faculty and students (O'Meara, 2006).

Mentoring: Creating Space in Diva Docs

It is important for students to see models of community-engaged scholars in their field, but we must also create a concrete space for professional and peer mentoring and support. Mentoring is a critical career development resource and can promote professional and personal growth. Often individuals with minoritized identities do not receive the mentoring they need to successfully progress in their careers. Women are more likely to engage in informal and spontaneous mentoring or professional friendship (Gardiner, 2008). These collegial friendships exist at the intersection of personal and professional and yield many benefits (Iverson, 2009; Seher & Iverson, 2015). Yet, collegial friendships also pose challenges to quality and consistency because they often lack formal institutional support. Incorporating formal spaces for mentoring therefore secures continuity of support for students.

Seeing this gap in the socialization of PhD students, Stephanie started a group for women graduate students she called Diva Docs. Creating this formalized space for students to interact, support each other as peer mentors, and be mentored by Stephanie was important to their overall success in the doctoral program. Angela discussed this, saying,

> Starting a group where we could support each other in authentic ways was important because it created a formal space that was supported by our institution. It makes me wonder how to continue to create these spaces of support moving forward.

Stephanie replied,

> "Well, I found that inviting people in is helpful. Just saying, "Come talk to me" or "Come join this group," it takes on its own life. I have a responsibility as a human being to teach and establish caring relationships with my students who will, in turn, become caring human beings who will work with all students and consider their work as part of a larger system on Mother Earth.

Stephanie's humanness (Wall, 2001) is reflected in inviting others in. She continued,

> I've offered opportunities to teach with me, to offer my experience as a first-generation, far-from-traditional-student experience in a gendered environment. I offered a relationship in which we were able to express emotion within the academy. The Diva Docs group was my response to the lack of support for a group of female doctoral students, but it also served as a space for me to learn from and find a sense of camaraderie and support. It mattered. My teaching, my relationship building, my sharing, all matters to students, the academy, and consequently, our world.

If we think about this experience as a key part of the graduate student socialization process, then by using strategic messaging, orientation programs can assist in the recruitment of students whose values and practices align with the mission of the institution. Program components such as possible assistantships, diversity in curriculum offerings, teaching and research opportunities, shared interests in faculty research agendas, networks, methodology, and pedagogy increase students' investment in the program (O'Meara, 2006). Unfortunately, these opportunities do not always exist across institutions. The next phase in the socialization process takes place most often in the classroom as a result of curricula and pedagogy and becomes integral in cultivating graduate students' self-perception as scholars (O'Meara, 2006). The use of diverse and intentional pedagogical tools cultivates specialized knowledge, educational ideologies, and opportunities to hone teaching, critical thinking, and research skills (Saltmarsh & Wooding, 2016). Curriculum offerings that offer outlets for critical reflection on one's role in educational systems and the roles of power, privilege, and relationships with the community are instrumental in cultivating a scholar's identity (O'Meara, 2006). The last phase of student socialization occurs in created opportunities to display mastery over disciplinary content. Faculty are increasingly incorporating experiential learning components such as internships, service-learning, and collaborations with community partners to enhance traditional curricula with opportunities to put theory into practice (Saltmarsh & Wooding, 2016).

Because Stephanie and her experience are not always validated in the classroom and higher education generally, her approach is to humanize the classroom based on relational knowing (Caine, Estefan, & Clandinin, 2013) and relationality (Wilson, 2008). Her lived experiences and the lived experiences of her students are the foundation of her teaching. Students make meaning and relationships that inform their understanding of higher education. Foundational to Wilson's indigenous research paradigm, relationality is based on the accountability we humans have to other people, the environment and land, the cosmos, and ideas. We are responsible for these relationships. As Wilson said, "We could not *be* without *being in relationship* with everything that surrounds us and is within us. Our reality, our ontology is the relationships" (p. 76). This philosophical grounding influenced Stephanie's work with Angela and Molly and the formation of Diva Docs. Stephanie saw that support was lacking, that student voices and experiences were silenced, and she provided a space for these students because of her responsibility to people and to ideas. She felt accountable to the relationship of instructor to student, that is, the human-to-human, community-to-community relationship.

The indigenous research paradigm was developed through Wilson's (2008) search for an indigenous methodology; he learned from indigenous people from around the world. Relationality is of course about people, but it is much more complex than that. We also have relationships to the land and our environment, spiritually, and as stewards. Wilson discusses our complicated spiritual relationship to the cosmos in which "everything is sacred" (p. 90). We also have relationships with ideas. We come to higher education with our own knowledge, we learn together about new ideas and come to a relationship with that knowledge. Stephanie brings a higher education doctorate of life in an indigenous territory, her spirituality, her teaching experience, and her experience in higher education to the classroom and to her work with students. In turn, Angela and Molly brought their own experiences to the classroom and higher education. As Wilson (2008) stated, "It is incumbent upon the other person to come to their own decisions on the shape that the new ideas will take and to make their own conclusions" (p. 94). Diva Docs was a form of mentorship to give these doctoral students a space to be mentored and to mentor each other, a space dedicated to dialogue.

The culmination of student and faculty investment through initial orientation, pedagogy, curriculum, and relationship building is often exhibited through comprehensive exams, dissertations, conference presentations, and securing grant funding and future job placements (O'Meara, 2006; Saltmarsh & Wooding, 2016). Although these forms of mastery are demonstrative of student learning and development, they should also be markers of exceptional faculty engagement. All this is only made possible by engaged faculty, who are deeply committed not only to their students but also to their communities and public scholarship. According to O'Meara, "There is no substitute for engaged faculty scholars who intentionally open doors to engaged ways of knowing, learning, teaching and discovering" (p. 30). Through modeling and mentoring, faculty are often the most significant resource for students cultivating their identity as public scholars, and yet despite the many benefits, it is not work that comes easily.

Pedagogy: Service-Learning, Higher Education, and the Public Good

Coupled with modeling and mentoring, purposeful pedagogy through meaningful classroom experiences that specifically investigate scholarship for the public good proved to be the lynchpin of Angela and Molly's training as community-engaged scholars. Molly notes,

> Community engagement was a fundamental theme in many of my courses and assignments, always coupled with critical analysis and an interdisciplinary lens. Each degree required me to explore the context of my own work through other disciplines and as a result, my idea of public scholarship, while rooted in higher education, is influenced by anthropology, social work, and policy.

Angela responded that "this course in particular encouraged me to think critically and focus on community-engaged approaches to social justice in my scholarship and practice." Judy reflected this in her intent for the course, noting,

> Angela and Molly mention a course I developed at the University of Rochester, Service-Learning, Higher Education & the Public Good. The intent of the course was to review the evolution and impact of service-learning

and complicate the relationship between higher education institutions and the community.

Molly made it clear that the topic of public scholarship and community engagement was important as well as the holistic way it was presented in the course. Molly stated,

> Public scholarship was cultivated through experiences within the classroom that not only covered disciplinary content, but allowed personal and professional discovery in the process. Students gained additional skills through inclusive pedagogies consisting of diverse and innovative teaching methods, readings, assignments, reflection, and discussions that allowed me to further cultivate my own identity as a scholar.

Judy discussed the ways she incorporated this approach into the course noting,

> Students worked directly with a community partner all semester and applied that knowledge to a final paper that focused on developing their own critical consciousness. In developing their ideas around critical consciousness, I asked students to write about developing a deeper awareness of self; developing a deeper awareness and broader perspective of others; and developing a deeper awareness and broader perspective of social, political, cultural, and historical issues and seeing one's potential to make change. I asked students to do this while considering the broader question of what education was for and as a public good meant for them.

See Cipolle (2010) for more about critical consciousness and community engagement.

Angela noted that this pedagogical approach gave the class a stronger sense of classroom engagement as well.

> Right from the first class the classroom had a great energy. The organization of the readings was perfect, with each week proposing questions and encouraging us to think more deeply and critically about community engagement, higher education, and the public good. Class discussions were heated and interesting, and often students were sad to have to stop the conversation at the end of class.

Judy discussed how her interest in teaching this course developed, saying,

> My interest in developing this course stemmed from these very same questions that I was grappling with as a community engaged scholar. For me

then, this class represented an exploration into critically examining the role of education in communities, most often marginalized communities, as a means of sense making for my own scholarship and evolution as a researcher.

The goals Judy set for the class included the following:

- understand the conceptualization and evolution of service-learning as a pedagogy,
- understand the multiple (and changing) definitions of *the public good*,
- explore and redefine *service-learning* as a means of serving the public good,
- engage in an ongoing service-learning project with Rochester community partners, and
- create a personal definition of *service* and the *public good* and understand how it affects one's roles as researcher and practitioner.

Molly noted in the following how this approach supported her learning:

My faculty members pushed me to think critically about systems that relieve or perpetuate inequities, and my roles within them. In doing so, they also created a space that welcomed the benefits of my own lived experiences as assets to the learning environment within the classroom. They shared parts of their own histories, and took opportunities to learn about me as well, making the classroom an extremely engaging and humanizing environment.

Angela agreed, noting,

These pedagogical approaches expanded my understanding of the public good in higher education. In this course we were able to draw on historical and contemporary issues in higher education as well as issues of race, class, gender, and privilege all through a community engagement lens. Feedback on course assignments was invaluable to improving my writing and thinking about citizenship, service-learning, and social justice education.

Judy discussed how she became aware of the precarious ways we train graduate students, saying,

What I quickly realized is that rarely do we talk to our students about what it means to develop a scholar-practitioner identity that integrates positionality, identity, and responsibilities like teaching, research, and service. All too often we, as an academic community, attempt to compartmentalize these elements that when understood together, make us even more authentic and influential in our work. I arrived to class each week eager to have these deeper discussions with my students, excited knowing that the course was going in a direction that was student-driven based on their own emerging ideas and identities on community-engaged scholarship. Together we pondered questions such as, When you think about democracy and public good, how should they evolve conceptually and operationally given shifts in racial and ethnic diversity? What would a revised social contract look like? Developing a deeper awareness and broader perspective of social issues is facilitated when dissonance destabilizes our worldviews and leads to self-examination and questioning. When did (or has) this dissonance occur for you? Can you think of a particular experience either before or during this class that allowed you to step back and question your original values and beliefs?

Angela noted the importance of this approach to her personal and professional development, saying,

> This course asked us to create a personal definition of how service for the public good affects one's role as a scholar toward a deeper understanding of the importance of community engagement. Of all the courses I have taken in my 27 years of education, Judy's course, Service-Learning, Higher Education & the Public Good, has had the most meaningful and profound effect on my scholarship. Having participated in this course as an early graduate student has helped me to continue to develop my work in this area. It has continued to inspire me through my dissertation and into my career as an assistant professor.

Finally, Judy discussed the importance of having available scholarship to understand the goals of community-engaged research.

> We compared and contrasted Dewey and Freire's foundations of engagement, were informed by Kezar, Chambers, and Burkhardt's (2005) earlier writings, and each week read narratives from faculty of color (see Gonzalez & Padilla, 2008) as they shared why doing community-engaged work was at the core of who they were as scholars. In the end, we developed ideas about what individual and institutional responsibility should and could look like when serving the public good and further developed our own identities as community-engaged scholars. The course remains one of my most powerful teaching experiences, and I am grateful for the journey that the students and our community partners shared with us.

Molly noted how this intentional approach to pedagogy enhanced her learning.

Although some of these experiences are common across some, or maybe even most, graduate programs, I feel my experience was heightened because of the intentionality, holistic curriculum, and critical application that was modeled by the faculty and required of me as a student. But however beneficial this technical development was (or is), the most relevant and important experiences in shaping my identity as a community engaged scholar are the wealth of opportunities for mentorship I've been lucky to have been involved in.

The conversation not only describes the collaborative reflection among faculty and students but also illuminates some of the integral components and the impacts of doing community-engaged work. Implementation of community engagement continues to evolve with greater understanding of its theoretical underpinnings, pedagogical and research methodologies, and the reciprocal benefits it brings to institutions, faculty, students, and communities (O'Meara, 2006; Saltmarsh & Wooding, 2016). Although the benefits of community engagement include increased student retention, it is also an integral element of building skills and knowledge directly related to the development of the professional self (Austin & McDaniels, 2006; O'Meara, 2006). Exposing graduate students to community engagement opportunities encourages students and faculty to cultivate their understanding of social issues, the relevancy of their work, their lived experiences, and their own personal and professional agency (Yapa, 2009). In turn, graduate student scholars become conduits for change between communities and universities, reinforcing the role of higher education as a public good.

Rethinking Graduate Preparation for Future Community-Engaged Scholars

Despite their differences in institutional support, personal backgrounds, and research expertise, Angela and Molly received mentoring, modeling, and classroom experiences with community-engaged pedagogy that has shaped their own scholarship. Angela's and Molly's understanding of practicing community-engaged scholarship was shaped by the examples set by Judy and Stephanie, their faculty advisers. This modeling of exemplary teaching and scholarship was demonstrated along each step of the graduate student experience. Having already been well-established community-engaged scholars, Judy and Stephanie exemplified what it meant to do meaningful and reciprocal research that celebrates the experiences and knowledge of their own communities while challenging dominant discourse about equity, access, and the history of education.

Our experiences illustrate that faculty and graduate programs in higher education should be provided with models of community-engaged scholars, formal spaces for mentoring that incorporate community engagement, and courses that include community engagement and that use community-based pedagogies. Modeling this work can help students visualize the work they want to be doing and learn reciprocal models of engagement. Formal mentoring and classroom experiences add to modeling by providing formal spaces of institutional and faculty support for students interested in community-engaged scholarship.

In closing, we want to stress through our experience that it is crucial for this work to be authentic. The authenticity of this work is key to avoiding ethical issues in community-engaged scholarship and to work reflexively and reciprocally with community partners. In addition, we want to encourage the continued use of faculty and student narratives about their experience participating in community-engaged scholarship as it can lead to a deeper understanding of the need for preparation for graduate students toward community-engaged work by creating an ongoing dialogue.

References

Austin, A. E., & McDaniels, M. (2006). Using doctoral education to prepare faculty to work within Boyer's four domains of scholarship. *New Directions for Institutional Research, 129,* 51–65.

Bloomgarden, A. H., & O'Meara, K. (2007). Faculty role integration and community engagement: Harmony or cacophony? *Michigan Journal of Community Service Learning, 13,* 5–18.

Caine, V., Esefan, A., & Clandinin, D. J. (2013). A return to methodological commitment: Reflections on narrative inquiry. *Scandinavian Journal of Educational Research, 57,* 574–586.

Chambers, T. C. (2005). The special role of higher education in society: As a public good for a public good. In A. J. Kezar, T. C. Chambers, & J. C. Burkhardt (Eds.), *Higher education for the public good: Emerging voices from a national movement* (pp. 3–22). San Francisco, CA: Jossey-Bass.

Chambers, T., & Gopaul, B. (2008). Decoding the public good of higher education. *Journal of Higher Education Outreach and Engagement, 12*(4), 59–91.

Cipolle, S. B. (2010). *Service-learning and social justice: Engaging students in social change.* Lanham, MD: Rowman & Littlefield.

Clandinin, J. D., & Connelly, F. M. (2006). Narrative inquiry. In J. L. Green, G. Camilli, P. B. Elmore (Eds.), *Handbook of complementary methods in education research,* (pp. 477–487). Mahwah, NJ: Erlbaum.

Collins, P. H. (1990). *Black feminist thought: Knowledge, consciousness, and the politics of empowerment.* Boston, MA: Unwin Hyman.

Gardiner, C. E. (2008). *Mentoring: Towards an improved professional friendship* (Unpublished doctoral dissertation). Birmingham, UK: University of Birmingham.

Gonzalez, K. P. & Padilla, R. V. (Eds.). (2008). *Doing the public good: Latina/o scholars engage civic participation.* Sterling, VA: Stylus.

Harding, S. (1987). *Feminism and methodology.* Bloomington: Indiana University Press.

Iverson, S. (2009). Crossing boundaries: Understanding women's advancement from clerical to professional positions. *NASPA Journal About Women in Higher Education, 2,* 140–166.

Kezar, A. J. (2005). Challenges for higher education in serving the public good. In A. J. Kezar, T. C. Chambers, & J. C. Burkhardt (Eds.), *Higher education for the public good: Emerging voices from a national movement* (pp. 23–42). San Francisco, CA: Jossey-Bass.

Kezar, A. J., Chambers, T. C., & Burkhardt, J. C. (Eds.). (2005). *Higher education for the public good: Emerging voices from a national movement.* San Francisco, CA: Jossey-Bass.

Mertova, P., & Webster, L. (2012). Critical event narrative inquiry in higher education quality. *Qualitative Approaches in Higher Education, 3*(2), 15–21.

New England Resource Center for Higher Education. (n.d.). *Carnegie community engagement classification.* Retrieved from www.nerche.org/index.php?option=com_content&view=article&id=341&Itemid=618

O'Meara, K. (2006). Graduate education and community engagement. *New Directions for Teaching and Learning, 113,* 27–42.

O'Meara, K., & Jaeger, A. (2007). Preparing future faculty for engagement: History, barriers, facilitators, models, and recommendations. *Journal of Higher education Outreach and Engagement, 11*(4), 3–27.

Pitre, N. Y., Kushner, K. E., Raine, K. D., & Hegadoren, K. M. (2013). Critical feminist narrative inquiry: Advancing knowledge through double-hermeneutic narrative analysis. *Advances in Nursing Science, 36,* 118–132. doi:10.1097/ANS.0b013e3182902064

Riessman, C. (2008). *Narrative methods for the human sciences.* Thousand Oaks, CA: Sage.

Saltmarsh, J., & Wooding, J. (2016). Rewarding community-engaged scholarship: A state university system approach. *Metropolitan Universities, 27*(2), 74–86.

Seher, C., & Iverson, S. V. (2015). From dialogue to action: Consciousness-raising with academic mothers. *NASPA Journal About Women in Higher Education, 8,* 17–28.

Shapiro, H. T. (2005). *A larger sense of purpose: Higher education and society.* Princeton, NJ: Princeton University Press.

Vaccaro, A., Russell, E. I., & Koob, R. M. (2015). Students with minoritized identities of sexuality and gender in campus contexts: An emergent model. *New Directions for Student Services, 152,* 25–39.

Wall, S. (2001). *To become a human being: The message of Tadodaho Chief Leon Shenandoah.* Charlottesville, VA: Hampton Roads.

Wilson, S. (2008). *Research is ceremony: Indigenous research methods.* Halifax, Nova Scotia: Fernwood.

Yapa, L. (2009). Transforming the university through community engagement. *Journal of Higher Education Outreach and Engagement, 13*(3), 131–146.

14

PUBLIC SCHOLARSHIP ACROSS FACULTY CAREER STAGES

Jaime Lester and David Horton Jr.

Faculty are at the center of the social charter, the informal contract, between the public and higher education as they are integral in producing the research and new knowledge, the scholarship, to fulfill higher education's responsibility to the public. The explicit relationship between faculty work and public scholarship in the literature has not extensively taken into account the impact of faculty career stages or institutional characteristics, such as resources, community relationships, and institutional prestige. How career stages aid or impede faculty's participation in activities such as public scholarship, which can connect the academy to social and environmental challenges, is a crucial area for consideration.

The career of a tenured faculty member can last more than three decades and often undergoes three major stages—early, midcareer, and late career—characterized by significant transitions that redefine faculty's institutional and disciplinary roles and responsibilities (Baldwin, 1990; Kalivoda, Sorrell, & Simpson, 1994). Research found that faculty redefine the relative importance of their activities over time, with service and research becoming more important as a faculty member progresses through career stages (Baldwin & Blackburn, 1981). Additionally, Baldwin and Blackburn (1981) found that once faculty reach the midcareer stage, they are confronted with a variety of career progression options, such as making choices about administrative appointments, leadership roles, and service in disciplinary or professional organizations.

Across career stages, faculty face different intrinsic and extrinsic expectations and often experience a period of reevaluation of activities or a

196

reenvisioning of their career contributions (Terosky & Gonzales, 2016). This period of reevaluation often leads to changes in faculty members' level of commitment to public scholarship. Terosky and Gonzales (2016) suggest that during periods of reenvisioning, "faculty reject, resist, or negotiate prescribed roles and power structures made evident through historical and social relations within and outside of their institutional contexts" (p. 244). The mere process of reenvisioning, which often occurs during career stage transitions, creates opportunities for faculty to exercise their agency to integrate public scholarship across their work of teaching, research, and service. We contend that although there are institutional and structural challenges to being a public scholar, there are also opportunities that complement the career stages of faculty. In the following, we review the research on faculty career stages, acknowledge the current challenges to engaging in public scholarship, and provide recommendations for how individual faculty can work in public scholarship.

Faculty Career Stages

The purpose of this section is to review the literature related to faculty career stages to set the stage for the following discussion on the challenges and opportunities in incorporating public scholarship at each stage. Although this information might be equally relevant to faculty on tenure track and nontenure faculty, we focus on tenure-track and tenured faculty.

Early Career Faculty

The first stage of faculty careers starts with the first year as an assistant professor and continues until tenure and promotion, six to seven years later (Lumpkin, 2014). The initial stage is characterized by many conflicting demands that are often new experiences (Wright, 2005). New faculty are responsible for teaching between two and four courses per semester and engaging in research activities, depending on their institution's focus on research or teaching. They also often participate in student advising activities and departmental service and are expected to increase the number and depth of those activities from year to year. During this first stage, early career faculty experience a range of challenges and conflicts as they make progress toward tenure and promotion. Wright (2005) found that having conflicting demands, such as high expectations to teach new courses and engage in intense research activities, often results in burnout and stress. Baldwin (1990) also noted that early career faculty are under the burden of learning about institutional resources, organizational cultures, and department norms, and go through changes in professional identity. Early career faculty are under the stress of starting a new professional position in a new organization and often a new community while navigating independent work as a teacher and researcher usually for the first time.

Midcareer Faculty

Midcareer faculty, those 1 to 10 years after receiving tenure, make one of their most substantial career transitions characterized by a time of reflection and reassessment (Hall, 2002). Midcareer faculty face "a career plateau where professional goals are less clear, even while an array of attractive personal and professional options may be available" (Baldwin, DeZure, Shaw, & Moretto, 2008, p. 48). The literature has further suggested that midcareer faculty experience posttenure blues, a slump, or a letting down (Austin, 2010; Mathews, 2014; Trower, 2011). Increased dissatisfaction can lead to remaining at the associate level for longer periods of time before seeking promotion, reaching retirement, or leaving the profession.

The reasons for the lack of satisfaction among midcareer faculty are related to several trends in higher education. For example, the changing nature of the professoriate with too few tenured faculty and an increasing number of contingent faculty leads to an increased workload for midcareer tenure-track faculty. Kena and colleagues (2015) note that from fall 1993 to fall 2013 the number of full-time tenure-track and non-tenure-track faculty increased by 45%, whereas part-time faculty increased by 104%. As Baldwin and colleagues (2008) found, midcareer faculty encounter higher workloads and expectations across all areas of their work (e.g., obtaining research grants), but especially in leadership, service, and management roles to support the efforts of the department and university. Complicating the issues facing midcareer faculty is the lack of professional development to help individuals navigate the transition, set new goals, and establish new skills. Although a small number of disciplines have created extensive professional development programs for midcareer faculty, these initiatives have not yet been adopted by institutions or departments as a whole.

Late Career Faculty

Very little research has been conducted on late career faculty, with only recent attention paid to issues associated with retirement. Often defined as those who are 10 years after promotion to associate professor, *late career faculty* are a large proportion of tenured faculty on many college campuses. Late career faculty include those who do not seek further promotion (lifetime associates) and full professorships. One of the few national surveys on late career faculty found that faculty maintain a high level of productivity through the age of 60 and high degrees of engagement in their institutions, disciplines, and with students (Trower, 2011). The same survey noted that late career faculty have more work-life balance and less stress, and tend to delay retirement because of high job satisfaction. O'Meara (2004) found that late career faculty tended to resist posttenure review in part because of a concern that evaluation expectations would be uniform across faculty ranks and inclusive of new higher research activity norms in the university. O'Meara also found that late career faculty were concerned that nonquantifiable activities regarding faculty leadership, such as mentoring, would be negated by posttenure review.

Contemporary Challenges of Conducting Public Scholarship

Current contextual conditions of faculty work have an impact on discussions of faculty career stages and public scholarship. Faculty are under increased pressure to produce a narrow set of valued academic products, have fewer tenured colleagues because of the rise of contingent faculty, and institutional reward structures that are increasingly reductive and quantified. In this section, we address some of the current trends in faculty work to situate the research on career stages and to identify the contemporary challenges of engaging in public scholarship.

Changing Faculty Composition

The composition of faculty is moving from primarily tenure-track or tenured faculty to a more contingent group defined by faculty contracts that do not have a tenure option. According to the National Center for Education Statistics, as many as 70% of faculty are in a contingent role (Aud et al., 2013). There is evidence that tenured and tenure-track faculty experience disproportionate service responsibilities because of fewer tenured and more contingent colleagues (Kezar & Maxey, 2014; Schuster & Finkelstein, 2006). Engaging in public scholarship becomes increasingly complicated when faculty experience increased service responsibilities posttenure, as noted in the research on midcareer faculty (Baldwin et al., 2008) because of fewer colleagues to share those service activities. Further complicating the pressure to avoid work on service activities is the lack of consideration this work is given in faculty evaluation processes. Research is a highly valued activity, with service having little value, and public scholarship being defined outside the historical three-legged stool (i.e., teaching, research, and service). How did we get to this point, you ask? A number of scholars have attributed the lack of value on service and public research to *academic capitalism,* defined as a "regime that entails colleges and universities engaging in market and market-like behaviors" (Rhoades & Slaughter, 2004, p. 37).

Neoliberal Academic Capitalism and Institutional Rewards

According to Slaughter and Rhoades (2004), academic capitalism refers to the characteristics of higher education institutions in the context of neoliberalism. The characteristics associated with academic capitalism are many (e.g., seeking patents, developing external partnerships, etc.) and have a significant impact on faculty, thereby altering the work activities that faculty engage in. Surveys on faculty productivity have found that the average number of hours a faculty member spends working has increased over the past two decades. In 1984 faculty reported working on average 40 hours per week; in 2004 they reported working on average 49 hours per week (Schuster & Finkelstein 2006). Another study of University of California faculty found that on average faculty worked 56 hours per week, with childless faculty working slightly more hours than their parenting counterparts (Mason & Goulden, 2004). Schuster and Finkelstein (2006) also found that faculty are producing 300% more publications than in 1970.

The activities that faculty are involved in while working longer hours are also related to academic capitalism. Research indicates that faculty are under increasing demands from institutions to control their output, such as producing peer-reviewed articles and writing grants as opposed to more diffuse ideas of scholarship, such as community development and engagement in the public via social media. At many institutions across the country, faculty are asked to complete annual reports to prove their worth, quantifying the number of publications produced, students taught, dissertations advised, and grants received (Flaherty, 2015). The increase in productivity standards makes it difficult for early and midcareer faculty to consider engaging in yet another activity—public scholarship.

O'Meara (2006) found that evaluations for tenure, in particular, inhibit faculty engagement in community or public scholarship. More and more institutions of higher education are competing for national or international rankings, such as that of *U.S. News & World Report,* which rank research-related activities higher (e.g., external research dollars, number of faculty citations, etc.). Institutions that have historically evaluated faculty based on their teaching and service have moved to hiring more research-oriented faculty and altering their tenure and promotion guidelines to emphasize, or even exclusively focus on, research endeavors. New metrics for research activities further discourage faculty to engage in public scholarship. It is important to note that the guidelines do not take an inclusive approach to scholarship as suggested by Rice (2002), among others. Rather, the three-legged stool of teaching, research, and service are separate, with differing levels of value in evaluation processes. We agree with Hurtado and Sharkness (2008), who said, "The future strength of the tenure system—and the survival of tenure itself—largely depends on the continuing support of faculty and the capacity of faculty to develop review processes that recognize emerging forms of scholarship" (p. 37).

Suggestions for How to Engage in Public Scholarship Across Career Stages

Although making changes to the tenure and promotion system is a long-term endeavor, faculty across career stages should not be discouraged from integrating public scholarship into their current efforts. In their research on faculty engagement and public scholarship, Colbeck and Weaver (2008) present a model of faculty motivation inclusive of personal agency that can be used to strategically engage in public scholarship. Essentially, they argue that faculty who acknowledge their skills and evaluate the contextual influences, such as what is valued in tenure and promotion, can identify activities that align skills with contextual considerations. They note, "Thus, a faculty member who perceived herself adept at communicating with multiple stakeholders might be more likely to engage in public scholarship than one who feels most comfortable talking to academic peers" (p. 11). Using this framework, we present a set of recommendations for how faculty at each career stage can integrate public scholarship into their practice and activities.

Early Career

Early career faculty have an opportunity to begin their faculty career as a public scholar by strategically identifying and working with their various publics to have an impact on policy and practice. The intentionality of a public scholar begins with identifying the individuals, groups, and organizations that would benefit from or become agents of change in policy and practice. Early career faculty then need to determine what those publics are and eventually connect with those publics. The process of identification will vary based on the experience and accessibility of one's publics but could include community-based organizations, policy groups, state or federal policymakers, local schools or universities, academic associations, and even international organizations. Defining and involving publics directly related to research creates an efficiency in workloads that is all too important for those tenure-track years and can include establishing relationships with publics to formulate integrated research projects and disseminating research findings to publics through conferences, meetings, and forms of media. In the first example, the intention is to establish more collaborative efforts to help publics establish data and research findings to support mutual goals, whereas the second is to share existing results and thereby is less collaborative. Early career faculty may take both these approaches and others as part of their intentionality as public scholars.

The opportunities to achieve the goals of an early career public scholar are many because the Internet and other communication technologies provide access to low-cost and accessible networking options. Social networking tools, such as Facebook and Twitter, now allow alternative ways to promote research in a timely manner. Early career faculty may be more adept at new social networking tools as they are more likely to have used them throughout graduate school. In addition to the ability to disseminate research, social media allows scholars to communicate with the larger community as a whole concerning important and pressing issues (Reddick, 2016). Faculty have found social media to be a valuable mode to communicate with audiences, such as politicians who typically do not read scholarly journals that have limited accessibility.

For example, faculty member Maria may begin her career with a research agenda related to identifying the barriers to low-income college students' success by completing a dissertation on the subject and pursuing academic publication. Maria is interested in working to change state and federal policy that is directly having a negative impact on low-income student financial aid, such as the lack of obtaining the federal Pell Grant in the summer. She identifies several policy advocacy groups in Washington DC and sets up meetings to inform the groups of her findings, discuss opportunities for collaborative research, and make additional connections to other pertinent groups. Maria then creates an infographic of her findings and publishes it on a new project-based website and through social media. She regularly sends out updates of her and others' research on the same topic using social media and also sends updates of her work to those policy groups. She also connects with local colleges and universities to help them identify research-based interventions to support low-income students and meets with her contacts once a semester, who work with her to develop checklists and tool kits to publish online, disseminate, and support the efforts on a national level. Dissemination also continues through academic associations and during invited talks on college campuses. Maria's long-term intention is to become more involved in helping individual students and more directly involved in politics once she feels more secure with tenure.

Midcareer

The literature on midcareer faculty identifies a significant career transition that can result in a slump or what is also termed *posttenure blues* (Austin, 2010; Mathews, 2014; Trower, 2011). This slump partially occurs because of the success (stress) of getting tenure, the accomplishment of a long-term goal (tenure), and an increase in service expectations that overwhelm other aspects of work, such as research activities. In addition, more institutions are reducing graduate assistantship and professional travel support to encourage faculty to obtain externally funded grants to support such perks. Research suggests a variety of interventions to reduce the likelihood of the midcareer slump, including mentoring programs, professional development, depart-ment-level planning of service roles, and the like (Baldwin et al., 2008). We suggest that engaging in or engaging more deeply in public scholarship by identifying new audiences and new platforms for disseminating one's work and working in communities will decrease the impact of the posttenure blues for faculty.

Midcareer faculty can begin to take advantage of their agency and power under the protection of tenure and take on more leadership roles in their committees, groups, or other units that are seeking to conduct research or have an impact on other communities or groups. By doing so, midcareer faculty can help protect early career faculty and serve as role models and mentors. We agree with O'Meara, Terosky, & Neumann, (2008) in arguing for a redefinition of faculty work that moves away from constraint to agency, and where leaders and faculty development specialists need to help faculty

> identify ways to foster, in faculty members, the desire and will to craft themselves as teachers, researchers, and partners in service and community engagement who have actively chosen—and continue actively to choose—the academic career as a way to lead their lives. (p. 19)

Faculty agency is contextual in the social structure that provides privilege and power, such as through granting tenure.

Midcareer faculty are also moving to a more prominent role in student advising, in service in the institution, and in mentorship of early career fac-ulty. Each of these new or more emphasized roles provides an opportunity to engage in or promote public scholarship. Midcareer faculty in their role with undergraduate and graduate student advising may find new opportunities to direct student research or help disseminate that research to reach other publics. For example, a graduate student may be interested in research in community colleges, which leads to meetings at the local college to discuss data collection and to new dissemination venues to reach community college practitioners. Institutional service that provides opportunities to bring in external speakers, engage in service-learning activities, or rethink cocurricular experiences are all additional ways to work with more publics.

For example, Maria received tenure and promotion after her probationary period and reevaluated her public scholar identity and activities, acknowledging that she now has the protection of tenure along with a certain level of academic freedom. Quickly Maria began to increase her social media presence with more direct discourse and advocacy language on how to support low-income college students. She wrote several opinion pieces for local and national newspapers (online and in print) and disseminated that work through her policy network and social media. Working with her college dean, Maria also pursued funding to create a research center and developed a new website with a blog that she updated regularly with the results from her research. Maria also began writing for more practitioner magazines and began attending conferences on academic advising and financial aid to try to work with practitioners to support low-income students. Most important, Maria developed a workshop on financial aid that she and her graduate students began conducting in local high schools and higher education institutions to assist low-income students and families. She is also mentoring several local students to help them get into college. Maria's work from her early-career years continues through her already established networks, but with tenure she has also become more public and more of an advocate.

Late Career

Late career faculty are often at a time of reflection, looking back at their career and determining how their work will sustain itself after retirement. This time of reflection does not preclude late career faculty from introducing public scholarship into their work lives, not does it suggest that late career faculty who are public scholars ramp down that work. Rather, these faculty have additional opportunities to model public scholarship and to set up sustaining structures to support faculty public scholarship in the future.

Late career faculty serve as role models on how to involve publics and extend their definition and role in the publics they reach and serve. For example, late career faculty may make more international efforts, seek to effect change in local communities, use existing relationships across campus, and lead disciplinary societies to consider addressing divides between research and practice. Time in the discipline often leads to more exposure on research and efforts as well as the development of a larger social network to rethink the opportunities and scope of engagement in public scholarship. Late career faculty may consider developing consulting opportunities to become more engaged with policy or advocacy organizations that are related to their areas of expertise. They may also take part in internationalization efforts and lead study abroad experiences for students.

Maria is now a late career faculty member who has achieved success in her research and public scholarship agenda. Although her initial desire to change federal policy to allow Pell Grant awards in the summer was not achieved, she had a positive impact on the lives of many low-income students and families, graduate students, early career faculty, and academic associations. Her efforts in late career have been to establish sustainable institutional funding for her financial aid and mentoring programs with local students. She is also serving as a mentor at her institution and nationally for early career faculty. Maria's work in leadership roles in her academic associations has also called attention to her work and prompted members of these groups to write legal briefs, reports, and policy papers in support of low-income students. Dissemination of her research to a broad audience through the Internet and speaking engagements continues as well as her work with individual colleges and universities in a consulting capacity. Maria has also been working on changing state-level policy with local representatives and senators. Finally, Maria is working to change the tenure and promotion guidelines at her institution to redefine research to be more inclusive of public scholarship.

Conclusion

The overall purpose of this chapter and this book is to explore the idea of public scholarship as a goal and a way to overcome the lack of impact on practice and policy for higher education. We specifically approached this topic by examining the relationship between faculty career stages and engagement in public scholarship. Understanding the potential challenges and barriers associated with various stages of faculty life, we provide concrete ways that faculty at all stages can engage in public research. Although time and space do not allow us to provide a detailed discussion of each recommendation, we are confident that they provide the starting point for those interested in beginning or increasing their engagement in public scholarship. As scholars we understand the importance of engaging with publics to share our knowledge and expertise to benefit citizens in general and those who do not have the capacity or voice to advocate for themselves more specifically. We strongly believe there is no greater time than now to live the words of Boyer (1990), that is, to connect our work in the academy to the social and environmental challenges beyond the campus.

References

Aud, S., Wilkinson-Flicker, S., Kristapovich, P., Rathbun, A., Wang, X., & Zhang, J. (2013). *The Condition of Education 2013* (NCES 2013-037). Retrieved from nces.ed.gov/pubs2013/2013037.pdf

Austin, A. E. (2010). Supporting faculty members across their careers. In K. J. Gillespie, D. L. Robertson, & Associates (Eds.), *A guide to faculty development* (2nd ed., pp. 363–378). San Francisco, CA: Jossey-Bass.

Baldwin, R. G. (1990). Faculty vitality beyond the research university: Extending a contextual concept. *Journal of Higher Education, 61*, 160–180.

Baldwin, R. G., & Blackburn, R. T. (1981). The academic career as a developmental process: Implications for higher education. *Journal of Higher Education, 52*, 598–614.

Baldwin, R., DeZure, D., Shaw, A., & Moretto, K. (2008). Mapping the terrain of mid-career faculty at a research university: Implications for faculty and academic leaders. *Change, 40*(5), 46–55.

Boyer, E. L. (1990). *Scholarship reconsidered: Priorities of the professoriate.* Princeton, NJ: Carnegie Foundation for the Advancement of Teaching.

Colbeck, C. L., & Weaver, L. D. (2008). Faculty engagement in public scholarship: A motivation systems theory perspective. *Journal of Higher Education Outreach and Engagement, 12*(2), 7–32.

Flaherty, C. (2015, October 23). Going through the motions? The 2015 survey of faculty workplace engagement. *Inside Higher Ed.* Retrieved from insidehighered .com/news/survey/going-through-motions-2015-survey-faculty-workplace-engagement

Hall, D. T. (2002). *Careers in and out of organizations.* Thousand Oaks, CA: Sage.

Hurtado, S., & Sharkness, J. (2008). Scholarship is changing, and so must tenure review. *Academe, 94*(5), 37–39.

Kalivoda, P., Sorrell, G. R., & Simpson, R. D. (1994). Nurturing faculty vitality by matching institutional interventions with career-stage needs. *Innovative Higher Education, 18*, 255–272.

Kena, G., Musu-Gillette, L., Robinson, J., Wang, X., Rathbun, A., Zhang, J., . . . Dunlop Velez, E. (2015). *The condition of education 2015* (NCES 2015-144). Retrieved from nces.ed.gov/pubs2015/2015144.pdf

Kezar, A., & Maxey, D. (2014). Faculty matter: So why doesn't everyone think so? *Thought & Action*, 29–44.

Lumpkin, A. (2014). The role of organizational culture on and career stages of faculty. *Educational Forum, 78*, 196–205. doi:10.1080/00131725.2013.878420

Mason, M. A., & Goulden, M. (2004). Marriage and baby blues: Redefining gender equity in the academy. *Annals of the American Academy of Political and Social Science, 596*, 86–103.

Mathews, K. R. (2014). *Perspectives on midcareer faculty and advice for supporting them.* Cambridge, MA: Collaborative on Academic Careers in Higher Education.

O'Meara, K. A. (2004). Beliefs about post-tenure review: The influence of autonomy, collegiality, career stage, and institutional context. *Journal of Higher Education*, *75*, 178–202.

O'Meara, K. (2006). Encouraging multiple forms of scholarship in faculty reward systems: Have academic cultures really changed? *New Directions for Institutional Research*, *129*, 77–95.

O'Meara, K., Terosky, A. L., & Neumann, A. (2008). Faculty careers and work lives: A professional growth perspective. *ASHE Higher Education Report*, *34*(3).

Reddick, R. (2016). Using social media to promote scholarship: Amplify, magnify, clarify. In M. Gasman (Ed.), *Academics going public: How to write and speak beyond academe*. New York, NY: Routledge.

Rhoades, G. (2009). From the general secretary: What we do to our young. *Academe*, *95*(3), 56.

Rice, R. E. (2002). Beyond scholarship reconsidered: Toward an enlarged vision of the scholarly work of faculty members. *New Directions for Teaching and Learning*, 90, 7–18.

Schuster, J. H., & Finkelstein, M. J. (2006). *The restructuring of academic work and careers: The American faculty*. Baltimore, MD: Johns Hopkins University Press.

Slaughter, S., & Rhoades, G. (2004). *Academic capitalism and the new economy: Markets, state, and higher education*. Baltimore, MD: Johns Hopkins University Press.

Terosky, A. L., Gonzales, L. D. (2016). Re-envisioned contributions: Experiences of faculty employed at institutional types that differ from their original aspirations. *Review of Higher Education*, *39*, 241–268.

Trower, C. A. (2011). Senior faculty satisfaction: Perceptions of associate and full professors at seven public research universities. *Research Dialogue*, *101*, 1–15.

Wright, M. (2005). Always at odds? Congruence in faculty beliefs about teaching at a research university. *Journal of Higher Education*, *76*, 331–353.

15

PREPARING HIGHER EDUCATION SCHOLARS TO ENGAGE IN PUBLIC SCHOLARSHIP INSIDE THE BELTWAY

Crossing Cultures, Building Bridges

Lesley McBain

Higher education associations in America are a varied lot. Academic readers may be most familiar with those that tend to be faculty centric, for example, the American Association of University Professors; limited to a subset of institutions, such as the Association of American Universities; or whose membership is restricted to research universities. Others are even more specialized, and their memberships are correspondingly limited, such as disciplinary associations like the Association for the Study of Higher Education.

However, as this chapter discusses, a larger world of American higher education associations offers opportunities for emerging scholars and established campus researchers to conduct public scholarship. This world may seem arcane or distant to campus-based researchers or doctoral students because it is by and large grounded in the physical and political arena of Washington DC. Yet these organizations generate independently distributed public research, policy analysis, and scholarship as part of their missions. They employ research and hire researchers in alternate academic positions to advocate for higher education policy as well as engage in political dialogue with lawmakers and act in coalition with other education advocacy groups.

In addition, they can form partnerships with members of policy think tanks and research institutes.

Why are these higher education associations and their policy research, as well as their advocacy efforts, important to public scholarship? Notwithstanding the valid critiques in chapter 1 regarding their position as elites and gatekeepers, for decades, higher education associations' advocacy, backed by research, has helped shape national higher education policy. Although some higher education associations are more concerned with practice (e.g., American Counseling Personnel Association) than policy, this chapter focuses on those with significant policy research components.

Thus for an academic interested in public scholarship or a doctoral student preparing to deal with the complexities of public scholarship after graduation, this chapter offers a perspective on how these associations conduct and produce public policy research that is more often disseminated in the form of a white paper, fact sheet, or infographic than in academic journals. Suggestions for established academics and doctoral students interested in working with associations on public scholarship are also included. A clearer understanding of this world by higher education researchers and those college and university faculty who, it is hoped, better prepare emerging scholars to accept public scholarship positions help advance the larger goals of public scholarship. This is increasingly important in a contentious and uncertain political climate. As John Walda, chief executive officer and president of the National Association of College and University Business Officers (NACUBO), and a long-time member of institutional boards, observes, "Public scholarship takes on more profound importance [in such a time]" (J. Walda, personal communication, November 9, 2016).

Understanding the World of Associations

The first thing scholars interested in the world of associations as an avenue for public scholarship should understand is that the Washington DC higher education policy advocacy and research community contains hundreds of associations whose memberships are classified as either institutional or individual (Ewing Cook, 1998). Ewing Cook's (1998) classifications encompass associations such as but not limited to the following: institutional researchers, university business officers, public institutions, private nonprofit institutions, and private for-profit institutions. Other independent think tanks and research institutes are also part of this space.

The sector expanded notably in the mid to late 1960s because of the amount of federal education legislation passed at the time (King, 1975). Institutional associations have historically been dominated by "the Six" or the "Big Six," which are the informal nicknames for the six higher education associations based in Washington DC, that individually and collectively represent all nonprofit sectors of higher education (Ewing Cook, 1998).

In alphabetical order, the Six are the American Association of Community Colleges, American Association of State Colleges and Universities, American Council on Education (ACE), Association of American Universities, Association of Public and Land-grant Universities, and the National Association of Independent Colleges and Universities. Higher education institutions may have membership in several of the Six; ACE plays the role of the coordinating or umbrella organization (Harcleroad & Eaton, 2005). However, each individual member of the Six has its own policy agenda, and although the Six conduct independent research on higher education policy, they focus heavily on federal relations, otherwise known as lobbying, on behalf of their members.

The Washington Higher Education Secretariat (WHES), formed in 1962, is an even larger advocacy force for higher education. Its membership incorporates not only members of the Six but also many other associations that Ewing Cook describes as individual membership associations. The WHES is coordinated by ACE and requires as a condition of membership that an association wishing to join "monitors and/or influences policy issues for its members" (WHES, n.d.). Its working committees take on various issues important to its higher education constituents.

Individual membership associations in Ewing Cook's classification, in contrast to the Six or the WHES, focus on those in particular roles (e.g., chief business officers, professors, or members of institutional governing boards) or who are interested in a common issue (e.g., graduate or international education; Ewing Cook, 1998). These individual memberships can be either truly individual (e.g., an individual pays for his or her membership in a disciplinary association) or institutional (e.g., a university pays for membership on behalf of the institution). This not only presents a dizzying array of options for a scholar interested in entering the association world but also complicates higher education advocacy.

In addition, political alliances continually shift among higher education policy stakeholders. What matters most to one single-issue association may be a peripheral part of another association's broad education policy portfolio. As associations respond to *policy windows*, defined by Kingdon (2003) as "opportunities for actions on given initiatives" (p. 166), they may become allies or divide over the initiatives' potential effect on particular sectors or subsectors. Further, as Parsons (1997) explains, these alliances are grounded in established, yet disputed, principles guiding federal interest in higher education as well as continually changing conflicts related to debates regarding that interest. Such alliances and tensions can also create or dissolve research partnerships.

In responding to policy windows, various association stakeholders can create what Roe (1994) refers to as *policy narratives*, the dominant stories (or narratives) that stakeholders use to establish and fix policy-making assumptions on particularly complex and contentious policy issues. These stories resist change even in the face of contradictory empirical data,, which can be supplied by public scholars, because they have become integral to decision makers' assumptions (Roe, 1994).

Why does this happen, and why are these stories so important not only to policy making but also to public scholarship? Because, as Roe (1994) stated,

> Many public policy issues have become so uncertain, complex, and polarized . . . that the only things left to examine are the different stories policymakers and their critics use to articulate and make sense of that uncertainty, complexity, and polarization. (p. 3)

But research and empirical data and public scholarship can be used to correct policymakers' anecdotal misperceptions of higher education and change Roe's (1994) narratives.

Hence, this complicated, sometimes volatile, world presents opportunities for emerging scholars to conduct public scholarship by offering research employment outside the ever shrinking tenure-track faculty job market. It also offers the chance for established campus-based researchers to work with association researchers to conduct public scholarship. In addition, depending on the association's mission and capacity, researchers may also work on research grant projects funded by federal or nonprofit entities. However, at present much of association research is often culturally and logistically very different from the university research world, even if associations' and universities' public scholarship research goals may be similar.

Comparing Academic and Policy Public Scholarship

The differences in working in the association and policy worlds are important to understand. This section points out some of these differences as well as opportunities in association research.

Mission and Goals

According to Bill Dillon, executive vice president of NACUBO, the major difference between public scholarship in the association world versus the university world is that "public scholarship in the association world is limited by the mission and goals defined by each association's membership. Much of this scholarship can benefit public entities but that is usually not its primary purpose" (B. Dillon, personal communication, December 19, 2016). An inherent tension exists between serving members' interests (including advocacy and providing professional development programs, data, and research that benefit their day-to-day work) and contributing to broader public scholarship. As associations have responded over time to the changing national higher education environment, and in the case of university and college presidents' associations, as the public role of college presidents has changed, balancing the public good and member needs has shifted back and forth depending on the association. Researchers who work at or with associations navigate this tension according to their individual ethical compasses.

Dillon's point is echoed by Jonathan Gagliardi, associate director of ACE's Center for Policy Research and Strategy. He said that the need to provide research that is valuable to association members "force[s] you to frame difficult [topics] in ways that are politically savvy and that can be translated by distinct audiences in their own ways" (J. Gagliardi, personal communication, December 19, 2016). This means the research is framed to also make it readable, accessible, and persuasive. Although this focus on messaging and framing and politics may seem distasteful or alien, it is now crucial to effective public scholarship in the fast-paced realpolitik world in which associations currently operate. Congressional staffers and association lobbyists do not have the time or training to wade through a regression analysis or conduct literature reviews; they expect association researchers to translate research into easily understood data points they can use to inform policy. A well-crafted infographic or PowerPoint slide with selected data points can be taken to a Capitol Hill meeting for immediate impact; the journal article or long white paper the data are drawn from are less effective for advocacy.

Also, the reality is that association members pay dues for services that include research specific to their policy and practice needs. These needs can simultaneously serve a public good and a narrower member benefit. However, the tension between the public good writ large and the necessity to conduct research that members can use to achieve policy and practice goals (which, to further complicate the dynamic, can serve the public good) is one that association researchers must navigate. This often has to do with a particular aspect of institutional stewardship as Dillon explains in the following:

> For example, the National Association of College and University Business Officers has studied endowment management practices at colleges and universities for over three decades. While the results may help inform public policy regarding spending policies and other matters of public interest,

the primary objective is to assist institutional members with endowment management practices. This is also the case with research into tuition discounting practices, profiling higher education business officers and other similar efforts. (B. Dillon, December 19, 2016, personal communication)

To put this in an academic context, association members are the equivalent of grant funders, and their needs, goals, and missions set the grant requirements that pay an association researcher's salary. An association researcher therefore must conduct research on a wide variety of topics related to an individual association's needs and may have to sign conflict-of-interest paperwork as a part of employment. This may raise ethical issues for particular researchers so they should clearly understand how associations operate before they commit to working with them.

Timing

Another important difference pointed out by Muriel Howard, president of the American Association of State Colleges and Universities, is that "there is a short window to conduct the research and a short window to analyze and report research especially in today's climate. Change is occurring so fast that long-term research projects may not seem valuable or useful upon completion" (M. Howard, personal communication, January 4, 2017). This means association researchers are required to work quickly and accurately on short-term projects using secondary data analyses or conduct surveys that go from design to data collection to analysis to final publication in a matter of months rather than years.

In addition, as Howard alludes to, association researchers can be asked to conduct topical research even more rapidly. For example, research on how a proposed piece of legislation might affect an association's membership may require advocacy staff to inform key congressional stakeholders about its impact in days or even hours. Yet this type of research combines public scholarship and the needs of an association employer.

Association-Driven Topics

Although a researcher can find ways to generate public scholarship based on an individual dissertation topic or areas of scholarly interest related to an association employer, it is harder, although not impossible, to generate public scholarship based on unrelated research interests. That research may have to be done in off hours and may be subject to conflict of interest policies. Functioning as an independent scholar outside a full-time job can be challenging. However, given declining immediate postgraduation employment for PhDs in all areas over time (National Science Foundation, 2015) and fewer tenure-track jobs for emerging scholars, support structures including associations for independent scholars (e.g., the National Coalition of Independent Scholars [NCIS]) are increasing. A researcher can also make the case to her or his association employer that an area of interest has the potential to benefit the public good and the association's members. Although this is not guaranteed (particularly if the association is narrowly focused), the possibility exists.

Opportunities

Despite the previously mentioned restrictions such as conflict of interest policies, the higher education association world offers opportunities for public scholarship including full-time employment possibilities for newer researchers, partnership opportunities for more established academics, and publishing of white papers or reports that are circulated more rapidly and broadly than peer-reviewed journal articles. According to ACE (n.d.), the "CPRS produces papers, issue briefs, and convenings that provide stakeholders with acute insight, rigorous analysis, and on-the-ground application" (para. 2). Other associations produce similar analyses and reports. Researchers thus have opportunities to personally benefit and to see their research used for a public good (e.g., advancing educational access and equity issues). Conducting research at an association can also potentially lead to becoming an expert resource for the media, further advancing public scholarship by enabling the researcher to communicate with the public. In terms of shaping an association's overall research agenda, Walda said, "One of the key things researchers can do is help associations think proactively about research, new ways to analyze a message or data. Projects are often couched defensively [because we are] trying to combat misperceptions." He also suggested the creation of a "cross-association, proactive research agenda designed to tell a data-backed story about the work we do," noting that NACUBO works with other associations that represent administrative offices on campuses to conduct research on common interests. Finally, he added, "The goal I like to promote and employ is to provide more factual information that underscores the work we do and the contribution of our institutions to the community" (J. Walda, personal communication, November 9, 2016).

Better Preparing Higher Education Researchers for Public Scholarship in the Association World

The Washington DC higher education association world may not appeal to every higher education researcher, whether emerging or established, as an avenue for public scholarship because of the structural differences described here and other political and methodological criticisms noted in chapter 1. But in view of the diminishing tenure-track faculty jobs over time, not all emerging scholars will obtain a full-time tenure-track faculty position immediately after graduation. Thus encouraging students to broaden their horizons and prepare themselves for the possibility of conducting higher education research in these associations can be part of public scholarship.

The following suggestions on how newer researchers can better prepare themselves to build bridges with the association world and do meaningful research might also assist emerging scholars in preparing for other alternate academic careers in which they can engage in public scholarship. They additionally address some ways campus faculty can form partnerships with associations to create public scholarship.

Get Practical Experience While in a Doctoral Program

Everyone interviewed for this chapter focused on the importance of practical experience for emerging scholars interested in the association world. This experience can range from campus jobs to policy-focused internships or large grant projects in which students can hone their project management and research skills. For instance, when asked about better preparation in doctoral programs for those interested in the Washington DC policy world, Howard suggested the following:

> I would provide students with an internship experience. I have had a number of doctoral students shadow me but the ones that are able to spend at least eight weeks working and shadowing in the organization, with some independent and/or team assignments to work on, seem to gain a better insight into associations, their mission and work. (M. Howard, personal communication, January 4, 2017)

Dillon added,

> Doctoral training should include multiple field experiences where the candidate doesn't just study policies and practices but actually works to implement them in real-life circumstances. The experiences should at a minimum require the student to: communicate complex concepts to diverse members of the public; lead change without authority; and practice the art of compromise to achieve practical results. A critical element of this experiential learning should be near continuous 360-degree feedback. (B. Dillon, personal communication, December 19, 2016)

Seek Interdisciplinary Experiences While in a Doctoral Program

Setting agendas for higher education policy focuses on higher education structures (e.g., accreditation policy) and specific policy issues from various academic disciplines (e.g., science, technology, engineering, and mathematics and technology transfer policy). In addition, researchers at broader-based associations such as those representing a higher education sector will be expected to develop at least a smattering of expertise outside their dissertation topic. Thus, emerging scholars interested in public scholarship inside the Beltway should take advantage of opportunities available to them for interdisciplinary study or experiences.

This suggestion was reinforced by Walda, who said, "I'm impressed when I see interdepartmental curricula designed [at institutions of higher education]. One example is the School of Public and Environmental Affairs at Indiana University—their interdepartmental culture, their skilled research and experts and messaging and public support, their academic collaboration" (J. Walda, personal communication, November 9, 2016).

Understand How to Write and Communicate Ideas for the Policy Audience

Although social media and other ways of communicating with multiple audiences as a public scholar are also covered in chapter 10, association work requires a different style of writing from a traditional academic article submitted to a journal. Gagliardi said that if he could change general preparation for doctoral students to better fit them to work inside the Beltway,

> I'd better prepare doctoral students to be ready to translate their academic voices into policy voices. Too often they come to DC and it takes them a long time to figure out what their policy voice is. Many lack the common touch, and often default to jargon and methodology when the reality is that it needs to be broken down into simpler terms. (J. Gagliardi, personal communication, December 19, 2016)

Where Association Researchers and University Researchers Intersect

Established campus researchers also have the opportunity to build public scholarship bridges between the association research world and the university research world. A few ways they can do so are presented next.

Investigate Existing Campus Memberships/Involvement in Associations

A large university most likely belongs to more associations than a smaller institution, but even a small campus has possibilities ranging from large associations (e.g., the Big Six or the WHES) to more specific focus areas (e.g., financial aid professionals). Some campus leaders list their association memberships in website biographies, particularly if they serve on association boards or committees. Speaking with them about their association work can give a campus researcher valuable information about the potential fit between their research and the association's work as well as possibilities for further engagement.

Identify Avenues for Engaging With Association Members and Researchers

Some associations issue a call for proposals for their annual meetings or smaller conferences. Thus, a campus researcher might submit a proposal alone or work with another professional on campus involved with the association in question. For example, a faculty member researching student affairs topics could work with a student affairs officer to submit a proposal to a student affairs conference). Association researchers also work with their members on research, so creating relationships among campus researchers, members on campus, and association researchers can build a bridge between the two arenas.

Identify Associations of Interest's Guidelines

Some higher education associations publish magazines, books, and reports. Depending on researchers' interests and the association, pitching a magazine article or book proposal can get their work into the hands of a different public from an academic journal audience.

Identify Researchers or Current Research Projects

Finding a researcher at an association or a current research project depends on a scholar's interests and particular associations because research functions and staff sizes vary widely. However, an outside scholar, as suggested by Walda, can help associations think more proactively and less defensively about data and research, challenge current orthodoxies, and create new public scholarship. One such example of research collaboration is the Council of Independent Colleges' report on changes in faculty composition at their member institutions, written by three faculty members and supported by the

Lumina Foundation as part of a larger project on the future of independent institutions (Morphew, Ward, & Wolf-Wendel, 2016).

Conclusion

The higher education association world and its work in higher education policy is relatively opaque for higher education scholars because it operates largely inside the Beltway and focuses on producing research and other material geared toward higher education policymakers rather than academic research. It can also be criticized, as the editors of this volume do in chapter 1, for gatekeeping and elitism. However, it can be a potentially fruitful public scholarship avenue for emerging and established scholars.

References

American Council on Education. (n.d.). *Center for Policy Research and Strategy*. Retrieved from www.acenet.edu/news-room/Pages/Center-for-Policy-Research-and-Strategy.aspx

Ewing Cook, C. (1998). *Lobbying for higher education: How colleges and universities influence federal policy*. Nashville, TN: Vanderbilt University Press.

Harcleroad, F. F., & Eaton, J. S. (2005). The hidden hand: External constituencies and their impact. In P. G. Altbach, P. J. Gumport, & R. O. Berdahl (Eds.), *American higher education in the twenty-first century: Social, political, and economic challenges* (pp. 253–283). Baltimore, MD: Johns Hopkins University Press.

King, L. R. (1975). *The Washington lobbyists for higher education*. Lanham, MD: Lexington Books.

Kingdon, J. W. (2003). *Agendas, alternatives, and public policies* (2nd ed.). New York, NY: Longman.

Morphew, C., Ward, K., & Wolf-Wendel, L. (2016). *Changes in faculty composition at independent colleges: A report for the Council of Independent Colleges (CIC)*. Washington, DC: Council of Independent Colleges.

National Science Foundation. (2015). *Doctorate recipients from U.S. universities*. Retrieved from www.nsf.gov/statistics/2016/nsf16300/digest/nsf16300.pdf

Parsons, M. D. (1997). *Power and politics: Federal higher education policymaking in the 1990s*. Albany, NY: SUNY Press.

Roe, E. (1994). *Narrative policy analysis: Theory and practice*. Durham, NC: Duke University Press.

Washington Higher Education Secretariat. (n.d.). *About us*. Retrieved from whes.org/index.html

16

PUBLIC SCHOLARSHIP

An Invitation, a Final Example, and
a Summary of Key Themes

Adrianna Kezar, Zoë Corwin, Joseph A. Kitchen, and Yianna Drivalas

This volume defines *public scholarship*, explores the ethical considerations behind this work, and provides examples of what public scholarship might look like from researchers using different approaches, methods, and modes of engagement. The preceding chapters recount public research conducted by scholars at different points in their careers and across different types of institutions and suggest ways to integrate and prioritize this work for current and future higher education researchers. Each contributor has his or her own way of making sense of public scholarship and engaging with it as best fits each one's expertise, methods, research questions, and level of comfort and familiarity. We hope our readers are able to engage in public scholarship by altering how they teach writing in their graduate courses, adding community members to research teams, involving and aligning themselves with current social movements, working in partnership with policy organizations, or taking another approach that best suits their research.

To close this volume, we want to highlight an important initiative we are all involved with at the Pullias Center for Higher Education at the University of Southern California's (USC) Rossier School of Education. This initiative, called Ensuring Just Higher Education, is public scholarship in direct response to the election of Donald J. Trump as president of the United States and the detrimental changes in campus climates that have since transpired. Each component of the project aims to resist the many policy initiatives he and his administration have proposed, each of which would fundamentally and negatively alter higher education and affect many of its varied stakeholders. The response of our center is mainly aimed at supporting students under the Deferred Action for Childhood Arrivals (DACA) immigration policy;

international, Muslim, or other religious minority students; and lesbian, gay, bisexual, transgender, and queer (LGBTQ) students who may now feel that college campuses and the United States, whether it is their nation of origin or otherwise, are no longer safe for them. As part of this initiative, we examine what it means for universities to serve as places of sanctuary and address larger federal policy issues, including the Higher Education Reauthorization Act and the potential for repealing DACA.

The work conducted as part of this initiative synthesizes and exemplifies many of the concepts authors have presented throughout the book. We begin by describing the Ensuring Just Higher Education project and how the Pullias Center conceptualized, organized, and executed the project plans. We then summarize key themes from across the chapters and explain how the themes are represented in the Ensuring Just Higher Education project. We hope that this chapter excites and invites you into the realm of public scholarship.

Social Justice, Federal Policy, and University Climate: The Pullias Center's Response

In the fall of 2016, Pullias Center faculty recognized a tangible change in climate at USC. Because of the political rhetoric targeting undocumented immigrants and religious minorities, students expressed to faculty their feelings of fear and high levels of anxiety. In addition, our home school, the Rossier School of Education, had been grappling with the desecration of a series of Black Lives Matter posters in the building hallways. We noticed a heaviness among faculty, students, and staff, many of whom expressed concern over the uncertainty of the future.

We decided to hold an emergency town hall meeting to present concerns, lend support to each other, and determine a plan for moving forward. Of the 31 people affiliated with the Pullias Center, almost our entire group of faculty, staff, and graduate students attended. In a basement classroom, squeezed into student desks, we formed an awkwardly shaped circle and spent a focused two hours brainstorming action items. This meeting resulted in the creation of an important public scholarship project: Ensuring Just Higher Education.

Our approach was to capitalize on the strengths of the Pullias Center in terms of content expertise and our ability to disseminate scholarship and think pieces to a broad audience. As a research center with only limited community connections, we knew we were not well equipped to directly provide services to communities in need. However, we could share information and help inform practice and policies. Within a period of several months, we were able to produce and disseminate the following products:

- *The University as a Sanctuary* (Pullias Center for Higher Education, 2017d), which highlights the complexity of the term *sanctuary*, discusses who should take leadership on fostering safe spaces on campuses, and offers 10 statements to guide an institution's legal and instrumental approaches to creating sanctuary environments;
- *Understanding DACA and the Implications for Higher Education* (Pullias Center for Higher Education, 2017e), which chronicles the history of DACA, defines terms, lists resources for individuals, suggests principles to guide universities' approaches to supporting DACA students, and includes a one-page infographic shared widely online;
- a memo to Secretary of Education Betsy DeVos (2017b) that expressed concern for the future of scholarly research and delineates five educational priorities to guide the Department of Education's approach to educational policy;
- a memo to Higher Education Taskforce Chair, Jerry Falwell Jr. (2017a), signed by the directors of higher education research centers across the country, that names seven critical challenges confronting higher education in the United States and underscores the importance of promoting academic freedom and free inquiry, institutional autonomy, and the distinctive roles of federal government, state government, and accrediting agencies;
- My Higher Ed Story (myhigheredstory.org), a blog that presents stories of students from historically marginalized communities in U.S. postsecondary institutions to educate policymakers, postsecondary administrators, and the general public about the varied experiences faced by students and thus to inform practice and policy; and
- a grant through the Bringing Theory to Practice program supported by the S. Engleman Center in partnership with the Association of American Colleges & Universities that supports a series of campus dialogues on the concept of understanding the university as a sanctuary; we have held 4 dialogues with more than 100 university stakeholders and are in the process of developing an action agenda to share with USC administrators and the field of higher education.

To ensure that the public scholarship we released was high quality, effective, and appropriately timed (i.e., came out quickly), we were guided by the following principles: identify, understand, and engage audiences and collaborate with stakeholders; capitalize on strengths; and create accessible and multiple research products. We also bore in mind the challenges associated with working in public scholarship as well as the opportunity to use this project to socialize graduate students involved in the initiative to public scholarship, which we elaborate on in the following summary of the book's themes.

Identify, Understand, and Engage Audiences and Stakeholders

Because many iterations of public scholarship exist, and because different arenas permit greater or lesser direct involvement with various communities, public scholarship may manifest itself across a spectrum of stakeholder engagement. As stated in chapter 1, we subscribe to an understanding of public scholarship as a continuum of levels of engagement with more or less engagement between researchers and the communities that provide the research material. All public scholarship has the intention of involvement with and support of the communities involved, but the work can vary on degree of mutual engagement. The contributors to this volume emphasize that it is important for the public scholar to involve stakeholders so they might share in the benefits of inquiry and discovery. Where a form of public scholarship falls along the spectrum is less about the mode of dissemination or the vehicle (e.g., policy brief, blog post) but more about the degree to which the work is mutually beneficial. We do not assume that some research is better or more important than other research simply based on where it falls on the public scholarship continuum. Different research questions and methodologies lend themselves to varying modes of public scholarship as do access to communities and sites, the vulnerability of certain populations, and so on. As Hurtado said in her chapter, her work is done "on behalf of marginalized communities, along with diverse communities, and in collaboration with those servants of the public good or the institutions intending to serve diverse communities" (p. 54). Finally, Sam and Gupton offer an insightful reminder to those reading this book that scholars engaging with their publics are not only sharing their knowledge with the public but are also learning from the knowledge, concerns, and values the public has to share.

The contributors to this volume engage their publics in various ways. For Dache-Gerbino, engagement happens in the classroom, in her research, and in her daily life as an activist in which stakeholders are organically part of the public scholarship process. Mull, Daniel, and Jordan describe the ways cooperative extension scholars are very intentional in stakeholder identification and engagement to solve community problems. These scholars are embedded in their communities and with their stakeholders working with agricultural staff, for example, as part of their research on an ongoing basis. Nehls and colleagues identify policymakers as their target audience and revised the writing and products they produced to reach their audience to inform decision-making on policies. Davis and colleagues and Bensimon describe collaboration in their research centers to develop tools as well as their work with communities to receive feedback on their center's publications and tools. Iloh uses social media as a platform to congregate with other scholars and find new and appropriate channels to disseminate her work. This is important to public scholarship because it creates another opportunity to find and work with communities that would benefit from research findings and that may be potential collaborators in the future. Iloh describes how this is especially important to underrepresented scholars, creating a platform for recognition that other outlets have not historically offered.

The contributors describe how collaboration among researchers and colleagues enhances public scholarship's impact, which is a key reason for additional levels of engagement. The impact of the Pullias Center's Ensuring Just Higher Education project will be measured by the extent to which audiences and stakeholders use the work. If our target audiences do not use our work, then we would have essentially wasted a lot of time for little more than practice. Although we cannot control the extent to which people apply our materials, we can ensure we have done everything we can to get public scholarship in the right hands and make it accessible in terms of comprehensible writing and different research products. Every public scholarship project will be different because the form it takes is dependent on many factors, as mentioned throughout this volume.

Historically, Pullias Center work has focused extensively on identifying and engaging stakeholders. Pullias Centers electronic mailing lists and outreach practices target leaders in the higher education community who include a diverse range of scholars, funders, and practitioners. When creating the public scholarship pieces as part of the Ensuring Just Higher Education project, we aimed to expand beyond the center's usual audiences to reach audiences important to supporting DACA, international, Muslim, and LGBTQ students. We intentionally did not take a combative tone in any of the publications that would give anyone a reason to turn away and discredit our work. Instead, publications were constructed to be accessible to conservatives and progressives alike, with a goal of informing practice and policy. For the campus dialogues, we at the center were very intentional about inviting participants from diverse stakeholder groups across the university to include faculty, staff, and student perspectives. Researchers seeking to similarly bring in members outside their own communities may consider making contact with community organizers, faculty from different departments, or others whose interests are aligned and whose audiences and contacts would benefit from contributing to or receiving this work.

As part of this initiative, the Pullias Center for Higher Education released a series of multimedia documents in response to the changing campus climate at USC and across other institutions. Some documents, such as those describing DACA and the university as sanctuary are static; they are based on research and have been well disseminated online and in other venues, but they are on the less mutually engaged end of the public scholarship spectrum. Conversely, the qualitative website My Higher Ed Story (Pullias Center for Higher Education, 2017c) is representative of more mutually engaged work. Members of the Pullias Center collected short narratives from underrepresented students and faculty across the country to create a tapestry of lived experiences that demonstrate the urgency of the dangers surrounding proposed changes to higher education and social and economic policy. My Higher Ed Story is updated as more narratives are collected, allowing members of collegiate communities to participate, giving them access to a wider audience than usual. The end product is just as relevant to how public scholarship takes place as the process.

Capitalize on Strengths

Many of the contributors mention working from or capitalizing on strengths. For example, Bensimon worked as a community organizer and drew from that experience to develop the Center for Urban Education, which uses the Equity Scorecard tool to address racism in postsecondary institutions. Her background as a community organizer and related skill set help her understand how to interact with different stakeholders on campus and advocate on issues of equity. Bensimon also describes involving strategic collaborators to enhance the strengths brought to a project such as Robert Rueda and Donald Polkinghorne, who have expertise in educational psychology, and Alicia Dowd, who has expertise in tool making. Kezar reviews how she also built on her strengths from long-time connections in the Washington DC policy community to create a network for the Delphi Project on the Changing Faculty and Student Success. She also used these long-standing relationships to create a partnership with the Association of American Colleges & Universities. Iloh calls on younger scholars and scholars savvy in social media to capitalize on this strength to make a larger impact across different types of communities that are linked to the Internet. Clark-Taylor and colleagues provide examples of scholars building from their own experiences to develop research agendas for public scholarship. They note how a scholar's own experiences can provide strength and insight to create public scholarship, whether an experience is racial discrimination, innovative forms of teaching and learning, lack of indigenous curricular content, positive mentoring, democratic leadership practices, or sexual harassment.

As part of Ensuring Just Higher Education, we provided an opportunity for people to volunteer to contribute to an area (or two) of the initiative. This approach allowed us to move quickly in creating public scholarship because we delegated work based on expertise and strengths: the memos and reports relied on content knowledge and policy experience, the blog drew on qualitative researchers' confidence in the power of storytelling to effect change, and the campus dialogues reflected the center's ability to collect and analyze focus group data to identify larger themes. Furthermore, we made use of Pullias team members' skill sets. Diane Flores, Pullias's front-end administrator, kept impeccable track of the people invited to contribute to written pieces or attend events. Her masterful follow-up and organizational skills were efficient and critical in ensuring the success of our efforts. Our efforts to publicize scholarship in a way that is accessible to the public would have not been possible without the skill sets of our undergraduate student workers, Phoenix Campos, Maria Ballon, and Myranda Montez. Campos spent hours programming and curating the blog. Monica Raad, the center's administrative project manager, oversaw the successful fruition of all the varied projects from managing the student workers to fielding countless questions from contributors to developing a public relations plan.

Multitude of Accessible Research Products

Public scholarship research products described in the preceding chapters were broadly conceived, and they are often framed as a public coproduction. Some chapters recounted what might be considered more tangible forms of public scholarship research products (e.g., journal publications or social media posts), whereas other scholars described less tangible, but equally valid, forms of research products (e.g., solved community problems, changed minds, community networks). Research products are a crucial area to consider in the realm of public scholarship because they represent the fruits of one's labor; they are the artifacts that signal whether the public scholarship is achieving the intended aims and objectives. Thus, research products are a critical measure to consider when evaluating the impact of one's efforts as a public scholar. The variety of public scholarship products described in this book is notable because it demonstrates that one does not have to rely on a single type of product to be a successful public scholar.

Lanford and Tierney's chapter contends that one of the primary barriers to understanding and developing trust between the university and scholars and the public is rooted in the university's or scholars' inability to effectively communicate the value of their work to broader audiences outside academe such as politicians, journalists, and other constituencies. They make the important argument that public scholarship, particularly communicated in an accessible manner, helps to convey the value of scholarly work to public constituencies. Building trust and understanding between the two rather than writing solely for one's peers in the academy is vital. We contend that it can be a both-and situation in which one can feasibly communicate research products to peers in academe and to the publics we serve. We simply must be intentional in the way we create products with our audiences in mind. Kezar's chapter describes how she has balanced serving both audiences by creating different written products from each research study, one written for other scholars and the other written for practitioners and policymakers throughout her career. Scholars involved in public research do not have to limit themselves to any one venue to communicate the product of their work; rather, the choice of venues are limitless, and the same work can be communicated in multiple ways (e.g., publication, social media, infographics, etc.). By effectively communicating public research products, strong bonds can be formed between scholars and the community, leading them to see each other as partners working together to solve problems.

Beyond traditional academic journals, Lanford and Tierney discuss communicating research to the public in magazines, newspapers, and other similar publications, all tangible forms of public research scholarship. Sam and Gupton add that one can share research findings from public scholarship through opinion pieces, policy briefs, grant applications that support local communities, and public practitioner-focused forums. Davis, Harper, and Smith similarly assert that in an ideal world, public research should be able to be translated into multiple formats to ensure wide accessibility and dissemination including reports, policy briefs, essays, infographics, and films.

Many of the chapter contributors also described less tangible products of public scholarship. Mull, Daniel, and Jordan describe one such product of public scholarship: the exchange and transference of knowledge between the public scholar (cooperative extension systems) and the publics they serve (farmers and agricultural workers). They emphasize that knowledge is learned in communities, not given to communities, which suggests that cocreation of knowledge is a product of public scholarship. Nehls and colleagues present a case study in which the product of their public research was creating a new model that could be adopted by other communities in becoming involved in a policy-making process that is more directly informed by research that could produce a progressive change in thinking, policy, and social norms.

The Pullias Center's Ensuring Just Higher Education project has resulted in many forms of public scholarship products. Consistent with the purpose of public scholarship, these products were designed to help inform practices and policies to support social justice and educational equity. Mirroring many of the products described in the preceding chapters, the initiative produced tangible research products that were disseminated through a variety of mediums including a think piece on the university as a sanctuary, an online blog where students from marginalized communities share their stories, and a DACA resource document and infographic. A number of products were aimed at informing progressive changes in thinking among policymakers. The center's initiative produced memos sent to powerful national leaders in education stressing educational priorities in an effort to inform education policy and describing the importance of the values we hold including academic freedom, free inquiry, and institutional autonomy. The center also successfully pursued a grant to fund campus dialogues about the university as sanctuary. These several products were intermediate steps working toward the ultimate less-tangible product goal: changed hearts and minds and convincing others of the value of our commitments and ideas.

Challenges and Wariness to Do the Work

Sometimes wariness to engage in public scholarship may present real challenges to the public scholar and the various publics that are involved in public scholarship. Scholars face challenges such as scrutiny over the value of public scholarship that may not result in products valued by traditional academic structures (e.g., tenure process). Publics may be reluctant to work with a scholar and may be wary of scholars' intentions. Despite the potential challenges one might face, we argue that the potential benefits of engaging in public scholarship far outweigh the challenges.

Lester and Horton, Clark-Taylor and colleagues, and Iloh raise a common concern about conducting public scholarship: It is often not recognized in current rewards structures for faculty, and sometimes these structures even undermine efforts to do this work. Clark-Taylor and colleagues call on leadership to take a feature role in encouraging and rewarding faculty and students engaged in public scholarship. Lester and Horton's chapter similarly calls on institutions and academic communities to incorporate the value of public scholarship into decisions on faculty promotion, awards, and rewards. Davis and colleagues answer those who are wary to engage in public scholarship with a call to reimagine our commitments as scholars and to remember the purposes of our work as a way to restore agency to the researcher and to the communities the scholarship intends to serve. They don't advocate doing away with traditionally valued forms of research products, they simply make an appeal to consider the value of scholarship in its many forms.

Hurtado's chapter argues convincingly that there is value in engaging in public scholarship beyond some of the traditional notions of rewards. She describes engagement in public scholarship as a way to satiate one's purpose in life; someone may not know the impact of public scholarship immediately, and there may be no immediate reward, but it can fulfill a person's sense of purpose. The Clark-Taylor and colleagues' chapter offers a philosophy emphasizing the role of the university and its scholars in serving the public good, recognizing personal responsibility for communities we belong to, which in turn nurtures growth and development in the scholars themselves. Mull and colleagues' chapter also highlights the role of faculty in public scholarship and appeals to faculty's sense of wonder, determination, and leadership in efforts to promote a better society and to help people solve their problems. Similarly, Lester and Horton's chapter notes that faculty are often motivated to seek progress in their communities through their work and may feel a responsibility to apply their knowledge toward societal progress. Intrinsic rewards, such as finding a purpose in one's work, can serve as a motivator to faculty in their efforts to improve society and engage in public scholarship. Lester and Horton argue that extrinsic rewards (e.g., tenure, evaluation) can detract from efforts to engage in public scholarship. Difficulty in integrating public scholarship into the three traditional spheres of faculty work (teaching, research, and service), can sometimes act as a bulwark in this work. They argue that it is important for public scholars to believe in the value of their work themselves, which can in turn serve as a source of motivation and inspiration to continue doing it in the face of discouraging messages.

Public scholarship is a two-way process that involves the scholar and their publics. It is noteworthy that in engaging in public scholarship, the public might also be wary, or stakeholders might experience difficulty in facing the truths uncovered by the public research process. Bensimon's chapter recounts the difficulty some individuals may face when confronted with the reality that their institution might be engaged in practices that place certain student groups at a disadvantage and may be perpetuating institutionalized racism. This truth may be difficult for stakeholders to face and may pose a challenge for researchers to communicate. Others such as Sam and Gupton acknowledge that although scholars may wish to address a problem in a community, they may encounter resistance from the public because of general mistrust of the scholar's intentions or because of prior work between researchers and the community that did little to solve problems or promote positive change despite what the publics or stakeholders may have been promised. This calls attention to the essential and primary responsibility of the researcher to the communities, the need to create co-ownership of the work, and to promote community acceptance and share in the benefits of public scholarship products.

The wariness on the part of scholars should not impede efforts to engage in public scholarship. Bensimon's chapter discusses the "seductiveness of the life of the mind and the privileges enjoyed by professors at research universities" (p. 81). Resisting complacency in traditional academic work and deliberately seeking opportunities to engage in public scholarship require intentionality on the part of the scholar. The information exchanged through public scholarship is too vital to societal change and progress to be left unaccounted for and avoided in favor of the comfort found in traditional academic spaces.

In the end, all the contributors to this volume suggest that those who are engaged in public scholarship must embrace the benefits and challenges of engaging in this work knowing that it serves a greater and essential purpose. This was a guiding notion for the Pullias Center initiative, to create change and proactively address challenges facing higher education in light of recent sociopolitical developments, enduring challenges, and desiring to celebrate achievements. Some of the students and staff involved in the initiative were wary about engaging in this work. Many are Hispanic (some undocumented), Muslim, international, or LGBTQ, which was a motivator that propelled their involvement in the first place. However, their involvement came with risks. Many of these individuals, from minoritized, marginalized, or oppressed groups, were fearful about retribution from powerful groups. Ultimately, the sense of shared common purpose, support from colleagues, and the sense of camaraderie working toward shared goals in the project strengthened their resolve to move forward with participation.

Learning About Public Scholarship: Socialization and Graduate Education

A variety of chapters examined how we might rethink graduate education to better socialize students to public scholarship. A very underrecognized area in discussions of graduate education that is so pivotal to altering the culture and structure of programs is modeling and mentoring as part of graduate student socialization, as suggested by Clark-Taylor, Sarubbi, Marquez Kiyama, and Waterman. Public scholarship is not learned passively or simply through conversation. Lanford and Tierney describe active engagement in learning new modes of writing. McBain also describes drawing students into internships or work with association and policy groups as a way to be mentored. Many students will not be fortunate enough to have been a community organizer like Bensimon, so they need a way to acquire the skills of stakeholder identification, community engagement, and new ways of writing and problem-solving while in graduate school. Creating online mentoring spaces is another way for graduate students to learn about public scholarship even if their own program may not offer opportunities, or they can be spaces that complement service-learning, community scholarship, and internships.

Socialization is also accompanied by values that underlie the public scholarship approach. Clark-Taylor and colleagues described their commitment to feminist standpoint theory and notions of intersectionality where class, race, sexual orientation, and gender are crucial for positioning oneself as a public scholar. These frameworks are important to understand our own perspectives and commitments, perhaps even challenging us to examine more issues affecting equity and a better understanding of oppression. We encourage grounding public scholarship in frameworks that acknowledge power dynamics inherent in society, such as critical race theory, noted in Bensimon's chapter, as well as indigenous perspectives, which are often overlooked. We need more opportunities for students to reflect on their positionality and to develop the commitments to public scholarship most aligned with these commitments.

McBain's chapter describes another important idea, that of gaining interdisciplinary training to think about problems in more complex ways. This point about interdisciplinary learning is touched on by other contributors as important for expanding students' theoretical repertoires so that they may see problems as practitioners and policymakers see the world, less bound by specific disciplines. As we rethink our curricula, providing opportunities to think in interdisciplinary ways is important within and across courses. Although not all programs may be able to offer interdisciplinary courses, they can provide freedom and opportunity for students to craft curricular plans to take courses in other units to develop this expertise. We encourage graduate students to also seek interdisciplinary course work across universities to build this expertise.

One of the most repeated themes was the importance of learning to write for practitioner and policy audiences, to write shorter and more accessible pieces in formats different from journal articles as McBain and Kezar implore. Lanford and Tierney not only note the need for opportunities to write in different ways but also suggest that such writing requires a different understanding of the writing process itself, a sociocultural approach that honors the way language and communication manifest themselves in different communities. Moreover, to reach these communities requires an understanding of their different approaches to communication. Learning to communicate effectively through writing could result from a seminar where students practice writing for many stakeholders, getting peer reviews and feedback from practitioners and policymakers and working with technologies, particularly social media.

Although many recommendations focus on rethinking graduate education, several chapters also addressed how scholars socialized in traditional research methods might learn public scholarship. Hurtado's, Kezar's, and Bensimon's chapters show how scholars evolve from traditional scholarship to public scholarship. McBain describes ways for scholars to team with associations and the requisite expertise to do so. Advice for shifting work toward public scholarship is addressed in each chapter.

The Pullias Center's work is modeling public scholarship for our graduate students. Our students have been directly involved as contributors across all policy briefs, included in planning dialogues, and engaged in collecting stories for My Higher Ed Story. Most students assigned themselves to projects aligned with their research and methodological interests. We hope these efforts are helping graduate students see the possibilities of public scholarship and how they might integrate public scholarship into their practice in a way that complements their course work and other research projects. The writing for this project draws on multiple disciplines to shape and frame arguments. The entire project serves many purposes, including promoting awareness and making important research findings that directly concern current events. At the same time, involved students observe, participate, and learn about this process while learning new approaches to writing and dissemination.

Conclusion

We hope this volume serves as an inspiration and starting point for researchers who want to find a different way to conduct their research, who feel drawn to greater engagement with the communities of people who play leading roles in their research studies, or who just happened to stumble across this volume and curiously began to read. The idea for this book came from Kezar's American Educational Research Association Division J Vice Presidential address in 2016. Her advisee Yianna Drivalas, ending the second year of her PhD program at the time, felt encouraged by the speech, saying that it felt more aligned to what higher education research was meant to be. When Kezar was invited to edit this book, she invited Yianna and Joseph, a postdoctoral scholar at the Pullias Center who had also expressed similar interest on public scholarship, to join in. As we came together to discuss goals for the book, we primarily hoped to make public scholarship accessible to higher education researchers while presenting great examples of that work, familiar or otherwise, through a public scholarship frame.

For researchers who want to engage in public scholarship, this book offers advice on how to identify stakeholders, different modes for engaging stakeholders, varying methodologies, ways to collaborate with colleagues, approaches to tangible and intangible research products, and ways to learn the skills of public scholarship. Those in higher education are situated in a time and place where they must constantly defend its relevance, purpose, and utility. Coupled with the uncertain and troubling political and social futures for the most marginalized and oppressed communities in the United States, higher education stakeholders have important decisions to make about their research agendas. We contend that public scholarship should be considered a valid, accessible, and useful way to ensure that research is striving to represent and include the experiences of participants while also making sure the work falls into the hands of all relevant audience communities.

References

Pullias Center of Higher Education. (2017a). *Memo to Jerry Falwell, Jr., Taskforce on Higher Education, Chair: Priorities for higher education in the United States.* Los Angeles, CA: University of Southern California. Retrieved from http://pullias .usc.edu/ wp-content/uploads/2017/02/Falwell-Memo-2-14-2017.pdf

Pullias Center of Higher Education. (2017b). *Memo to U.S. Secretary of Education Betsy Devos: Educational priorities and decisionmaking.* Retrieved from pullias.usc .edu/wp-content/uploads/2017/03/Educational-Priorities-and-Decision-making.pdf

Pullias Center for Higher Education. (2017c). *My higher ed story.* Retrieved from myhigheredstory.org

Pullias Center for Higher Education. (2017d). *The university as a sanctuary.* Retrieved from http://pullias.usc.edu/wp-content/uploads/2017/01/The_University_as_a_Sanctuary_Final.pdf

Pullias Center for Higher Education. (2017e). *Understanding DACA and the implications for higher education.* Retrieved from pullias.usc.edu/wp-content/uploads/2017/02/understanding_daca_final.pdf

EDITORS AND CONTRIBUTORS

Estela Mara Bensimon, the founding director of the Center for Urban Education, is professor at the University of Southern California. Her current research is on racial equity in higher education from the perspective of organizational learning and sociocultural practice theories. Her most recent publications include *Engaging the Race Question: Accountability and Equity in US Higher Education* (with Alicia C. Dowd; Teachers College Press, 2014) and *Critical Approaches to the Study of Higher Education* (with Ana Martinez Aleman and Brian Pusser; Johns Hopkins University Press, 2015). Bensimon is a fellow of the American Educational Research Association and a member of the National Academy of Education. She is the recipient of the Research Award from the Association for the Study of Higher Education, and in 2017 she received AER's Social Justice in Education Award. Her opinion pieces have been published in *Inside Higher Ed, Huffington Post, Los Angeles Times, Denver Post, Sacramento Bee,* and *Zocalo.*

Wilmon A. Christian III is director of the National Equity Network for the University of Southern California Race and Equity Center. He is also a student in the doctorate of education in educational leadership program at the University of Southern California's Rossier School of Education. A practitioner, Christian's work and research are praxis focused, aiming to improve higher education outcomes, environments, and conditions for people of color. His professional experience and background weave an emphasis on race, student success, and equity in educational contexts.

Angela Clark-Taylor is on the Rochford Leadership Initiative faculty in the department of leadership and higher education at the University of Redlands. Her research centers on the relationship between college and career readiness, university-community engagement, and critical pedagogies with a particular focus on exposing systemic inequities and expanding opportunities to educational access. Clark-Taylor's current research projects explore the development of students' greater awareness of social issues and the belief that they can effect change through career development and service-learning that uses a critical pedagogical approach.

Zoë Corwin is associate professor of research with the University of Southern California's Pullias Center for Higher Education. Her research examines the role of college preparation programs and college guidance counselors in supporting historically underrepresented students, college pathways for foster youth, and the role of social media and games in postsecondary access and completion. Corwin directs the Pullias Center's First in the World project funded by the U.S. Department of Education's Fund for the Improvement of Postsecondary Education, which uses game-based strategies and social media to engage students in learning about college and following through on college application and admissions processes.

Amalia Dache-Gerbino is an Afro-Cuban American scholar and an assistant professor of higher education at the University of Missouri. She is also an Isabelle Lyda Endowed Professor for the College of Education. Dache-Gerbino serves as affiliate faculty in Black studies, the Afro-Romance, Institute, and peace studies. Her major research areas include the postcolonial geographic contexts of higher education, community and student social justice activism, and discourses contributing to urban and posturban college accessibility. Her research has been published in journals such as *Teachers College Record* and *Community College Review*, and articles are soon to be published in *Review of Higher Education* and *Equity & Excellence in Education*.

Jenna B. Daniel is a public service faculty member at the University of Georgia. As a College of Agricultural and Environmental Sciences Extension 4-H specialist, her work centers around grant and fund development and county extension faculty community engagement. Her research interests focus on the organizational challenges, adaptation, and capacity of the Cooperative Extension Service.

Charles H. F. Davis III is an assistant professor of clinical education in the Rossier School of Education at the University of Southern California. He also serves as the chief strategy officer and director of research at the university's Race and Equity Center. Davis's research primarily focuses on issues of racial justice and educational pathways toward freedom and liberation in K–12 schools, higher education, and their social contexts. In addition to publishing in peer-reviewed journals, Davis's work has been published in the *Los Angeles Times*, *Chronicle of Higher Education*, and *Inside Higher Ed*. He has also served as an on-air contributor to FOX News, NBC, NPR, and TVOne.

Yianna "Joanna" Drivalas is a PhD student at the University of Southern California's Rossier School of Education. Prior to graduate school, Drivalis studied creative writing and theater and taught at the community college and high school levels. She is a research associate at the university's Race and Equity Center under the advisement of Shaun R. Harper. Her dissertation work examines White male faculty consciousness and contributions to departmental climate, with a specific focus on race and gender.

Lorelle L. Espinosa serves as assistant vice president for American Councinl on Education's (ACE) Center for Policy Research and Strategy, where she is responsible for the codevelopment and management of the center's research agenda, which focuses on issues of diversity and equity in twenty-first century higher education, public finance and higher education systems, and transformational leadership. Espinosa has served the higher education profession for nearly 20 years, beginning in student affairs and undergraduate education at the University of California, Davis; Stanford University; and the Massachusetts Institute of Technology. Prior to ACE, she served as a senior analyst at Abt Associates, Inc., and as director of policy and strategic initiatives for the Institute for Higher Education Policy.

Oscar Espinoza-Parra is a September 2017 PhD graduate of Azusa Pacific University. His dissertation examined the interrelated factors that promote student learning and success among Latina and Latino undergraduate students at four-year colleges and universities. He currently works for the Association for the Study of Higher Education as director of finance and communications. His research agenda focuses on international students, campus climate, sense of belonging, Latina and Latino undergraduate students, public policy, and the role of student-faculty interaction and academic engagement on student success.

Jarrett T. Gupton is an assistant professor of organizational leadership, policy, and development in the College of Education and Human Development at the University of Minnesota. His research focuses on educational equity and opportunity for marginalized populations.

Shaun R. Harper is a provost professor in the Rossier School of Education and the Marshall School of Business at the University of Southern California. He also is the Clifford and Betty Allen Chair in Urban Leadership, founder and executive director of the university's Race and Equity Center, and a past president of the Association for the Study of Higher Education. Harper's research focuses primarily on race, gender, and other dimensions of equity in an array of organizational contexts, including K–12 schools, colleges and universities, and corporate environments. The *New York Times*, *Washington*

Post, *Wall Street Journal*, *Chronicle of Higher Education*, and over 11,000 news outlets have published Harper's comments and featured his research, and he has been interviewed on CNN, ESPN, and NPR.

David Horton Jr. is an associate professor in the higher education and student affairs program at Ohio University. Horton's research primarily centers on the curricular and cocurricular experiences of marginalized groups at community colleges, with a special focus on student athletes. Horton's research also focuses on faculty at two- and four-year institutions. Horton received his PhD in higher education administration at the University of Florida and has been working at Ohio University for the past nine years. Horton regularly teaches graduate courses that include Community Colleges in America, Leadership and Change, Diversity in Higher Education, and Critical Theories in Higher Education.

Sylvia Hurtado is a professor in the Graduate School of Education and Information Studies at the University of California, Los Angeles and directed the Higher Education Research Institute for more than 10 years. She is a former director of the University of Michigan's Center for the Study of Higher and Postsecondary Education. Her research includes transformative paradigm approaches, using mixed methods, campus climate, equity and diversity in higher education, and student talent development in diverse learning environments.

Constance Iloh is an assistant professor of higher education at the University of California, Irvine. Iloh's research on college access, opportunity, and educational stratification has been published in *Teachers College Record*, the *American Educational Research Journal*, and the *Journal of Negro Education*, with her forthcoming new model of college-going in the *Harvard Educational Review*. One of Iloh's latest articles, "Exploring the For-Profit Experience: An Ethnography of a For-Profit College" was the *American Educational Research Journal's* second-most-read article for the year 2016. Iloh is one of the only academics named to the Forbes 30 Under 30 list.

Jenny Jordan is a retired public service and outreach faculty member at the University of Georgia. She previously served as senior public service associate at the J. W. Fanning Institute for Leadership Development for three years and as Volunteer and Teen Program specialist for the College of Agricultural and Environmental Science Extension 4-H Program. She currently teaches a first semester seminar as an adjunct instructor for Athens Technical College. Her research and professional interests include boundary spanning, youth-adult partnerships and engagement, community leadership, and risk management for youth programs.

Adrianna Kezar is a professor of higher education at the University of Southern California and codirector of the Pullias Center for Higher Education. Kezar is a national expert of student success, equity and diversity, the changing faculty, change, governance, and leadership in higher education. Kezar is well published with 18 books and monographs, more than 100 journal articles, and more than 100 book chapters and reports. Recent books include *Envisioning the Faculty of the 21st Century* (Rutgers University Press, 2016), *How Colleges Change* (Routledge, 2013), *Enhancing Campus Capacity for Leadership* (Stanford Press, 2011) and *Organizing for Collaboration* (Jossey-Bass, 2009). She is the project director for the Delphi Project on the changing faculty and student success and was just awarded a grant from the Teagle Foundation for institutions that better support faculty and create new faculty models.

Joseph A. Kitchen is a postdoctoral scholar for the Pullias Center for Higher Education at the University of Southern California. Previously, he was a postdoctoral fellow at Harvard University and a postdoctoral researcher and program coordinator at Ohio State University. His work focuses on the role of programming and institutional supports in promoting access, successful transitions, and college success among underrepresented and underserved student populations.

Judy Marquez Kiyama is an associate professor in the higher education department at the University of Denver's Morgridge College of Education. Her research is organized in three interconnected areas: the role of parents and families in developing college-going cultures in the home, equity and power in educational research, and underserved groups as collective networks of change. Kiyama's current projects focus on the college-going and transition experiences of first-generation and low-income students and families of color and their role in serving as sources of cultural support for their students.

Michael Lanford is a postdoctoral research associate in the Pullias Center for Higher Education at the University of Southern California. Before that, Michael worked as a college writing center coordinator and humanities instructor. His research explores innovative approaches to secondary and higher education, focusing on student development, educational policy, and the impact of globalization. Over the past three years, his work has appeared in the *American Educational Research Journal, Higher Education, Higher*

Education: Handbook of Theory and Research, and *Policy Reviews in Higher Education*, among other publications.

Jaime Lester is an associate professor of higher education at George Mason University. The overarching goal of her research program is to examine organizational change and leadership in higher education. This focus has led to examinations of nonpositional leadership and tactics to promote local and institutional change and the role of individual identity in creating equitable workplaces in colleges and universities. Her latest research on learning analytics and pedagogy in computer science is funded by the National Science Foundation and Google.

Lesley McBain is an assistant director of research and policy analysis at the National Association of College and University Business Officers. In this role, she works on higher education finance-related research studies. She has also held various research and analysis-related positions at the U.S. Department of Education; the Cooperative Institutional Research Program in the Higher Education Research Institute at the University of California, Los Angeles; and the American Association of State Colleges and Universities.

Casey D. Mull is a public service faculty member in the University of Georgia's College of Agricultural and Environmental Sciences. His work focuses on leveraging land-grant university resources to support military organizations, service members, families, and youths statewide and nationwide as a 4-H and Air Force specialist. His research interests include boundary spanning, youth development, residential camping, and university-community engagement. He is president of the largest association of youth development professionals in the United States and president-elect of the Joint Council of Extension Professionals.

Kim Nehls has served as the executive director of the Association for the Study of Higher Education since 2008. She earned a Global MBA from Duke University, a PhD and a master's degree from the University of Nevada, Las Vegas, and bachelor's degrees in political science and speech communication from the University of Illinois at Urbana-Champaign. Her research and professional interests include university philanthropy, leadership, and student engagement.

Elena Nourrie serves as the coordinator of the Native American Student Center at California State Polytechnic University, Pomona. She completed her BA at California State Polytechnic University, Pomona and her MEd at the University of Nevada, Las Vegas. She is passionate about advocating for social justice and inclusion with a particular focus on Native American students in higher education.

Cecile H. Sam is an assistant professor of educational leadership in the College of Education at Rowan University. Her research interest focuses on the interconnections among ethics, leadership, and education in a K–20 setting.

Molly Sarubbi is a PhD candidate in higher education at the University of Denver and a policy researcher in the Postsecondary and Workforce Development Institute at the Education Commission of the States. Her current research focuses on access for traditionally underserved students and families, specifically on educational pathways for foster care youths, and the resulting imperatives for higher education policy and practice. In her role at the Education Commission of the States, Sarubbi serves as a resource for state constituents on a variety of postsecondary education policy issues and also remains an active foster care advocate by serving on multiple boards in service to youths and families in care.

Holly Schneider is the director of conference and events for the Association for the Study of Higher Education. She earned her PhD in higher education from the University of Nevada, Las Vegas (UNLV) in 2015, her master's in sports education leadership from UNLV in 2008, and her bachelor's degree in kinesiology from California State University, San Bernardino in 2006. Her research interests include mattering in the doctoral advising relationship and first-generation students' college experiences. Schneider enjoys spending her free time hiking, swimming, and watching Netflix with her husband and four children.

William G. Tierney is university professor, Wilbur-Kieffer Professor of Higher Education, codirector of the Pullias Center for Higher Education at the University of Southern California, and past president of the American Educational Research Association. His research focuses on increasing access to higher education, improving the performance of postsecondary institutions, and analyzing the impact of privatization on postsecondary education. He is a fellow of the American Educational Research Association and a member of the National Academy of Education. His latest book is *Rethinking Education and Poverty* (Johns Hopkins University Press, 2015).

Travis Tyler received his BA in English with a concentration in creative writing from Dartmouth College. While completing his undergraduate course work, Tyler was a member of the Dartmouth Men's Swimming and Diving Team. He earned his MEd in higher education from the University of Nevada, Las Vegas. An academic vagabond, his research interests include gender issues, masculinity, media (video games in particular), popular culture, and athletics.

Stephanie J. Waterman, Onondaga, Turtle Clan, is an associate professor at the Ontario Institute for Studies in Education, University of Toronto, where she coordinates the Student Development/Student Services stream. Before moving to Tkaronto she was a faculty member at the Warner Graduate School. Her research interests are First Nations and Native American college experiences, First Nations and Native American Student Affairs units, the role staff play in student retention, indigenous methodologies and pedagogy, and critical race theory. She is a coeditor of *Beyond the Asterisk: Understanding Native Students in Higher Education* with Heather J. Shotton and Shelly C. Lowe (Stylus, 2013) and *Beyond College Access: Indigenizing Programs for Student Success* (Stylus, 2018).